THE WORLD'S MODERN COOK BOOK

For The Busy Woman

Including a Complete Guide to Kitchen Management

by MABEL CLAIRE

The WORLD SYNDICATE PUBLISHING Co.

CLEVELAND, OHIO   NEW YORK

Copyright, 1932 by
GREENBERG, PUBLISHER, INC.
New York

Manufactured in the United States of America

CONTENTS

	PAGE
LIST OF ILLUSTRATIONS	9
INTRODUCTION	11

SECTION ONE
The Kitchen

CHAPTER
- I. GLOSSARY OF COOKING TERMS. MEASURES COMMONLY USED 13
- II. A WORKSHOP OF COLOR AND CHARM . . . 18
  Advice on Furnishing the Kitchen
- III. A COLOR AND CONDIMENT SHELF 22
- IV. KITCHEN WARE 25
  How to Select Pots and Pans of Iron, Chromium Steel, Aluminum, Enamelware, Tin, etc.
- V. ELECTRIC, GAS AND OIL RANGES 28
  Models in Modern Stoves and Comparative Cost of Using
- VI. ELECTRIC TABLE STOVES AND KITCHEN CONVENIENCES 32
  Motors, Mixers, Beaters, Egg Cookers, Waffle Irons, etc.
- VII. CASSEROLES AND OVEN BAKING DISHES . . 53
  Glass, China, Clay, Aluminum, etc.—Care of Oven Dishes
- VIII. ROASTERS AND BROILERS 57
- IX. INVENTORY OF KITCHEN FURNISHINGS . . 59
  All You Will Need to Equip Your Workshop and Approximate Costs

CONTENTS

CHAPTER		PAGE
X.	AN EMERGENCY SHELF . . . . How to Provide for the Unexpected Guest	62

SECTION TWO

Good Meals Well Served

XI.	MENU MAKING . . . . Secrets of a Well Balanced Diet	64
XII.	SERVING MEALS PROPERLY	69
XIII.	TABLE DECORATIONS	74

SECTION THREE

Cooking

XIV.	COOKING FOR THE BUSY WOMAN	76
XV.	COURSE DINNERS IN FIFTEEN MINUTES . . Complete Menus and Cooking Instructions for Eight Dinners That Can Be Prepared in a Quarter of an Hour	87
XVI.	COURSE DINNERS IN TWENTY MINUTES . . Ten Menus and Full Instructions	97
XVII.	COURSE DINNERS IN THIRTY MINUTES . . Choice of Twelve Menus	111
XVIII.	ADDITIONAL TIMED RECIPES . . . . . . Full Instructions for Preparing Ham and Potatoes; Calves Liver and Bacon; Smoked Sturgeon with Egg Sauce; Pork Tenderloin Frenched; Baked Chicken with Mushrooms; Mashed Potatoes Sauté; Potato Soup; Lyonnaise Potatoes; Creamed Rice; Potatoes O'Brien; Candied Sweet Potatoes; Cauliflower; Creamed Celery; Scalloped Onions; Creamed Cabbage; Summer Squash; Vanilla Soufflé; Blueberry Pancakes; Scones; Jumbles; Hot Frosted Gingerbread; Date Custard; Berry Pudding	129
XIX.	PLATE DINNERS FOR THE BUSY WOMAN . .	138
XX.	PLATE DINNER MENUS AND COMPLETE COOKING INSTRUCTIONS	143

CONTENTS

CHAPTER		PAGE
XXI.	PLATTER DINNER MENUS AND COMPLETE COOKING INSTRUCTIONS	176
XXII.	PLANK DINNERS	183
XXIII.	CASSEROLE DINNERS	189
XXIV.	DINNERS PREPARED AHEAD OF TIME	194

SECTION FOUR

Entertaining

XXV. COCKTAILS 196
  Including Recipes for Making White Grape Juice Cocktail; Grapefruit and Prune Cocktail; Cranberry Cocktail; Grape Juice; Loganberry Juice Cocktail; Lime Cocktail; Pineapple Crème de Menthe; Currant and Raspberry Cocktail; Sauerkraut Juice; Tomato Juice Cocktail; Clam Juice Cocktail; Clam Juice and Tomato Cocktail

XXVI. HORS D'ŒUVRES AND CANAPÉS 200
  Including Recipes for Antipasto; Stuffed Tomato; Stuffed Eggs; Salami or Smoked Salmon; Potato Chips with Pimento Cheese; Stuffed Pickled Beets; Cucumber; Stuffed Radishes; Tiny Sausage Rissoles; Sausage and Almond; Dried Beef Hors d'œuvres; Celery Stuffed with Shrimp; Celery Stuffed with Chicken; Celery Stuffed with Avocado; Caviare Canapé; Asparagus Tip Canapé; Cheese and Onion Canapé; Peanut Butter and Bacon; Sardine Canapé; Avocado Canapé; Anchovy Canapé; Surprise Canapé; Prunes and Bacon; Apple and Cheese; Cheese and Mustard Butter; Stuffed Olives and Bacon; Mushroom Canapé; Lobster Canapé; Pickled Mussels; Water Cress and Shrimp; Blini

XXVII. FANCY SANDWICHES AND COOL DRINKS . . 225
  Includes Recipes for Anchovy Sandwich; Pâté de Fois Gras Sandwich; Avocado Sandwich; Cheese and Ginger; Pimento Cheese and Nuts; Lobster Sandwich; Chicken Sandwich; Sweet Red Pepper Sandwich; Cream Pistachios; Summer Club Sandwich; Deviled Ham Sandwich; Bar-le-Duc and Cream Cheese; Decorative Ice Cubes. Also the following Delicious Summertime Drinks: Logan-

CONTENTS

CHAPTER		PAGE
	berry Punch; Grape Juice and White Rock; Grenadine Delight; Stonewall Jackson; Raspberry Soda; Golden Glow; Iced Chocolate and Iced Tea	
XXVIII.	SUMMERTIME SUPPERS	235
	Complete Menus and Suggestions for Such Pleasing Things As, Tomato Cocktail; French Dressing; Pear and Pineapple Cocktail; Shrimp Cocktail; Salads Such As Moulded Potato; Stuffed Pimento; Moulded Ham and Chicken Moussé; Alligator Pear; Moulded Cucumber	
XXIX.	HOT WEATHER ENTERTAINING	239
	Various Menus for Summer Parties Including Recipes for Fruit Cocktail; Cheese Sandwich Loaf; Iced Chocolate; Chicken Almond Sandwich; Sandwich Delight; Lime Rickey; Sweetbread and Cucumber Salad; Currant Cup; Frozen Tomato Salad; Tiny Bran Muffins	
XXX.	HALLOWE'EN PARTIES	244
	Among the Recipes Given are the Glorified Club Sandwich; Shrimp Wiggle; Orange Cream in Orange Baskets; Chicken or Oyster Patties; Orange Cake; Orange Frosting; How to Decorate Cake	
XXXI.	HOLIDAY ENTERTAINING	250
	Recipes Include Such Joyful Dishes as Southern Sandwich; Snappy Sandwich; Rolled Salamagundi; Biscuits; Sandwich Biscuit; Holiday Cookies; Gingers; Holly Cakes; Icing; Mulled Loganberry Juice	
XXXII.	HOLIDAY DINNERS	255
XXXIII.	BUFFET SUPPERS	257
	Among the Recipes Given Are Those for Vegetable Salad; Fried Chicken; Asparagus Salad; Chicken with Mushrooms and Sweetbreads; Macaroni Salad	

SECTION FIVE

Recipes

XXXIV.	SOUPS	262
XXXV.	SEA FOOD AND FISH	270

CHAPTER		PAGE
XXXVI.	MEATS	276
XXXVII.	VEGETABLES	292
XXXVIII.	LUNCHEON DISHES	305
	Aids in the Preparation of Light Repasts	
XXXIX.	SALADS	310
	How to Make Various Delectable Salad Dishes, With Numerous Ingredients	
XL.	ELECTRIC WAFFLE IRON DISHES	318
	Full Instructions for the Preparation of Waffles; Cornmeal Waffles; Raised Waffles; Short Cake; Chocolate Waffle Cake; Maryland Cream Waffles; Gingerbread Waffles; Waffle Cake	
XLI.	HOT BREADS	322
XLII.	YEAST BREADS	330
	Recipes Given Are Those for White Bread; Cinnamon Bread; Date Bread; Cinnamon Cake; Sally Lunn; Graham Bread; Ice Box Rolls	
XLIII.	PIES	334
XLIV.	CAKES	342
	Instruction Also Given in Preparing the Icing for a Variety of Cakes	
XLV.	COOKIES	358
	Ingredients Used for the Preparation of Different Varieties	
XLVI.	DESSERTS	363
	Including a large Variety of Up-to-Date Recipes	
XLVII.	QUICK DESSERTS	375
XLVIII.	CANDIES	379
	Recipes Given Are Useful in the Making of Some Toothsome Bits	
XLIX.	JAMS, JELLIES AND PICKLES	383
L.	COFFEE, TEA AND CHOCOLATE	388

SECTION SIX
The Mechanical Refrigerator

CHAPTER		PAGE
LI.	Care and Use of the Mechanical Ice Box	390
LII.	Frozen Refrigerator Desserts	395

LIST OF ILLUSTRATIONS

	Page
THE OUTDOOR LUNCHEON. A simple yet colorful table setting.	33
DINNER IS SERVED. An attractive table setting. Also settings for each individual course.	34-5
AN INFORMAL BUFFET SUPPER. Table arrangement.	36
CHINA AND GLASS FOR COOKING AND SERVING.	37
A WELL PLANNED KITCHEN.	38
AN EFFICIENT KITCHEN CABINET.	39
A GOOD KITCHEN SINK ARRANGEMENT.	40
THE COSY BREAKFAST CORNER.	41
ELECTRICAL HELPS IN COOKING. A modern stove and a mixer—beater—juice extractor.	42
REFRIGERATOR DISHES. They save space and hold flavors.	43
MODERN STOVES. Table top and console types.	44
HANDY CONTAINERS. They make for a compact kitchen.	45
A VENTILATING FAN.	46
MODERN WASHING AND IRONING MACHINES.	47
SANITARY REFUSE CONTAINERS.	48
UTENSILS FOR MAKING COFFEE. Boiled, perked and drip.	209
PROPER UTENSILS. For frying, broiling, boiling and roasting.	210
TABLE COOKERY. An electrical stove, a percolator and a grill for table use.	211

	Page
CLEANING ACCESSORIES. Three handy electrical aids.	212
HOUSE CLEANING AIDS. Polishes, cleansers, mops and brooms.	213
GOOD CUTLERY. To make your cookery easier and more efficient.	214
SPECIAL TOOLS TO SPEED WORK. A number of handy utensils.	215
MOULDS. For puddings, jellies, ice creams, cakes, etc.	216
MIXING EQUIPMENT. A number of up-to-date tools.	217
SPECIAL EQUIPMENT. For preparing food for the baby or the invalid.	218
UTENSILS FOR SALAD MAKING.	219
TOOLS FOR DEEP FAT FRYING.	220
UTENSILS FOR "WATERLESS" COOKING.	221
TOOLS FOR FIXING FRUITS.	222
SMALL TOOLS. A number of handy kitchen helps.	223
PAPER ACCESSORIES. They reduce laundry bills.	224

INTRODUCTION

Never let anyone tell you that cooking is not an art. It takes creative ability to be a good cook and it takes a degree of culture to appreciate good cooking. Good cooks and critics who can distinguish good cooking when they find it are as highly cultured as good artists or writers and their discriminating critics.

A good cook feels that same urge that makes an artist want to paint a picture or a writer write a story and incidentally some of the greatest artists and writers have been famous cooks.

There is need for more beauty in the world, more graciousness and glamour in our daily living. Money cannot buy it, but a clever woman can create it in the home which is the best of all places for starting reforms. She is responsible for the things that make the home a pleasant place to go into; for the kind of meals that make people happy and contented. She originates most of the pleasant details of daily living.

There is no profession in the world that a woman should be prouder of than that of home maker. Nor is there one of more service and importance to civilization. It is a profession that takes knowledge and brains, embracing the arts and sciences. The pursuit of it is full of fascinating problems.

Whether a woman does her own housework or hires it done, she should understand the business of running her home and understand it from experience, not theory.

So many women labor under the erroneous impression that members of their sex are born cooks. They do not think women have to learn cookery. "It comes naturally," they say.

Some persons may be born with a special enthusiasm and aptitude for cooking as others have such an aptitude for medicine or sculpture or poetry, but the preparation of properly balanced meals in which every dish is ready at the proper moment is a science as exact as the compounding of drugs and requiring, in addition, the vision of an artist.

More than half the fun of cooking is in creating new dishes. Any woman can be an artist and enjoy the artist's thrill without stirring out of her kitchen. But first she must learn the rudiments of the science by following recipes and learning to be accurate, by experimenting with the new recipes other cooks create, by keeping up with the modern household machinery and reading the magazines. One cook book is not enough; she should have many and use them. In this her training is no different from the training of the writer or the painter, for it is only when these brother artists have a thorough grasp of their mediums through practise and knowledge of what is known that they can venture into the delightful fields of new ideas with any hope of experiencing the thrill of discovery.

If you are going to be a cook, be a good cook. Get some fun out of it.

SECTION ONE

THE KITCHEN

CHAPTER I

GLOSSARY OF COOKING TERMS

All the measurements in this book are level. A standard measuring cup holding ½ pint is the one meant whenever a "cup" is mentioned as a quantity in recipes. These cups may be purchased wherever cooking equipment is sold. They are divided into quarters, thirds and halves. Use an ordinary tablespoon, not a mixing spoon for measuring tablespoonfuls; and a teaspoon for measuring teaspoonfuls. A set of standard measuring spoons can be purchased in any house furnishing store.

When measuring dry ingredients fill the cup or spoon above the rim and level with a knife. Do not pack dry ingredients into the cup. Flour and confectioners' sugar should be sifted before measuring.

When measuring liquid ingredients a "cup", "tablespoon" or "teaspoon" means to fill the utensil as full as possible or so that it will not spill when moved.

One Cup	= ½ Pint
16 Tablespoons	= 1 Cup
3 Teaspoons	= 1 Tablespoon
A Pinch	= Less than ⅛ Teaspoon

Cooking Thermometers

The use of cooking thermometers has added greatly to the accuracy of cooking. Purchase a set and there will be no more guess work about the heat at which the different foods should be cooked. You will always be sure of uniform results. The three different thermometers commonly used are the oven thermometer, the fat thermometer and the candy thermometer. A roasting thermometer may be added to these to insure the accuracy of roasting meats. A stove with heat control does not require an oven thermometer.

How to Use an Oven Thermometer

When the heat is turned on, place the thermometer in the center of the oven three inches from the front. When it registers 25 degrees above the temperature you wish, place the food in the oven. The reason for the higher temperature is that the cold food reduces the heat slightly. Regulate the oven burners to keep the heat constant for as long as you wish that heat. To lower the temperature reduce the heat of the burners. To raise the temperature apply more heat.

How to Use a Deep Fat Thermometer

When the fat is melted and before it reaches a high temperature place the thermometer in it. This is to insure against breakage. The bulb of the thermometer should be covered. Do not let the bulb rest on the bottom of the kettle. Fat should be heated at least 15 degrees higher than the temperature wanted because the food cools it.

How to Use a Candy Thermometer

Place the thermometer in water. Bring to the boiling point. Transfer it to the syrup. The bulb of the thermometer should be covered. Do not let the bulb rest

GLOSSARY OF COOKING TERMS

on the bottom of the kettle. In reading the thermometer read it on a level with the eye. The candy thermometer temperature corresponds to the cold water test used for sugar syrup.

Oven Temperatures

200° to 300° F.	Slow Oven
325° to 375° F.	Moderate Oven
400° to 450° F.	Hot Oven
450° to 550° F.	Very Hot Oven

Deep Fat Frying Temperatures

360° to 370° F.	Fish and Meat
360° to 370° F.	Croquettes and Fritters
360° F.	Doughnuts
350° to 360° F.	French Fried Potatoes
380° to 390° F.	Potato Chips

Candy Making Temperatures

238° F.	Thread Stage or Soft Ball
250° F.	Firm Ball
260° to 270° F.	Hard Ball
290° F.	Brittle

Cookery Terms

Boil: To bring any liquid to a heat where it is kept in violent motion.

Braise: To cook in a covered pan with a very small amount of liquid.

Baste: To dip over a food spoonfuls of the liquid from the bottom of the pan in which it is cooking.

Broil: To subject a food to direct, live heat as live coals gas flame or electric coils.

Pan-Broil: To cook in a hot pan with barely enough fat to keep the food from sticking.

Blanche: To pour boiling water over food, followed by cold.

Beat: The object of beating is to introduce air into a mixture. It should be done violently with a lifting motion of the spoon or beater.

Dredge: To sift a light coating over food, usually used in connection with flour or powdered sugar.

Fry: To cook in deep fat.

Fold in: To cut in gently with a sidewise motion of the spoon, being careful not to drive out any air. Usually applied to whipped cream, stiff egg whites, flour or sugar.

Mince: To chop fine.

Marinate: To cover with French dressing or a spiced liquid.

Mask: To just cover or coat the top of food, usually in reference to a sauce, mayonnaise or whipped cream.

Parboil: To partly cook a food in liquid.

Rice: To put cooked food through a vegetable or fruit press.

Steam: To cook a food in a covered steamer over continuously boiling water.

Simmer: Liquid brought to a heat where it barely moves.

Sauté: To brown in a small quantity of fat. Do not confuse this term with "Fry".

Stew: To cook gently in a small amount of water.

Stir: A rotating movement of a spoon or beater to blend ingredients.

Measures Commonly Used in Cooking

1 cup	= ½ pint
½ cup	= 1 gill or ¼ pint
2¾ cups brown sugar	= 1 pound
2 cups granulated sugar	= 1 pound
3½ cups confectioners' sugar	= 1 pound
4 cups sifted flour	= 1 pound
1 pint liquid	= 1 pound

1 pint solid fat = 1 pound
1 pint solid chopped meat = 1 pound
10 eggs = 1 pound
2 tablespoons butter = 1 ounce
4 tablespoons flour = 1 ounce
16 tablespoons dry ingredients = 1 cup

CHAPTER II

THE KITCHEN, A WORKSHOP OF COLOR AND CHARM

The kitchen should be the pleasantest room in the house. There is no good reason for the millions of ugly kitchens in the world. Nor is there any good reason for kitchens that look like white tile lunchrooms. In a kitchen that is gay, cozy and pleasant, half the labor of cooking seems to be eliminated.

In many houses that have been restored and kept in memory of another day, the kitchen is a most interesting and delightful room. When the tour of the house has been made and the kitchen reached, there is always a sigh of pleasure. A sense of comfort and jollity pervades the place. The mellow walls, the lovely old containers for flours and spices, the gay platters, bowls and cups, the gleaming copper, the rocking chairs!

A kitchen I shan't forget is one in the Thomas Bailey Aldrich Memorial house in Portsmouth, N. H. There the author spent the boyhood he describes so vividly in "The Story of a Bad Boy". Walls and floors are painted a rich pumpkin color. It has a copper sink and pump gleaming with polish. A corner cupboard is filled with the gayest of quaint platters cups and plates. Copper pans hang about the enormous old fireplace. Kitty's rocker is drawn near, and one imagines the wraith of that devoted soul returning to it at night to spend an hour remembering happy days long dead.

Near the fireplace on the wall hangs an almanac of

ancient date containing the most entrancing recipes and remedies.

Old-fashioned picture blinds hang at the sunny windows which look into the garden. The shelves along the walls hold gayly decorated spice containers, flour and sugar canisters. All sorts of jolly dishes and utensils fill the odd spaces.

The modern housewife should try to get in her kitchen the same jolly atmosphere, while preserving a convenient arrangement of furnishings and utensils. The best arrangement for labor saving is one where all operations move from left to right: Refrigerator to work table, table to stove, stove to serving table, and to sink.

This has been the subject of an interesting survey made by the Herald Tribune Institute (New York) and the results of this study have been published in a pamphlet issued by them.

A visit to the kitchen furnishing department of a modern store sets the mind teeming with ideas that will add charm and convenience to your kitchen. Most kitchens can be improved and whether you wish to add the largest or the smallest item, it will be an inspiration to wander through these departments and get new ideas for the present or some future shopping.

The new iceless refrigerators and new designs in gas and electric ranges are finished now in lovely plain or tiled effects and a variety of colors. Since they are the most important and largest of single items their color will determine your kitchen color scheme to considerable extent.

Kitchen cabinets have so many built-in conveniences they are well worth owning. Both the kitchen and utility type cabinets give space with doors to hide whatever seems unsightly or is "out of the picture". This space is also convenient to store the less used articles. Keep the kitchen workshop free from the confusion of too many things. Both types of such cabinets come in a variety of colors to match your kitchen plan. Utility cabinets may be purchased in separate units and enlarged by adding units as they are needed.

Then there are the hanging shelves that fit into odd space and make such a difference in the convenient arrangement of your supplies or equipment. They might hold your cook books, for you should collect cook books if you wish to improve your cooking technique—and who doesn't? Cook book collecting is one of the most fascinating hobbies in which a woman can indulge.

The floor linoleum should be considered as an essential part of your kitchen color scheme. There is a wide variety in this field and the modern oil cloth that is useful to cover some shabby shelf or table also comes in patterns that are charming and beautiful. Shelving in strong or delicate colors and edging is another intriguing item of kitchen furnishing. The shelf edgings are made also in attractive paper designs.

The modern gleaming metal ware kitchen utensils are works of art in design and finish. Enamel ware comes in a great variety of colors. The color and shapes of waffle pitchers, sets of mixing bowls, containers for dry groceries and spices in metal and glazes and painted tin are varied enough to suit every person's artistic instinct.

Remember that the several metals and enamel finishes as well as glass and china are each suited best to certain uses. One must not lose sight of utility while satisfying the desire for color and charm. The various advantages of different wares are discussed a little farther on in a special chapter. Here we are speaking only of their highly decorative effect.

The size of a kitchen has nothing to do with its charm. My own kitchen is a small one, but it is so pleasing to me that I never enter it without a glow of satisfaction. At the window hangs a gay India print in which blue predominates. Shelves of assorted sizes are everywhere. Their edges are painted lacquer red. On the broad shelves are gayly patterned serving platters, tureens, colored glass dishes, fat casseroles, blue and amber drinking glasses and pitchers. Jolly flasks of Venetian glass contain vinegar and oil. Keeping these in the kitchen saves many steps. On the narrower shelves the supplies are kept, but in interesting containers that are easy to acquire.

The tiniest set of shelves holds the spices and colors for decorating and garnishing. Blooming plants line the window sill. Several decorative trays hang on the walls. Everything has been arranged with an eye for effect, but is also placed in the most convenient spot, nearest to where it is most used.

Above my stove I have hung a mirror in a green and gold frame. It reflects all the jolly kitchen as well as the cook. A cook should consult a mirror often. For what use is a decorative kitchen without a decorative woman in it! At least a woman as decorative as is humanly possible!

This chapter has dealt so far largely with the color and charm of the kitchen workshop. But a kitchen is, first of all, a workshop. Like the efficient modern factory it must produce a maximum of results with a minimum of labor. It is not so complicated a problem as might appear at first glance.

CHAPTER III

A COLOR AND CONDIMENT SHELF

On a set of shelves in my kitchen stands the very life and soul of good cooking. Without their contents the preparation of food would be an uninspired drudgery. Those shelves are devoted to the spices, flavoring, decoration and color which make food interesting.

The knowledge of how to use these materials constitutes the difference between monotonous cooking and good cooking. Unflavored, colorless food casts a blight over any meal. The variety that proper flavoring and decoration give to a dish assures the enjoyment of it.

To obtain benefit from a food, you must want to eat it —not eat it from a sense of duty, nor because it is supposed to be good for you.

Attractive, well-flavored dishes, then, are the first requisite for a delightful table.

In my kitchen gay spice jars hold most of these condiments.

The neat rows present an inspiring sight. They suggest all sorts of ideas for creating cookery of distinction. Even their names are fascinating and bring visions of the far-off places from which they came:

Mace, ginger, cinnamon,

Nutmeg, cardamon, cloves,

Saffron, sweet basil, marjoram—

The list grows. The very names suggest swinging caravans, ships discharging their aromatic cargoes, old-fashioned gardens. More particularly my own garden by the sea, where I grew so many of the herbs that fill my jars. Of course, modern shops carry all of these spices.

But if the condiments suggest these things, they also remind us of something nearer home: Cinnamon, cloves and mace whisper of fat mince and pumpkin pies sending out their spicy sweetness as they bake—and of mulled drinks, brewed in winter by the open fire. The sage, marjoram and thyme bring to mind plump, brown turkey, roasted and bursting with stuffing. Cardamon, curry and coriander bring up visions of East Indian curry, that delightfully hot dish introduced to me by a writer who had spent years in that colorful land. And saffron speaks of Spanish chicken, a recipe given me by a Spanish poet whose culture recognized the function of pots and pans as a part of the beauty of life.

The jars holding small, sparkling spiced gum drops are especially good for birthday cakes. The colored drops are cut into petals and arranged as flowers over the frosting, while the green slices make the leaves. The red cinnamon candies are to color and flavor cooked apples and pears or to color watermelon pickles. The preserved cherries and the green angelica, cut into small bits, decorate the top of lemon foam puddings, served with yellow custard. The preserved pineapple, the citron, the kumquats, the candied orange peel, the nut meats, the marshmallows, and the tiny glasses of preserves and jellies decorate and flavor desserts. Pickles, olives, capers, garlic, anchovies, walnut ketchup, chili sauce, chutney, mushroom ketchup, Worcestershire sauce are to flavor sauces and salads.

On another shelf there are bottles. They contain peppermint, almond, vanilla, orange, lemon, grenadine and orange flower water. They are for cakes and desserts.

All of these are the things that make a cook into an artist. Every good cook has something of the great artist about him. It needs as much ability to create and serve a fine dish as it does to paint a fine picture. And it needs something of the great artist's culture properly to appreciate a fine dish!

It is a vulgar notion, that the appreciation of good cooking is plebeian. And it is not true. One who appreciates and distinguishes between the different flavors in cookery has highly developed taste and discernment. What is more, he has culture, which is a sensibility to the finer and more beautiful things in this world.

CHAPTER IV

KITCHEN WARE

If you are going to keep house, a considerable part of your days is going to be spent in company with your kitchen pots and pans. For this reason the kitchen ought to be a bright, attractive workroom and the metal dishes and utensils that line its shelves or hang from its hooks should be either polished to a shine or covered with bright colored enamels that help carry out the kitchen color scheme.

Enamel ware is especially good for foods that should have a low heat in cooking. Be sure to include a double boiler in this ware for creamed dishes and those with eggs. An enamel dish pan is the best type because it does not clatter and does not scratch the sink.

The china-like surface of this ware makes it extremely easy to keep clean. In buying enamel ware select the heavily coated kind which does not burn or chip easily.

Aluminum has a hard, bright surface that is kept polished without difficulty. It is impervious to acids and does not form any chemical reaction to foods cooked in it. All aluminum utensils discolor. This discoloration is harmless. It can be entirely removed by cleaning with a *good* aluminum cleanser. Since it is the pride of most cooks to keep their pots and pans shining you may find your aluminum needs brightening occasionally.

Proper Care of Cast Aluminum

Do not let utensils stand in any water, as this will cause

them to tarnish. Also do not use soda, lye or any cleaner which contains a strong alkali, as they will discolor the utensil.

For best results clean the utensil while it is warm or hot even if it is necessary to boil water in it.

Do not let food stand in them from one meal to another, as this causes them to discolor.

Do not put hot utensils in cold water; this causes them to discolor and may cause them to warp.

Heat utensils gradually and prevent warping.

Always use as low a flame as possible.

When not in use keep the utensil in a dry place with the cover off.

Ironware has its place in the kitchen. One thing is important to remember about ironware pots and kettles and skillets: They must be seasoned when first purchased and before they are used for cooking. Coat the sides and all inner surfaces of the utensil with oil or cooking fat and warm up at a low heat. Wipe off surplus oil with a soft paper napkin. It is often necessary to season ironware articles twice before they are well broken in. Ironware utensils will serve a lifetime.

Directions for Seasoning Dutch Ovens

Cover and pot should be seasoned separately. Fill utensil with a strong solution of washing soda, boil for at least half an hour, scour thoroughly. Grease with unsalted fat and place in warm oven for one hour. Remove and scour thoroughly again with scouring powder and steel wool.

Dry and grease with plenty of unsalted fat and leave in warm oven for about four hours, swabbing the side and rim occasionally with a cloth dipped in the fat.

Wipe out grease and pot is ready for use.

Wash, but do *not* scour the pot the first few times after using it.

Tin and Chromium Steel Ware

Tin is the least expensive of metals used in kitchen ware and serves very well for most purposes. The plating should be heavy. Tinware can be kept clean with a metal brush or steel wool and scouring powder. Baking dishes, steaming dishes and moulds made of tin are a good investment. There is some controversy as to the action of acids on tinware. Better avoid cooking fruits and such vegetables as tomatoes in tin dishes, or at least do not let such foods stand in tin.

The aristocrat of kitchen ware is the new chromium nickel steel. This hard, bright metal will avoid chemical action from any food. It will not tarnish and it will last a lifetime. The designs are handsome and it is easily kept clean.

If food has been burned in a chromium nickel steel dish, a brush and scouring powder will remove the traces from the bright metal surface and leave no discoloration not injure the metal in any way.

CHAPTER V

ELECTRIC, GAS AND OIL RANGES

Which type of range you are going to use must depend a great deal upon the public service facilities in the section where you live and also upon the cost of service.

If you have neither electricity nor gas there is the useful oil stove to be considered and that old stand-by, the wood or coal range.

The most convenient, cleanest and attractive form of cooking power undoubtedly is electricity. But in many cases electric power for cooking is expensive. Second in desirability —and a very close second thanks to the improvements in modern ranges—is gas. While nobody has yet discovered an inexpensive way to supply heating electricity without a central power plant, gas can be purchased now in containers which hold months' supply. The modern ranges are easily hitched up to these supply tanks and people who live in communities without public service gas endorse the method enthusiastically. If you are without gas in your community I can recommend that you consult your favorite department store's expert on gas ranges and learn about these new ideas before deciding that gas cooking is out of the question for you.

The cost of cooking electricity varies greatly in different parts of the country. Clever cooks who plan their meals to conserve power can keep the monthly bills lower. Experts for Good Housekeeping Institute have calculated that a family of four can cook with electricity by using 125 to 200 kilowatt hours per month. At a rate of five cents per kilowatt hour this would mean a monthly bill of between six and ten dollars. In some localities the cost of electricity is no more than the cost of gas.

If you are going to use an electric range study the suggestions and directions the manufacturer will send you with the stove. His domestic science engineers have been working out all sorts of practical and money-saving methods, even to planning the menus for your meals. Oven cooked meals are particularly to be recommended for the electric range. If they are properly planned all the oven space will be utilized at one time. The modern electric oven is under perfect heat control and time control. It is possible with such a range to place the dishes in the oven several hours before you wish cooking to begin, set a master clock and go about your business. At the proper moment the heat will be turned on and kept on until the cooking is finished. Electric oven regulation does away with all opening of the oven door to see how food is cooking. The automatic machinery takes care of that and the housewife who opens the door after that warning is merely wasting money.

Like the gas range, the electric stove has beside its oven and broiling unit, open heating elements for cooking on top of the stove. When you use these be sure that the pans and pots selected are broad enough to cover the heat element, so that no heat is wasted.

Proper heat insulation makes the electric range the coolest of stoves. They do not produce the soot or hot gasses due to faulty combustion. A turn of the control switch starts or stops them and the thermostat controls and clock devices will even attend to that detail for you.

In both appearance and usefulness the modern gas range

is far ahead of anything our mothers used a few years ago. It is possible now to buy a gas range of the cabinet or console type with a solid color finish or a tile finish that is a thing of beauty in the kitchen. Built on flat tops cover the open flame burners. Oven doors fit flush and except for a few small knobs there is no resemblance to the old-fashioned gas stove remaining.

The gas stove of today has the same automatic timing service to offer cooks that the electric range offers. Master clocks will control the length of cooking if you desire. Also the automatic control will take care of regulating heat for you. If you are buying a new gas range it is well to learn all about these new devices in control which give such great aid to the busy housekeeper and cook.

Several of these modern ranges are made with a built-in closed top like the top of the old coal range. Stove lids give access to the burners and there is a fine table surface on which foods may be kept hot. All the new models, even when they have open top burners, now add a handsomely enameled table surface which will be appreciated by anybody who has juggled pots and pans on the old grill topped stoves.

Some of the new ranges have automatic lighting devices which light the burners and have the additional recommendation of igniting gas if by accident the cocks were turned on. The ovens are thoroughly insulated against loss of heat and many have heat control devices. The new drawer type of broiler is a convenience since it makes the entire broiler and contents easily accessible without burning the hands.

The newer types of kerosene ranges generate gas from coal oil. This gives the advantage of a much hotter flame. The designs have been greatly improved with the various units made more accessible and better insulation of ovens.

Whichever type of range is selected, make sure it will fit your kitchen space conveniently. For the average family the stove with four open flames, an oven and broiling accessories or separate broiler drawer is ample. If you use a gas range it is best to connect its escape pipe with the chimney flue and eliminate all odors and unconsumed gasses from the house.

CHAPTER VI

ELECTRIC TABLE STOVES AND KITCHEN CONVENIENCES

With the help of electrical conveniences some of your cooking can be done at the table. The method is not only a labor saver and a help, but it furnishes certain sorts of food hotter, fresher and more delightful. There is added interest and pleasure in seeing the breakfast eggs and bacon, the waffles or the coffee prepared at table and served hot and fresh the moment they are done.

While the electric cooking ranges are still expensive to operate in parts of the United States where the power rate is high, the smaller table stoves, percolators, toasters and broilers are not. They use less current and their efficiency has been increased remarkably.

A change in the National Electric code now makes it possible to plug in appliances of high wattage in service outlets which means hotter electric plates. The use of special wire for heating elements has speeded up these stoves. Automatic heat control makes such delicate operations as the making of toast or cooking of eggs just right a certainty instead of a guess.

An electric percolator is one convenient way to prepare coffee. The percolation method insures getting all the best of the coffee bean and none of the grounds. It serves coffee which has all the delightful elements of that drink and none of the indigestible dangers of the old boiled variety. Percolators come in all sorts of models and while the price range is large, even the cheapest of them (which don't cost a great deal more than the old-fashioned coffee pot these days) has

The OUTDOOR LUNCHEON

table should be set with colorful, casual simplicity. You can achieve it with gay peasant ware; glassware of unusual colors, and bright hand-woven linens.

DINNER IS SERVED!

With the charm of candle-light, with the gleam of glass, of lovely linen damask, of simple beautiful silver—your table is sure to look its loveliest.

The table pictured was planned for a not-too-formal dinner party for eight. Many hostesses, these days, have endorsed the smart and amusing fashion of changing china with each succeeding course, so that there is no monotony —and that's the way we've photographed this dinner party. On the opposite page, we show one place, course by course, with the correct silver and china for each.

1—The first course, in clear crystal.

2—The soup appears in a colored cup.

3—The entrée is served on a patterned plate.

4—Below—For the meat, a lovely, creamy-white plate.

5—Salad plate like one used for entrée but smaller.

6—Dessert plate and demitasse to match, finger bowl of crystal.

An informal Sunday BUFFET SUPPER

Set for eight

China and glass
for COOKING and SERVING

A—This type of casserole is invaluable in preparing many recipes. It may be had in oval or round shapes and is useful with and without the cover. In ovenproof glass, or as shown in B, in deep brown earthenware.

C—Many confirmed tea-drinkers will have nothing but a pottery pot, for they claim it imparts a delicious flavor. Illustrated is an English Rockingham, as well as a Japanese decorated teapot.

D—Real seashells come all the way from France to make pretty baking dishes for your entrées.

E—Custard cups are made of ovenproof china, in plain rich brown, or green, or with decorations.

Is your KITCHEN planned to make your work easier?

This picture shows how a well-planned kitchen looks when a cake is in the making. See how handy the refrigerator is—how conveniently close to it the table is placed, with the mixer attached to a nearby wall-socket. And note that the stove is only a few steps away—so that in the shortest possible time and with the least possible effort, you can have your cake mixed, and popped into the oven. The table on wheels is pushed out of the way when not in use.

Three important units make

THIS KITCHEN CABINET

For flexibility, it is more convenient to have three separate pieces, and when you're working in the kitchen, it is best to have all of your supplies and utensils in one place —as in this kitchen cabinet. The doors are strong, solid panels, close-fitting, so they don't catch dust. The base is bakelite right to the floor, another good feature. And if you want additional storage space, you can get detachable eighteen-inch cabinets to set on top of these units, building them higher.

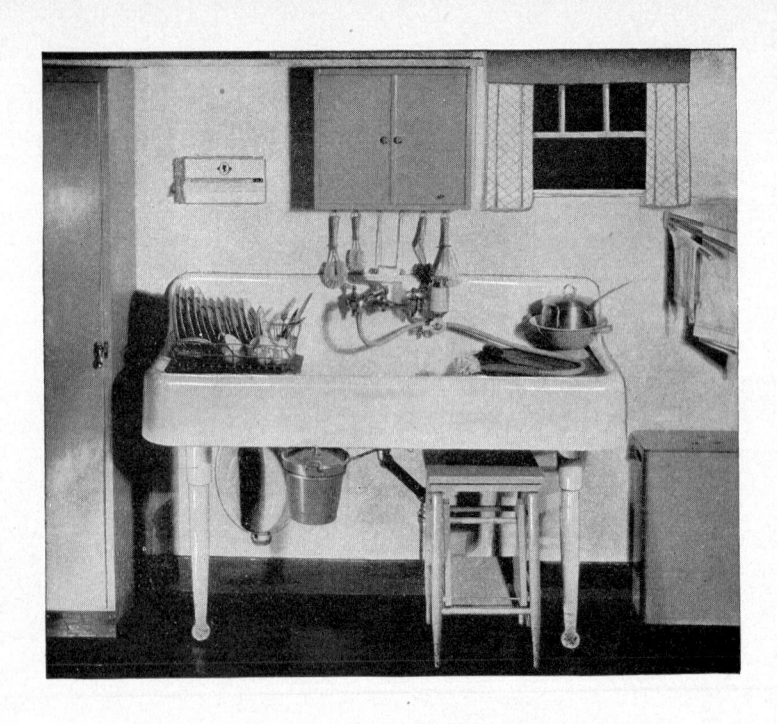

This is the way your KITCHEN SINK should look—

Right above the sink, there's a small but adequate cabinet for your scouring powders, and cleaning compounds, with a rack for brushes. At the left, a box of easily accessible paper towels. Under the sink, a kitchen catch-all swung at a convenient height to avoid back-bending. And a step-ladder stool without which no kitchen is complete. And last, but not least, the dish washer attached to the faucet, ready for work.

Nowadays, almost every KITCHEN has space for a cosy BREAKFAST CORNER

It saves steps, it can be made a very attractive spot, and it saves wear and tear on your dining-room. This Colonial type of furniture is effective and can be kept clean easily. On the table, is everything you need to make breakfast; waffle iron, a toaster, a special glass coffee maker; all electric of course, and on the corner chest, a sandwich toaster, for night raids on the kitchen, or for after-school rations.

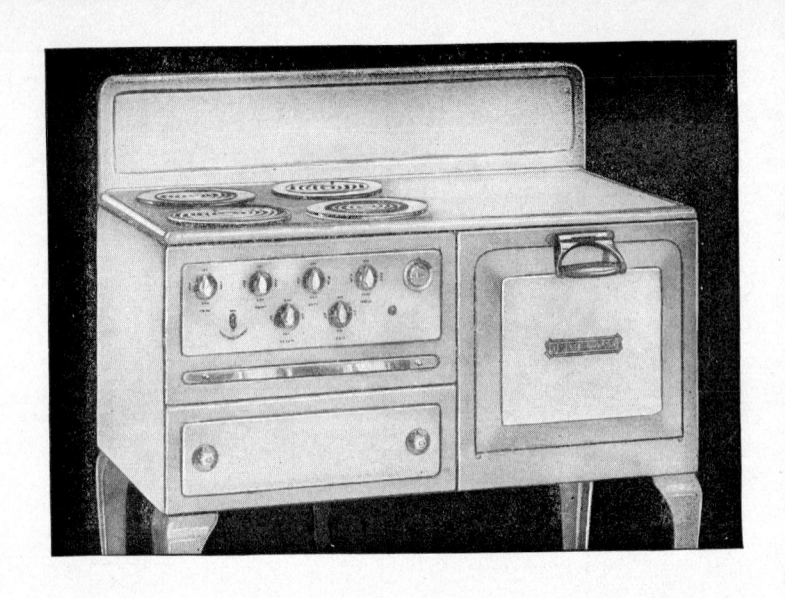

ELECTRICITY is the housewife's staunch ALLY
—in these, for instance

Above:—The new version of the stove. An electric range with automatic operation and various clock controls which make it almost human.

Left:—The mixer-beater-juice extractor that seems magical in its efficient performance, will simplify a dozen household duties. It whips cream, mixes cake, smoothes out cereals, extracts fruit juices, mixes soft drinks with no fuss and very little bother.

REFRIGERATOR DISHES

for Orderliness

Refrigerator dishes conserve space—and keep the flavors of foods from mixing. They may be had in plain and tinted glass and in white enamel. There are also useful wire baskets for eggs and fruits.

A table-top stove is a new idea, and it certainly is convenient. It provides you with a nice big, flat working surface whenever the stove is not in use. Lots of drawer space in this model, too.

These MODERN STOVES

make cooking a pleasure

This is a console stove—it also provides a flat working surface, but the oven is placed higher than in the table model, so that you have two levels.

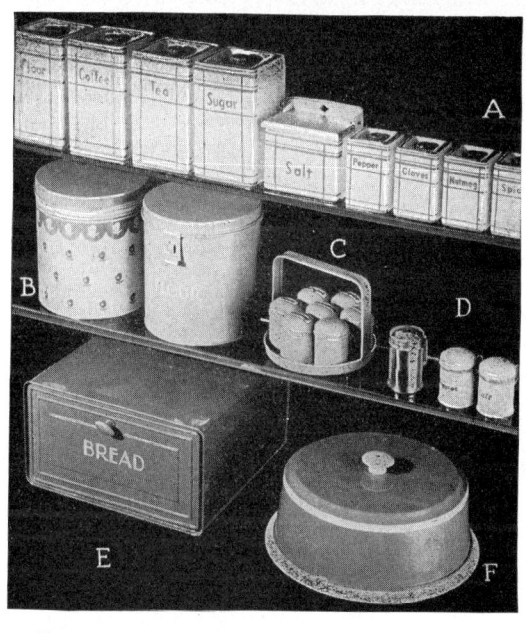

Keep your KITCHEN compact and colorful

Storage space is always at a premium, however large the kitchen. So that these containers serve a very useful purpose in addition to being decorative.

A—Is a typical cereal set of pottery with colored stripings and clearly lettered names.

B—Canisters like this come in various sizes for tea, coffee, sugar, flour, and the amusing flower pattern is effective in an otherwise simple kitchen. Next to it is a pastel solid-color one for conservative tastes.

C—Here's a handy little tray with tiny canisters for all your spices, in pretty painted tin.

D—Single individual salt and pepper and spice container can be had in painted tin or in shining aluminum, all legibly marked.

E—You need a good bread-box—perhaps one like this, of enameled tin.

F—This is a cake board and cover—the board of wood, the cover of painted tin with a handle.

Keep your KITCHEN COOL
even on the "dog" days—

A ventilating fan like this one will prove worth its weight in gold, if you have a large family to cook for. Not only in summer, but all year round, it will keep a stream of fresh air circulating to rid the kitchen faster of cooking odors and smoke. It may be had for alternating and direct current, and can be changed from house to house when you move. Even an ordinary oscillating electric fan will do a great deal to keep the air in the kitchen clear and cooler.

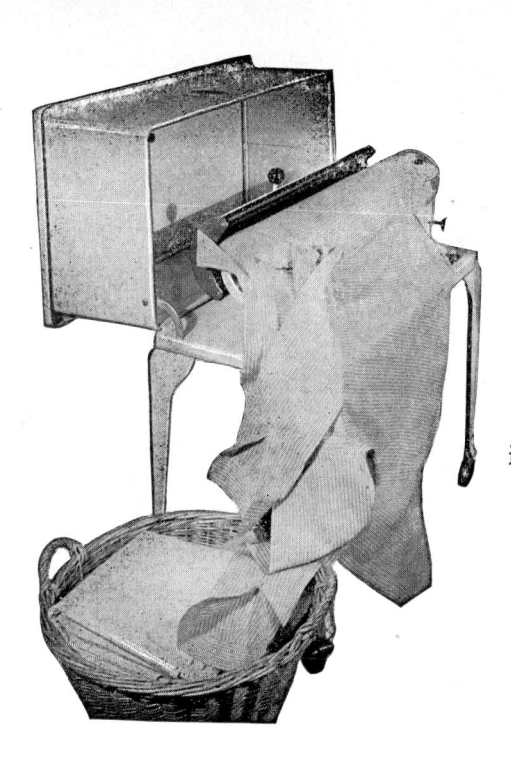

With these MODERN MACHINES "blue Monday" isn't the bugbear it used to be

At the right, the electric washing machine, which in its quiet, quick way does a grand job with the family laundry. All moving parts are completely housed, there's a pump to take the water out, the wringer is easily adjustable.

Above, the electric ironer which is automatically controlled with the knee, leaving your hands free to guide pieces through. Flat pieces go swiftly, and you soon get the knack of finishing more complex articles.

Neat solutions to the REFUSE PROBLEM

Indoors—You'll find a kitchen catch-all attached to the sink, and comfortably high-placed, an excellent addition to your equipment, illustrated A. And, shown B, is an enameled sanitary can with a foot lever. This comes in various kitchen colors, and has a separate galvanized iron insert which can be taken outdoors to be emptied.

Outdoors—Illustrated C—is an ample-size galvanized iron can which is strong and practical, for the back porch. And illustrated D, is the best type of container for the suburbs. It is buried in the ground—only the cover emerging, regulated by a foot lever. This type of can comes in large sizes.

You'll find a rubbish burner practical, too. They are made of heavy sheet steel, and painted.

proved highly efficient in my own tests. There are, however, several other methods of preparing good coffee.

Manufacturers of waffle irons often include in their instructions the statement that it is not necessary to grease the waffle iron or steel plate stove. My own long experience teaches me that one can avoid much trouble from burned or sticking food by light oiling when the iron is new.

Electric waffle irons are now equipped with heat indicators that tell you when to pour in the batter, that is, after the iron is sufficiently pre-heated. This has always been a source of trouble because, if the iron was not just hot enough, the waffle would stick and burn or else would not brown at all. There is also now an automatic feature added that gives you the desired brownness and crispness.

A new table grill that made its appearance recently is a particularly handsome article and has numerous uses. The cooking unit consists of two hinged, shallow plates of very heavy aluminum, oblong in shape with slightly rounded corners. Heat units are in the base and the cover. Sausages or bacon and eggs can be grilled in this dish and an outlet will drain off the grease of their cooking. Small meat cakes can be grilled. The machine is ideal for hot, toasted sandwiches and it could be used for making hot cakes. Because of the two heat units and the heavy, close fitting cover it will operate rapidly and at little cost in power. It has a generous cooking surface.

A toaster for table use that will take bread slices, sandwiches or even half rolls is made in chromium plate. Another refinement in the modern toaster is selective heat. A small trigger with an instruction dial enables you to set the heat for pale, medium or dark toast and the automatic shut-off stops the toasting as soon as the desired color is reached.

More ingenious still is the electric egg cooker. Eggs are among the most nutritious of our foods, but the egg cooked in boiling water, while it loses none of its nutritive values is difficult to digest. The electric cooker cooks eggs in live steam.

If you wish, you can buy the machine with a tray and a service of handsome egg cups. Eggs are placed in a little rack in the device and covered with a dome shaped cover. The machine is plugged into the current. The amount of water poured in determines whether the eggs are to be soft, medium or hard.

Addition of water completes the electric current and cooking starts in five seconds. When all the water in the machine is converted to live steam the electric current is shut off and the eggs are done.

There is a combination toaster and percolator on the market which includes a toaster and a hot plate to heat a percolator or cook any small breakfast dish. The base contains the heat unit and underneath is a drawer type of bread toaster. On top is the plate at the summit of a truncated pyramid, over which the percolator fits.

When you buy electric table stoves and devices it is well worth considering how many uses they can be adapted to. As a cook of many years experience I have found one small single plate table stove and one electric percolator a good elemental equipment. Add to this a waffle iron, an egg cooker and substitute one of the stoves which combines the functions of a toaster and grill and the average woman with a small family would have equipment enough to save her a great deal of work and add immeasurably to the pleasure and digestibility of meals. If you wish to carry the electric idea still further, add to the above one of the chafing dish type of electric cookers. For Sunday night suppers and for evening refreshments one of these or an electric waffle iron is splendid.

All small electric stoves are not meant to come to the table. There is, for instance, a very handy kitchenette electric grill that will handle all the cooking except baking. Its toasting drawer takes eight slices of bread at one time. On the open plates one can percolate coffee, broil a steak or fry or boil anything wanted. The stove includes a seamless alumi-

KITCHEN CONVENIENCES

num pan, a wire toasting rack and an aluminum griddle.

A more elaborate and highly useful type of small electric stove is a portable affair with a handle like a pail. This electric cooker can be used as a stove or a refrigerator if ice is added. A meal can be cooked in it and the whole device can be carried on a picnic where it will serve the foods piping hot miles from the light socket that is the only necessary connection to start it going. The cooking space is large enough and so ingeniously fitted with the proper pans that the cooker will prepare a 4½ pound roast, eight potatoes and 2 separate quarts of vegetables at the same time. A large chicken or joint of meat can be roasted in it. The equipment included in the outfit consists of 3 extra heavy aluminum pans adapted to many uses. The cooker has a selection of 2 degrees of heat. A broiling and frying attachment has been added to this cooker. The attachment is an open coil burner that can be fitted, hot side down, into the top of the cooker so that meat will receive heat from both sides at once. If you wish, the broiling device can be used hot side up as a separate electric plate, that will heat a percolator or serve any of the purposes of the top burner of a range.

When considering the uses of electricity in housekeeping do not fail to investigate the kitchen utility motor-driven mixer of which there are several brands that can be highly recommended. These motor-driven machines can be bought for a moderate price; their maintenance cost is extremely low. Any woman who has whipped cream, mashed potatoes or beaten up one of the cake or pudding recipes that demand muscular labor will bless a machine of this sort. The motors are light and easily carried about. They can be detached from their standard if you wish and used for mixing or beating or mashing over any dish or pan. On the standard they will mix up drinks, handle cake batter to perfection, mash potatoes, beat up delicate whips and puddings or muffin and various bread batters, make a meat loaf or extract the juices from oranges, grapefruit, etc. The various units of the machine are easily separated and easy to keep clean.

The sturdy electric motor needs no attention between long periods of time and the manufacturers maintain a helpful service which takes care of the few replacements necessary.

Before I leave the subject of household electrical helps let me add that if you have a baby in the house, better get one of the electric bottle warmers which cost very little and which do a lot toward eliminating that most difficult and annoying little task in the wan, dark hours when we would like to slumber.

All of the electric aids mentioned in this chapter can be found in the housefurnishing department of your favorite store. Their prices are remarkably low and their cost of use is low, too. Housekeepers with a very moderate budget can afford to make them part of the kitchen and table equipment and their ingenuity will eliminate a hundred tiring and difficult tasks of the day.

CHAPTER VII

CASSEROLES AND OVEN BAKING DISHES

Cooking of meals in the oven, using the special baking dishes designed to be brought to the table has several marked advantages. It is economical, since various items of a menu can be cooked at one time, saving gas or power. The vitamins of oven cooked foods are conserved best because little water is needed for oven cooking. Food is served in the same dish in which it is cooked and extra dish washing avoided.

Casseroles and heat proof oven dishes are made of glass, china, clay and metal. There is a great variety in size and design but it may be said of all the stocks carried by the modern housefurnishing stores that in color and design they are thoroughly delightful. You may have dishes of colored clay; fragile decorated china which it is hard to believe will withstand baking temperatures but does; transparent or colored glass or aluminum or similar metals. In size they range from the dish big enough to bake a chicken down to the little individual ramekins that hold about a quarter cupful. In all of them food may be baked and brought to the table in its original container.

When you buy casseroles there are a few important things to remember. Most important is the size of your oven. These dishes are intended only for oven use and most ovens are apt to waste more space up and down. For the small oven the narrow, deep dish saves the most space and heat. A number of these can be set in at one baking.

Oven dishes should have a flat, solid base and handles which are firm and dependable.

They should be well balanced so they can be moved about if necessary with the least inconvenience.

The surfaces should be smooth, nonabsorbent and easy to clean.

Covers must fit securely.

A last consideration is the variety of uses the individual dish may be put to.

There is a special chapter in this book devoted to casserole cooking which gives menus for dishes and even entire meals prepared in this way. There is very little, in fact, which cannot be prepared in oven baking dishes and the added flavor and nourishment of this kind of cookery is its greatest recommendation. A list of the possibilities must include soups, stews, soufflés, puddings, baked eggs, scalloped eggs, all the vegetables and meats, fruits, fish, macaroni and spaghetti, au gratin dishes, custards and fruit puddings.

Generally speaking, the wide, shallow oven baking dish is best adapted to macaroni and cheese, au gratin vegetables and similar recipes. The bean pot and the bean pot type is excellent for soups, fowl cooked with vegetables and stews. The little ramekin is one of the most charming of the whole list and splendid for serving individual portions of creamed mixtures, individual puddings, custards, eggs, etc.

Manufacturers have designed many of these dishes for several uses that should make them appeal particularly to the housekeeper whose purse is slender or shelf space scarce. For instance, a glass casserole has a deep, flat cover which can be used as a tile to set the dish on later, or can be turned upside down and used as a separate dish for some au gratin

CASSEROLES, OVEN BAKING DISHES

recipes. The aluminum casseroles are fitted with sturdy handles of a heat proof composition. Some have separate bases to protect the table which are also useful as trays. Confronted by the bewildering charm of so many designs and such variety in decoration, the shopper should remember always that these are oven dishes, meant to be used in the confined space of the usual range oven and let that consideration determine her choice.

There are a few things to remember in the use of oven baking dishes made of glass which will avoid disappointment and trouble. No manufacturer of these dishes guarantees them against use over an open flame. They are intended only for the oven.

Dishes of this sort should be handled when hot with a dry cloth, never a wet or damp one. They should never be set on a cold or wet surface when hot or transferred when hot to the ice box or from the ice box to the stove. The same is true of clay or china dishes.

Before the food is placed in any casserole for baking the dish should be brushed with oil or melted butter to prevent sticking.

When food sticks to your casserole fill the dish with warm water and add a dash of soap powder or flake and soak well. Aluminum has a tendency to discolor from boiling of water or from foods containing iron or alkali. So long as the dish is washed clean with hot water and soap it is safe to use, no matter how discolored. The coloration does no harm, but housekeepers like to keep these dishes bright. For this purpose any cleanser that does not injure the hands will serve to bring back the brightness. Sal soda, caustic soda, potash lye and ammonia discolor aluminum and should never be used either plain or in manufactured products to polish such ware.

A little understanding and care will make your shelf of casseroles and ramekins one of the most useful and pleasing units of your kitchen equipment.

CHAPTER VIII

ROASTERS AND BROILERS

The old-fashioned iron roasting pan was useful for its purpose, but it is not adapted to some of the oven uses of the newer covered roasters made to use in the oven or on top of the stove. The old-fashioned pan was a space waster for one thing and oven space should be utilized as fully as possible to keep down cooking costs. Nor could the old open pan be used for water cooking or baking fish.

The most useful type of roasting pan is one fitted with a flat topped cover. It should have convenient heat proof handles and the cover should have a vent for the escape of steam.

Glassware roasting dishes are easy to keep clean and retain heat for a long time. When hot they should be handled with a dry cloth only. Cold water cannot be poured into them while hot nor should they ever be set on a wet or cold surface or transferred to the refrigerator until cooled off.

An oblong shaped metal ware roaster with rounded corners and a flat top is excellent. Some come equipped with a built-in thermometer in the cover. An enamel ware roaster of oval shape has a removable perforated tray that stands off the bottom so that water can be put underneath and meats cooked by steaming as well as roasting.

A heavy oval aluminum roaster can be used in the oven or over an open flame. One model contains a movable tray on which the roast is set. This allows the juices to drain off the meat, insuring dry cooking. It is also a great convenience for cooking fish.

A meat thermometer is a handy little accessory for roasting. It is designed so it can be thrust deep into the roast, insuring accurate cooking.

Modern gas and electric ranges are equipped with built-in broilers but there are times when a separate broiler to be used under an open flame is a convenience.

Before you buy any roaster or other dish for oven use make sure by measuring the interior of your own oven that it will fit there.

CHAPTER IX

AN INVENTORY OF KITCHEN FURNISHINGS

My favorite department store has devoted a section of shelves to complete inventories of kitchen furnishings. Each complete outfit of kitchen equipment has been priced as a whole and it is quite simple to see at a glance just how far your money will go.

While there is bound to be some variation in prices of such articles in different parts of the United States, due to freight charges and cost of handling, I believe the two kitchen inventories given here are fairly accurate as to cost.

These lists cover just about everything a person would need in the kitchen aside from stove, icebox and the electrical and ingenious mechanical helpers mentioned in other chapters.

Kitchen Equipment for Small Apartment

Cost from $25 to $115 (Items marked with asterisk not included in $25 Kitchen).

Sauce pan with cover, 2 qt.
Sauce pan with cover, 4 qt.
Sauce pot with cover, 6 qt.*
Lip sauce pan, 1½ qt.
Lip sauce pan, 1 qt.*
Roasting pan *
Large fry pan
Small fry pan
Double boiler, 1 qt.
Coffee percolator, 6 cups
Colander
2 Gem pans, 6 each

Pie pan
Oblong utility pan
Cake cooler *
Mold for gelatine jelly *
Casserole
4 Ramekins *
Teapot *
Nest of bowls
3 Ice box containers *
Covered pitcher *
2 Cup measures
Large basting spoon

Paring knife
Bread knife
Slicing knife
Fork
Spatula
Broad spatula cake turner
Can opener
Knife sharpener *
Apple corer *
Corkscrew and bottle opener
Bread board
Set wooden spoons
Rolling pin
2 Butter paddles
Bread box
4 Storage canisters
Pastry brush *
Percolator brush *
Circular utility brush
Dish mop *

2 Dish cloths
2 Pot holders
Measuring spoons
Egg beater
Grater
Potato ricer
Biscuit cutter
Flour sifter
2 Strainers, assorted sizes
Juice extractor
Dough blender *
Towel rack
Wooden sink protector
Rubber drainboard protector
Sink brush *
Sink shovel *
Dish pan
Dish drainer
Sanitary garbage can with foot press

Additional Equipment for More Complete Kitchen
Cost approximately $40 to $110.

Sauce pot with cover, 10 qt.
Teakettle, 4 qt.
Coffee pot, 12 cups
Dutch oven
2 Layer cake pans
Loaf pan
Square cake pan
Tube cake pan
Cookie sheet
Griddle
Food chopper
Chopping bowl
Chopping knife
Deep frying kettle with basket
Extra double boiler
Quart measure
Electric roaster and percolator
Covered mold
Timbale iron

Potato masher
Salt and pepper shakers
Egg slicer
Extra paring knife
Utility knife
Butcher knife
Long handled fork
Ladle
Grapefruit corer
Grapefruit knife
Vegetable scoop
Set of shredders and graters
6 Custard cups
Fat thermometer
Candy thermometer
Egg poacher
Set of sandwich and cookie cutters
Extra pie plate

INVENTORY—KITCHEN FURNISHINGS

Funnel
Kitchen shears
Scales
Clock
Vegetable bin

Waste basket
Ice cream freezer
Ice bag and mallet
Rack for pots and covers

CHAPTER X

AN EMERGENCY SHELF

The emergency shelf is the solution for the inevitable domestic crisis of unexpected company. The modern hostess prides herself on being prepared for any emergency whether it is the dropping in of the casual guest, the late supper when you return from an automobile jaunt or the casual guest your husband brings home for dinner. It gives most men the keenest satisfaction to bring the unexpected guest and the modern hostess, in contrast to the old-fashioned wife of the funny stories, should feel calm and secure in the knowledge that her little shelf will solve the problem. If it is well stocked she is prepared for anything.

Whenever you use a jar from your emergency shelf replace it.

Always keep a plentiful supply of eggs, bacon, parsley, lemons, celery and tomatoes on hand. With a modern refrigerator this is an easy matter. These vegetables form the basis of many emergency dishes.

The shelf should be stocked with mayonnaise, French dressing, pickles, all sorts of plain and stuffed olives, chutney, pickled walnuts, relishes, catsups, pickled watermelon and cantaloupe. There should be jellies, jams and cooking wines. These things will dress up an ordinary meal and make it into a feast.

There should be canned soups and clam bouillon and bouillon cubes; canned chicken, lobster, shrimp, tuna fish, salmon, crab, clams and pickled oysters. These are old standbys and should always be kept on hand.

Antipasto is another useful item since it is complete in itself and makes an interesting first course.

The canned or bottled vegetables and fruit juices are useful in an emergency and form another type of first course. Of course you should have the staple canned vegetables and it is wise to add some of the fancier ones such as artichoke bottoms, tiny ears of corn, pimentos, peas, tiny lima beans, asparagus tips and mushrooms.

Keep cheese on hand and tins of cookies. The canned fruits are indispensable and when chilled in the ice box can be served in compote glasses, offering a delicious sweet course.

For the late supper or luncheon prepared welsh rarebit, chicken à la king, sardines and even buttermilk biscuit all mixed and ready for baking can be had. Ready mixed buttermilk biscuit must be kept in the refrigerator, by the way. These things are a boon to the housewife who would entertain with a minimum of preparation and manufacturers have done their utmost to prepare products that are the equal of those made in your own kitchen. While they cannot hope to equal the best home cooks, their prepared foods are delicious and provide variety.

Shop around. See what's new or what you have forgotten. Looking about the stores is one of the greatest inspirations to a good cook.

SECTION TWO
GOOD MEALS WELL SERVED

CHAPTER XI

MENU MAKING

There have been such great strides made in the science of diet that modern menu making has become a different art from the old-fashioned assembling of meals. Now we know that for the maintenance of health and the happiness which naturally follows, we must include certain foods every day in our meals. They are: Milk, butter, eggs, cereals, raw vegetables as well as cooked ones, fresh fruits or fruit juices beside the meat, starches and fats which are necessary for heat, energy and body building. The vitamin has taken a big place in diet. It provides the minerals or elements that the body must have to maintain life. While foods with a vitamin content do not always provide nourishment they must be included.

Another recent discovery is that the appearance and attractiveness of food play as big a part in the diet as the vitamin. We must want to eat, or have an appetite for the food that is before us, or it is useless. So there is the big reason for the housewife to serve attractive looking dishes that make her family want to eat them. Food forced upon them because they should eat it does them no good. If your family doesn't like some food they should have, fuss it up in some attractive style, add ingredients to it so that they can't resist it and they will have an appetite for it. In other words, the emotions enter into the amount of nourishment we derive from what we eat. What we like nourishes us; what we don't like does not.

There is a certain peace which follows the eating of a well chosen meal. Nothing equals it. A feeling of relaxation and pleasure descends upon every one.

There should be seven different types of food in a well chosen dinner. They are appetizer, liquid, starchy food, green vegetables, meat, fat and sweet.

I have worked out a test to apply to a menu. By using it anybody can easily determine if a menu is correctly proportioned. Each of the seven types of food is allotted a letter from the word VARIETY. When each letter is represented in your menu, the meal will be well balanced and eating it will be a pleasure. If one letter should appear too often in your list, the result is dismal failure. The table on a following page explains my methods.

By way of illustration, I have listed a few of the foods under each class. Notice that each class has its own class letter. All appetizers, for instance, are represented by V; all fats, by the letter T.

In choosing a menu you may test it by applying the letters to it. Each letter in the word VARIETY should be represented in a properly varied menu.

If you are serving a simple dinner, one of each letter should appear. A more elaborate menu calls for two of each letter. Read these menus over. Don't they sound good? Here are two sample menus:

Using 1 item of each group
E   Lamb Chops
R   Mashed Potatoes
I   Spinach
V   Chili Sauce
T-Y Ice Cream
A   Coffee

Using 2 items of each group
A   Clear Soup
E   Steak
T-R Creamed Potatoes
I   Baked Tomatoes
V   Jelly
V-I Salad, French Dressing
E   Cheese and Crackers
T-Y Floating Island
V   Macaroons
A   Coffee

V Appetizers	A Liquids	R Starches	I Green Vegetables	E Meats	T Fats	Y Sweets
Ginger	Coffee	Rice	Lettuce	Fish	Cream	Dessert
Mint	Grape Juice	Potatoes	Spinach	Fowl	Butter	Sugars
Jelly	Grapefruit	Noodles	Celery	Meat	Milk	Etc.
Pickles	Oranges	Breads	Tomatoes	Dried Beans	Gravy	
Chili Sauce	Soup	Crackers	Radishes	Lentils	Ice Cream	
French dressing	Tea	Etc.	Cucumbers	Cheese	Cream sauces	
Etc.	Etc.		Etc	Eggs	Etc	
				Etc.		

Some foods are a combination of 2 types, as ice cream, which is both a fat and a sweet.

Here is a sample of bad menu making:

R-T Potato Soup   R   Bread
R   Rice   R-Y Cornstarch Pudding
E   White Fish

This selection is practically all starch. Aside from being unhealthy to eat, it is uninviting in appearance. Everything is of the same uninteresting color. I can imagine nothing more dismal than eating this meal, especially if it were served on a white table cloth! The gloom and depression sure to follow would be ghastly.

In addition to variety in the combination of foods, one must have a variety of color. To make a meal appetizing, try to think how the meal will look on the table. Use bright china, glass, linens, besides a variety of color in the food itself.

Referring again to the first two sample menus with proper variety, here is a chart of the colors represented:

Menu No. 1   *Menu No. 2*
Brown   Brown
White   White
Green   Red
Red   Green
Pink   Yellow

Variety and color, these are the ingredients the cook must furnish. They mean more than health. Given the proper companionship at table, they mean happiness. Isn't it a worthwhile profession, that of creating happiness? Certainly there is none more worthy of respect. Every good cook deserves the applause due a great artist.

Don't laugh at the art of cookery. If you treat and think of this art as it deserves, you will inspire others to give it the respect which is its due.

If you form the habit of thinking about menus in this way, cooking becomes an interesting game. And it gives you the satisfaction of feeling that your meals are triumphs.

CHAPTER XII

SERVING MEALS PROPERLY

If you are so fortunate as to have a staff of servants or even one well trained maid, the proper serving of meals is a matter of small worry and this chapter need not concern you. If you have no servant or are in doubt as to the fundamental rules governing table setting and the serving of courses, it may be relied upon as coinciding with the correct usages of American etiquette. There are plenty of clever American wives of today who do not find their lack of a maid a handicap to entertaining their friends, even to giving formal dinners in which every worth while tradition of proper service is followed.

The foundation of all table etiquette is utility and common sense. A knife is placed so and a fork otherwise for the simple reason that these implements are thus most convenient to the hand of the person using them. What might appear at first glance to be complicated and highly formal rules are nothing more than the application of efficiency that is meant to reduce confusion and make the enjoyment of food and socicty possible.

China and Glassware

The home where proper entertaining is done and where the family may enjoy properly served meals requires certain fundamentals in the way of dishes and table implements. The equipment of china would include bread and butter plates, service plates (which are used in the servantless house for the main course), soup plates, double handled bouillon cups, coffee cups and saucers and dessert plates. Glassware must include water glasses, dessert dishes and, if formal dinners are given, finger bowls. Of course there would be in addition the usual platters, covered dishes for hot foods, baskets or plates for breads, compotes, salt and pepper service and a decorative bowl or bowls for floral centerpieces.

It is not necessary that table china should consist of one solid "set." Even in the serving of a formal dinner, the most rigid of our meals so far as etiquette is concerned, it is not a violation of good taste to use plates of different color and pattern for different courses and often this variety in color and pattern is used by clever hostesses to give an added attractiveness to the meal. Brightly colored dishes, colored candles (for a dinner table) and the use of colored glass and blooming flowers help greatly in making the serving of any meal a happy occasion.

Table Silverware

Designers and manufacturers offer a wonderful variety in silverware today. While the solid service which has been handed down from one generation to the next has beauty and charm and the added romance of long association, it can be replaced by any of a large number of excellent patterns in solid silver or silver plate and even the most inexpensive of these have the charm of good design.

In knives the modern hostess must have the main course or meat knife, and the small butter knife or spreader. A small knife for fruit is desirable but not necessary.

Two sizes in forks will take care of the courses of the average menus. The large fork is the sister of the meat knife and its equal in size. A shorter fork is splendidly adapted to salads, desserts and luncheon use. When oysters are served the little oyster fork should be included among these necessities. Of course there is the salad fork with a cutting edge if you wish it.

Spoons should include the serving spoon also proper as a soup spoon when soup is served in a bowl; the tea spoon and the little after dinner coffee spoon.

Table Linen

Good taste dictates a "bare" table for breakfasts and luncheons. Doilies are put under plates and for luncheon a pretty runner or lunch cloth with matching or contrasting napkins is correct. The variety in these is endless, and color and gay patterns are permissible. It is only the formal dinner which requires the all-covering cloth whose folds reach almost to the floor and white damask or ecru damask or faintly tinted damask with drawn work cloths or embroidered cloths are recommended.

Correct Table Setting

Each place or cover at the table is a complete unit in itself governed by the simple rule of "Knife to the right, forks to the left." Its center is, of course, the service plate which is the plate discovered at place for any of the three formal meals of the day. Since one uses forks with the left hand and knives with the right, the reason for the rule is apparent. But there is one fork used with the right hand, that is the small, useful oyster fork that picks oysters from their shells and when that is to be used it must appear with the knives at the right of the plate.*

Spoons also being a right-handed tool, appear at the right. The glass of water appears at the right at the tip of the knife where it can be reached most easily.

The order for placing forks and spoons never varies. The tool used first is placed at the outside of the row. Thus if

---

* It is etiquette to change the fork from left hand to right whenever more convenient. This modification is peculiar to America.

a dinner included a soup, fish course, roast, salad, dessert and fruit the arrangement would be as follows:

Center, the service plate. To the right of the service plate, on the extreme outside, the soup spoon, next and nearer the plate, fish knife; next to that the main course knife and should the salad require a knife, next to the plate the salad knife. (The use of a knife to cut salad when necessary is good form.) To the left of the plate the outermost fork would be the fork for fish, preferably one of the shorter, luncheon fork kind; next to that the main course fork and next to that the salad fork.

The spoon or fork necessary for dessert course does not appear when the table is set, but arrives with the dessert on the individual plate and the fruit knife appears last of all on the small individual fruit plate.

It is on this last plate that the finger bowl makes its appearance, set on a thin doily. Each guest removes the bowl and doily for himself and uses his plate for the fruit or dessert.

Exactly the same rule governs table setting for breakfast or luncheon. What tools are necessary to a course are set to right or left of the service plate with the implements wanted first on the extreme outside.

When the table is set and ready for guests the service plate and implements for all but the dessert course are in order at each cover. The water glasses are just filled. In the center is whatever arrangement of flowers or decorative china or fruit the hostess has chosen. And on each service plate is the individual napkin, the large napkin for dinner, the smaller ones for breakfast or luncheon. While the etiquette of proper service demands that the napkin should appear neatly folded on this plate when the table is set, common sense has altered this in the house without servants, because it is convenient that the first course should be set on the service plate before guests are seated. In this case the napkin is placed to the left of the forks. When these rules have been observed a table is correctly set and the hostess need not fear comparison with the smartest household in the land. Then, if the meal be a dinner, the candles may be lighted. Candles are only used for dinners never for luncheons and naturally not for breakfasts.

When there is a maid to pass the courses she should serve each individual from his left. It follows as a simple and easy modification of this rule in the servantless house that such dishes as are passed, breads, vegetables, etc., be handed from right to left. In such an establishment it is simplest to have the first course of the meal, fruit cocktail, salad, soup or hors d'œuvres ready on the service plate when guests are seated. When the first plates are removed the service plate is ready for the meat course or main course that follows. In such a household the host usually carves and always serves. If the man of the house dislikes carving or is not a proficient carver of roasts it is convenient to carve a roast in the kitchen, but place it together again so that it appears as a handsome entity. It avoids much confusion of passing plates if the host not only carves, but serves on the plates such vegetables as the meal includes excepting only wet vegetables that must be served in small, individual dishes.

The woman who entertains without a servant often uses a member of her own family or a friend to assist her in removing plates after a course. Many such a hostess has found cause to bless the useful tea wagon which may be left by her own place. Its top tray may hold salad and even dessert courses and its lower trays accept the soiled plates as they are changed.

In Section Three of this book, under the chapters dealing with Platter and Plate Dinners a number of very useful labor and confusion saving hints will be found.

CHAPTER XIII

TABLE DECORATIONS

There are such numberless ways to decorate the modern dinner table the housewife need never be at a loss for variety.

The combination of colored table linen and colored glassware is often so pleasing that no other decoration is necessary. If in addition to this you consider the color combinations of the food served in connection with the scheme of the table decoration the result will lend distinction to your dinner table.

Keep an assortment of different colored candles on hand. They are inexpensive and vary the monotony of your decorations.

Red and white checked linen table runners, blue glasses and yellow candles make a gay looking table. A yellow linen damask cloth with red glasses and apple green candles is another interesting combination. Rose colored runners, pale green glasses and lavender candles make a pleasing color scheme. Plum colored glasses on a green cloth in combination with yellow candles and a bowl of daffodils is a delightful arrangement.

The usual arrangement of fruits for a centerpiece which is such a decorative one may be varied. A single rich red pomegranate on a small dull blue pottery plate is beautiful. Two or three orange colored persimmons on a rich dark green plate might be used. Pale green clusters of grapes on a chinese red lacquer tray; orange tangerines in a pale yellow bowl; purple grapes on a pewter plate are highly decorative arrangements.

An unusually beautiful centerpiece is made with the gay colored balls used for decorating a Christmas tree in combination with a unit of Christmas tree lights. The balls are piled in the center of a large round dish or tray. The lights arranged as a border. Ivy or any dark green foliage is used to cover the cord so that only the colored lights are visible.

Small Dresden figures grouped on a tray holding a bowl of flowers makes an attractive center for a table. One of the amusing modern figures in glazed china may be used alone with good effect.

A Japanese water garden may be constructed with little labor. A low copper, brass or pottery dish is used. The bridges, pagodas and small Japanese figures are purchased at a store where Japanese goods are sold. A horseradish root is cut into pieces. The dish is filled with water, the garden furniture arranged and the horseradish root set in place. Dark green leaves grow rapidly from the root and the garden is complete.

SECTION THREE

COOKING

CHAPTER XIV

COOKING FOR THE BUSY WOMAN

The average woman is the busy woman nowadays.
If her day is taken up by other matters than those pertaining to her house, she may dine at a restaurant or eat food purchased at the delicatessen. These methods pall in time.

The purpose of this chapter is to present menus that may be prepared in from fifteen to thirty minutes.

It is meant to show the busy woman how she may come home, purchase materials for a meal and in a short time sit down to an appetizing dinner that has not taken hours to make ready.

The menus have been chosen with an eye to their color variety, which is important because of its psychological effect.

They contain the proper proportions of fats, starches, proteins, roughage, etc.

The quantities given are meant to serve two rather hungry people. Adding to the quantities should not add to the time needed for preparing or cooking.

These menus all have been prepared in the writer's kitchenette on a three-burner gas stove with an attached oven and a broiler. Electrical stoves are a convenience for using at the table.

The modern woman's time may be spent more profitably than in hours of pot-watching.

The writer has spent from six minutes to six hours in preparing a dish, and the one needing the shorter time was the more successful. At least, those at the table seemed to enjoy it more. The cook certainly did because she was not wearied by cooking.

One of the pleasantest dinners I remember was one given by two artists who were very busy women.

It was cooked on a small electric grill. The kitchenette was made from two trunks, piled one on the other, and concealed by a gorgeous gold screen which had been evolved from a burlap screen covered with gold paper.

That dinner included:

Grapefruit	Bananas Sauté with Cream
Lamb Chops, Broiled	Bread and Butter
Creamed Potatoes	Coffee
Combination Salad	

It included also, as a delicious sauce with every course, a great deal of lively conversation about art, books and people; the companionship of cooks who were not tired.

Because the menus in this section can be prepared rapidly, it does not follow that they should be eaten rapidly. They should be lingered over as all good meals deserve to be.

In an old cook book in my collection is a recipe that has never failed to arrest my attention. It is entitled, "A Good Cake" and includes the following instructions:

Ten Eggs	One Cup of Flour
One Cup of Sugar	Beat ONE Hour

People are always sighing for the good old days. I wonder!

I have always cooked ever since I used to beg my grandmother for a piece of dough to make biscuits with. And in the beginning of my culinary attempts nothing was too complicated for me to tackle. I courted difficulties, and time was nothing. But I have yet to try "A Good Cake."

In the left-hand column, under the menu, is a list for shopping. This does not mention such staples as flour, seasoning, etc., which, it is assumed, are in any woman's kitchen.

To the right of the shopping list is an enumeration of the utensils and seasonings and staples which should be assembled conveniently on the kitchen table before the cook starts preparing the food. If the reader will take the trouble to follow this list I am sure that anywhere from five to ten minutes usually spent in hunting for things in a hurry may be saved.

The writer also has tried to arrange the actual cooking directions in their chronological order. In her mind's eye she has seen the cook spreading out this book on her kitchen table and following out its paragraphs step by step. In this, too, the hope was to save a few minutes for the busy woman.

The reader may disagree with the author concerning the actual length of time it needs to prepare some of the meals described. The author can answer only that she has prepared every meal listed in somewhat less than the time allotted; but she realizes that varying degrees of experience and skill will vary the speed of the performance.

Of one thing the reader may be sure: The actual cooking time given for various dishes is correct for a gas range and may be relied upon implicitly.

Do not think that because these dinners are prepared rapidly the table should reflect it in any way.

The simpler the meal, the gayer the table should be. There should be an air of festivity about every meal.

Variety of color both in the table decorations and in food are indispensable. They aid digestion and avoid monotony. For instance, a dinner where the table was set with a white cloth and consisted of Potato Soup, Rice, White Fish, Corn, and Cornstarch pudding would be indigestible and unpleasant.

Bright colors and happy surroundings are worth any number of bottles of medicine. They are a real tonic that aids digestion and makes every meal what it should be, a recreation.

Colored linens, bright china, candlesticks and candles and flowers are inexpensive and add immeasurably to the looks of the table. Whole fruits arranged on a gay dish, grapefruit, jellies and green vegetables may be used to advantage with no extra trouble. The use of a few of these things at each meal lends a party atmosphere to the simplest dinner.

Mistakes Common in Cooking

So many people do not know the reason for their failures in cookery. Of course there is usually an answer in chemistry, but you do not need to know chemistry. A few rules and reasons will be sufficient to correct your errors.

Cakes: A light cake of even texture and height is the one desired by cooks and achieved by the expert cake baker. The reason for a cake that is uneven in height or that humps up in the middle is too hot an oven when the cake begins to bake. The batter has had no chance to rise before the cake browns. The sides bake too quickly in too hot an oven, becoming solid. The gasses which cause the cake to rise have nowhere to go, so if the cake is browned before it bakes in the interior, these gasses will cause a hump and often break the crust as a means of escape. This is particularly inconvenient in a layer cake. Some cooks put a cake in a cold oven. The gradual warmth causes the even raising of the cake. As the heat increases it bakes and in the end, browns.

Too much flour is another cause of humping and cracking in the center of a cake. This cause also is to blame for a coarse grained cake that will soon dry because of lack of moisture.

Too much fat or too little flour will make a cake fall.

A cake in which the ingredients are not well blended will be heavy and coarse grained. That is why you should cream the butter and sugar thoroughly, beating the cake vigorously as the ingredients are added in order to blend all of them.

Pie Crust: A light, flaky pie crust is the mark to aim for. Too much water makes pie crust tough. Use just enough liquid to barely hold the dough together. Too slow an oven causes a heavy, tough crust. For the first 10 minutes baking the oven should be very hot (450°-500° F.).

Lightness in handling after the flour and shortening have been blended is essential. Also thoroughly chilled ingredients. If the finished dough is allowed to chill in the refrigerator before rolling, the action of the oven heat is more effective on it and makes a lighter crust.

Custards: The secret of smooth baked custard is a moderate heat in cooking. If the custard is cooked in the oven, the dish it is cooked in should be placed in hot water that is under boiling. Egg recipes should never be cooked at an intense heat because the eggs will coagulate before becoming blended with the other ingredients. The correct temperature for baking custards is 325° F. Too intense heat or over-cooking is the cause of watery custard. Custard should be watched and removed from the oven just as soon as it is done. To test this, insert a silver knife in the center of the custard. As soon as the knife comes out clean the custard is finished.

Boiled Custards: When the custard is not smooth and there are bits of egg through it, it is because the egg was added to the milk when it was too hot. Always cook custard in a double boiler. Heat the milk and add the hot milk a tablespoonful at a time to the egg and sugar beaten together. Beat the mixture between each addition. After adding ½ cup of milk to the egg and sugar add it to the milk in the double boiler and keep the water in the double boiler under boiling point. Stir constantly until smooth and clear. Beating with a rotary beater while custard is cooking helps to blend and keep the mixture smooth.

Cream Sauce or Gravy: A cooked mixture including fat, flour and liquid should have an equal proportion of flour and fat. Too much fat makes the liquid and flour separate. Too much flour makes a thick, opaque mass. In making gravy pour off the excess fat and add an equal amount of flour. Two tablespoons of fat, 2 tablespoons of flour and 1 cup of cold water or milk is the proper proportion for gravy or thin cream sauce. A larger proportion of fat and flour is used to make thick cream sauce. Three tablespoons of flour, 3 tablespoons of butter and 1 cup of milk cooked in the double boiler is the recipe.

Welsh Rarebit: If Welsh rarebit separates add 2 well beaten eggs for each pint of rarebit. The rarebit mixture should have been cooked in the double boiler and the eggs are added to the hot liquid. Beat vigorously with the heat turned off. The hot liquid will cook the eggs.

Frozen Desserts in the Mechanical Refrigerator: The reason for grainy, hard desserts that are frozen in a mechanical refrigerator is that they are prepared without stirring. Stirring while they freeze makes all of these desserts smoother and lighter in texture. The simplest way to do this is remove the pan from the refrigerator and stir the mixture from the back toward the front. Freezing begins at the back. Repeat this process three times at half hour intervals. After this allow the dessert to become firm. Stir for the first time as the dessert just begins to freeze, usually about half an hour after it is put in the refrigerator. Desserts made this way should have less sugar than ordinary frozen desserts. Too much sugar or flavoring prevents them from freezing properly. An excess of these ingredients prevents rapid freezing. It is rapid freezing that makes a smooth product. Do not freeze ice cubes when freezing desserts.

Before putting a mixture in the freezing trays, chill it thoroughly. Gelatine is added to keep it smooth, prevent it from getting icy and to keep it from melting too fast when served.

Whipped cream and whipped egg whites are added to make a thicker mixture. This reduces time needed for freezing and makes a smooth dessert.

Too long freezing makes a hard, icy product.

Ices should be frozen for a shorter period of time than ice creams, parfaits or mousses to prevent granulation.

Fruits or desserts with fruits in them should be removed before the fruit becomes icy and hard.

Candy and Frosting: Both candy and frostings which have a sugar syrup base are subject to the same mishaps. The finished product in either case should be smooth and creamy. When they are granulated or sugared the chef has failed.

The sugar, water and cream of tartar should be thoroughly dissolved before the mixture reaches the boiling point. After it boils do not stir it, or even move the saucepan in which it is cooking. This causes granulation. Just the right amount of cream of tartar is necessary. Too much will prevent the mixture from becoming creamy when stirred. It will be of a runny or too liquid consistency. Too little cream of tartar causes frosting or candy to be sugary.

Meringues: There are two methods of making meringues. Each is equally successful, but the finished product is slightly different in texture. Try each and choose which you prefer, or alternate them for variety.

For either method the egg whites should be beaten very stiff. For each stiffly beaten egg white add 2 tablespoons of granulated sugar. Add the sugar gradually, beating between each addition.

The difference in method is in the baking. One style meringue is piled on the dessert and baked in a very hot oven (500° F.) for 3 minutes, or until a delicate brown. Watch it constantly.

The other meringue is placed on the dessert and baked from 15 to 25 minutes in a moderate oven, (325 ° F.).

Omelettes: Whether you beat the eggs separately or together the success of an omelette depends on the cooking. A light, fluffy omelette should be cooked quickly and served immediately. The successful omelette requires the cook's undivided attention when cooking.

Heat the fat in the pan until it is a bubbling, light brown.

Turn in the mixed omelette. It should begin to brown instantly. Lift the edges with a spatula and let the uncooked liquid from the top run under. Repeat this until all the liquid is cooked.

Too long cooking makes an omelette dry and leathery.

When the omelette is finished the outside should be a delicate brown, the inside should be creamy. Then fold it once and turn onto a hot dish.

Mayonnaise: Mayonnaise should be thick and smooth, the ingredients thoroughly blended. If the oil separates from the other ingredients it is because it has been added too rapidly when mixing began or because the other ingredients are not thoroughly chilled or because the beating between each addition has not been vigorous enough.

Chilled ingredients, vigorous beating, gradual addition of oil and the thickening of the mayonnaise between each addition of oil is the secret of perfect dressing. The bowl and the beater should be ice cold, like the ingredients. Beat the eggs and seasoning thoroughly. Add the oil in small quantities. Some cooks add it a drop at a time, but a teaspoonful at a time is not too much. Beat between each addition. When the mixture is thick, lemon or vinegar may be added gradually between additions of oil. After the first thickening has been accomplished oil may be added in large amounts, as much as 1/4 cup at a time.

Mechanical mayonnaise mixtures that add oil a drop at a time are a convenience. An electric mixer is excellent because of the vigorous beating it gives.

Mashed Potatoes: Nobody likes gray, lumpy mashed potatoes. Fluffy, white potatoes are achieved by thorough mashing before adding liquid and hard beating after milk has been added. A vegetable press may be used instead of a masher to insure against lumps. Heat the milk and press the hot potatoes into it. Beat until light and fluffy. An electric mixer is excellent to accomplish both processes. The mixer will break up and mash the potatoes, then beat them light after the milk is added.

Baked Potatoes: Potatoes should be baked until thoroughly done. When you remove them from the oven roll the potatoes lightly in a towel to make them mealy. Split the skin on one side to allow steam to escape. Press gently from the bottom, insert a teaspoon of butter. Dust with salt and paprika.

Broiling and Roasting: Any meat, no matter if it is tender or tough may be reduced to a leathery mass by improper treatment at the beginning of cooking. The juices of meat should be kept in by quickly searing and browning the outside. This is done by subjecting the meat to intense heat when cooking begins. It is finished according to the type of meat being cooked. If the meat juices escape only fiber remains, dry, tough and unappetizing.

In broiling place meats close to the flame. Sear on one side quickly. Turn. Sear the other side. Brown all over. Reduce the heat or move farther from the flame and finish cooking. Roasts should be browned in the same way or browned in a very hot oven, (500 to 550° F.). When brown reduce the heat and finish cooking.

Meats for broiling and roasting are from the tender cuts, but this principle of quick searing and browning applies also to the tougher cuts used for pot roasts and stews.

Waffles: Tender, crisp waffles depend largely on the baking. The pre-heating of the iron is all important. If the waffle iron has no heat indicator, heat it for 10 minutes before baking waffles. The indicators on any of the modern electric irons sold in reliable stores can be trusted to tell you when the machine is hot enough for use.

Waffles should begin to brown the minute they strike the iron. They should bake quickly and be brown in from 3 to

5 minutes. Test your iron to find just the length of time this takes. Once you know, don't raise the lid until the waffles are done. Waffles will not stick if the iron is hot enough when the batter is poured in.

Insufficient shortening is another reason for sticking waffles.

When pouring the batter, just fill the sections and smooth until level. This leaves room for the batter to raise. Too much batter makes a thick, moist waffle.

Hot Biscuits: For white, light, tender biscuits sift the dry ingredients and blend them thoroughly with the fat before adding liquid. Light kneading for 15 seconds makes a finely grained biscuit. Too much baking powder makes a coarse grained biscuit with holes through it.

Roll biscuit dough ¾ inch thick. Bake in a hot oven, (450° F.) for 10 to 15 minutes, until brown.

Selection of Meats

In selecting meat it is well for the inexperienced cook to choose a dependable butcher. Question him carefully. He will be glad to instruct you. If you find he has misled you in any way select another one you can depend on.

The tender cuts of meat come from the less muscular part of the animal. The tougher ones have muscle and cartilage that must be broken down. In cooking any meat the surface should be seared quickly to keep in the juices. If the meat is tender the rule is to cook it rapidly. If it is from the tougher portions, sear quickly and thoroughly. Then cook at a low temperature, under boiling point to break down the muscle and cartilage. This slower cooking takes several hours according to the weight of the meat. There is no difference in the nutriment of the tough and tender cuts. Follow the instructions and the time for cooking in this book and you should have no trouble with the tenderness of the finished dish.

The best beef, that which has been well fed, is bright red in color and has yellowish streaks of fat running through it.

In selecting spring lamb the meat should be firm and pale pink, the fat white and flaky. This is the lamb that is a few months old. The flesh of the older lamb is darker in color. When the lamb is a year old the flesh darkens so that mutton becomes a dull red.

Veal is the very young calf, a few weeks old. It is nearly white in color and of a delicate flavor. It requires slow and thorough cooking and should have additional fat added because of the deficiency in the young animal. The flesh of older calves has a deeper color.

The pork of a young animal is almost white. It deepens with the age of the animal, when it becomes light red. Select pork with little excess fat on the edge for there is fat running through the flesh.

Fresh poultry should be yellow. The blue white or darker variety denotes a cold storage product. The breast bone of young poultry is pliable. The older birds have a harder breast bone. Of course, the older birds need longer cooking to make them tender but they are not inferior except in that way. This is true of all meats.

In purchasing meat and computing the cost, take into consideration the amount of cartilage and bone you have paid for. The higher price per pound denotes either a tender cut or one with no excess bone or cartilage which you have paid for and cannot eat.

In buying meat without bone allow ¼ pound to the person. In meats with bone like steak allow ½ pound to the person. A good rule for chops is 2 to each person. In poultry you will need 1¼ pounds per person on account of the weight of the bone.

The amounts needed for serving are given in the recipes in this book. Following them will give you knowledge as to the amounts to purchase.

CHAPTER XV

COURSE DINNERS IN FIFTEEN MINUTES

Ham and Eggs
Tomatoes, Peppers and Onions, Sauté
Bread and Butter
Baked Bananas with Cream
Coffee

Shopping List	Have Ready
Slice of Ham	3 Frying Pans
Four Eggs	Fork
Two Tomatoes	Tablespoon
Three Green Peppers	Knife
Three Onions	Sugar
Half Pint Cream	Butter
Four Small Bananas	Cinnamon
Loaf Bread	Salt
¼ Pound Butter	

Light the gas oven.

Light two gas burners. On one put frying pan with tablespoon of butter. On second burner heat frying pan for the ham.

When the butter in frying pan is hot, peel and slice into it the onions, next the peppers cut small, with the seeds removed, last the tomatoes, cut in dice. When these are hot, cover closely and cook over moderate flame until wanted.

When the frying pan is hot for ham, add 1 tablespoon of butter; brown the slice on both sides. Cook 8 minutes. Dish on to a platter and put into the oven.

Break four eggs into the pan the ham has cooked in and cook until done, about 5 minutes.

Heat the third frying pan and melt in it 1 tablespoon of butter. Peel and halve lengthwise the four bananas. Sauté on both sides. Sprinkle over these 3 tablespoons of sugar and a dusting of cinnamon and let this melt into them. Cooking time, about three minutes. Remove the bananas to the oven to keep hot until wanted for dessert.

Turn off the oven.
Prepare the coffee.
Set the table, 5 minutes.

Melon
Thin Sirloin Steaks
Toasted Rolls
Corn on the Cob
East Indian Chutney
Raspberries and Cream
Cake
Coffee

Shopping List	Have Ready
1 Melon	Frying Pan
1 lb. Sirloin Steak cut thin	Large Saucepan
3 Round Soft Rolls	2 Melon Plates
1 Bottle Chutney	Sharp Knife
Box of Raspberries	Dish for Raspberries
Cake	Tablespoon
½ Pint Cream	Butter
4 Ears of Corn	Opener

Heat water in large saucepan for the corn.
Cut the Melon. Put in refrigerator.
Set the table.
Wash the raspberries and arrange in dish.
Cut the cake.
Split the rolls and toast the soft sides. Butter them,

COURSE DINNERS—FIFTEEN MINUTES

cover and keep warm in oven. (The rolls may be toasted at the table, if you use an electric toaster.)

Husk the corn and drop into the boiling water.

Heat 1 tablespoonful of butter in frying pan for the steak.

Cut the steak into 4 inch squares and flatten them out, so that they are very thin.

Sauté the squares of steak for 5 minutes, turning them often.

Broiled Ground Steak
Potatoes with Onions
Romaine Salad
Ice Cream with Honey
Cake
Coffee

SHOPPING LIST	HAVE READY
1 lb. Ground Steak	Frying Pan
2 Potatoes	Covered Saucepan
1 Small Onion	Salad Plates
Head of Romaine	Tablespoons
Bottle Grated Parmesan Cheese	Butter
Garlic	Salt
1 Pint of Ice Cream	Pepper
Bottled Strained Honey	
Cake	

Put ice cream against the ice.

Heat water for the potatoes and onions in saucepan.

Slice potatoes and onions thin and start boiling.

Light broiler.

Make meat into one big cake and place in frying pan. Broil this under gas flame in oven and turn every 3 minutes. Salt and pepper.

Arrange the romaine on the salad plates.

Set the table, putting on a bowl rubbed with a bit of garlic and containing the dressing for the salad to be mixed at the table. Proportions for the salad dressing are:

Three tablespoons olive oil; 1 tablespoon of vinegar; ½ teaspoon of salt, pepper. Beat until creamy. Dress the salad and sprinkle it with Parmesan cheese.

Drain the potatoes. Add 1 tablespoon of butter, salt and pepper to taste.

Beef
With Vegetables
Poppy Seed Rolls
Mustard Pickles
Cornmeal Dodgers with Maple Syrup
Toasted Angel Cake and Jam
Coffee

SHOPPING LIST	HAVE READY
6 Strips of Bacon	2 Frying Pans
1 Pound Ground Round Steak	1 Saucepan
¼ Pound Mushrooms	Flour
2 Tomatoes	Bay Leaf
1 Onion	Salt
Poppy Seed Rolls	Pepper
Cornmeal	Opener
Mustard Pickles	Sharp Knife
Maple Syrup	Tablespoons
Angel Cake	Butter
Jam	Eggs
	Measuring Cup

Heat on the flame, in the saucepan, 1½ cups of water. Stir in ½ cup cornmeal. When slightly thickened, remove from the fire and add ¼ cup of sifted flour. Beat into this 1 egg.

Brown six strips of bacon. Remove from the pan to a

place where they will keep warm. Pour almost all of the fat into the second frying pan to be used presently for the corn dodgers.

Into the first frying pan, slice the onion. Brown this. Next add the mushrooms, after they have been washed and cut in small pieces. Add tomatoes cut small. Add ground steak and a small bit of bay leaf, salt and pepper. Cook for 8 minutes.

Heat the bacon fat in the second frying pan and add 1 tablespoon of butter. Drop the cornmeal batter, about 1 tablespoon to the cake and brown on each side.

Heat the rolls in the oven.

Start the coffee.

Set the table.

The angel cake either may be toasted on an electric plate at the table or toasted in the gas oven when wanted for dessert. Serve with jam.

Kidneys on Toast
With Poached Egg
Cooked Endive with Cream
Mustard Pickles
Sliced Peaches with Cream   Cake
Coffee

SHOPPING LIST	HAVE READY
6 Lambs' Kidneys	Frying Pan
¼ lb. Endive	2 Saucepans
Mustard Pickles	Dessert Dishes
2 Slices Bacon	Knife
2 Peaches	Butter
Bread	Tablespoon
Cake	Cream
1 Lemon	Flour
2 Eggs	Enamel Pan
1 Orange	Onions
½ Pint Cream	Bay Leaf
Parsley	Measuring Cup

In one of the saucepans heat 1 cup of water.

Wash the endive. Cut in very thin slices across. Add to boiling water and cook until the water is nearly evaporated. Add ½ cup of cream and 1 teaspoon of butter. Do not cook for long after cream is added.

Toast 3 slices of bread, butter them, cut into cubes and cover in a pan. Keep warm in the oven.

Slice the peaches.

Cut the cake.

Set the table.

Make the coffee.

Cut the bacon in squares. Brown in frying pan and add ½ tablespoon of butter, 2 slices of onion and a bit of bay leaf.

Cut the kidneys into small pieces and cook in the frying pan with above mixture until kidneys are seared. Then add 1 tablespoon of flour, stirred into the juices. Add 1½ cup of water, salt and pepper and cook until this is thickened. Add the juice of 1 orange and 1 tablespoon of minced parsley. Cook slowly until wanted.

Heat water for eggs and poach the eggs.

On the serving platter, put squares of toast, next the kidneys and gravy and, on top, the poached eggs.

Slice the lemon, dust the slices with paprika and use them to garnish the platter.

Mushroom Soup
Dried Beef with Scrambled Eggs
Whole Wheat Bread
Sliced Tomatoes
Loganberry Jam with Cream
Frosted Cake
Coffee

COURSE DINNERS—FIFTEEN MINUTES

Shopping List	Have Ready
¼ lb. Mushrooms	Small Saucepan
¼ lb. Dried Beef	Frying Pan
4 Eggs	Bowl
Parsley	Sharp Knife
2 Tomatoes	Opener
Loganberry Jam	Butter
Frosted Cake	Tablespoons
½ Pint Cream	Sherbet Glasses
Whole Wheat Bread	Flour
1 Pint Milk	Measuring Cup
	Salt
	Pepper

Set the table.

Arrange the loganberry jam in the sherbet glasses.

Make the coffee.

Slice the tomatoes and dust them with salt, pepper and minced parsley. These are to be used to surround the beef and eggs.

Melt a tablespoon of butter in the frying pan. Brown the dried beef in butter.

In the bowl, break 4 eggs. Add 4 tablespoons of cream and beat slightly.

Wash the mushrooms. Cut them fine.

In the saucepan heat 1 tablespoon of butter and cook the mushrooms in this for 5 minutes. Do not brown. Sift 1 teaspoon of flour over this. Add 1 cup of thin cream or milk and heat again for serving.

When the soup course is finished, stir the egg mixture into the dried beef and cook, stirring constantly until done; cook about 3 minutes. This may be cooked while the rest of the meal is preparing and kept warm if desired.

Serve the eggs and beef on a platter surrounded by the tomatoes.

Spiced Ham
Noodles with Butter Water Cress Salad
Parker House Rolls Grape Jelly
Orange Compote
Coffee

Shopping List	Have Ready
1 Slice of Cooked Ham, ½ Inch Thick	Frying Pan
1 Package of Noodles	Saucepan
Grape Jelly	Sharp Knife
6 Parker House Rolls	Opener
1 Bunch of Water Cress	Dessert Plates
2 Oranges	Salad Plates
Orange Marmalade	Butter
Preserved Cherries	Brown Sugar
Small Jar of Honey	Cloves
	Salt
	Paprika
	Measuring Cup
	Tablespoon

Heat 4 cups salted water in the saucepan for the noodles.

Heat 1 tablespoon of butter in the frying pan. Add the ham and sprinkle over all 4 tablespoons of brown sugar and ⅛ teaspoon of cloves. Turn often.

Put the noodles into the boiling water. Cook for 10 minutes, drain and dress with butter, salt and a sprinkling of paprika as it is sent to the table.

Peel and slice the oranges. Arrange on dessert plates. Over each portion put 3 tablespoons of honey, 1 tablespoon of orange marmalade and, on top, 1 teaspoon of preserved cherries.

Heat the rolls.

Set the table and start the coffee.

The water cress may be dressed at the table. Things needed for the dressing are:

One bowl with a small piece of ice; 3 tablespoons of olive oil, 1 tablespoon of vinegar and ½ teaspoon of salt. Beat together in the bowl until creamy and thick. Dust top with paprika.

Omelet
With Mushrooms, Celery and Onions
Hot French Rolls   Strawberry Jam
Tomato Salad
Sliced Bananas with Cream   Fruit Cake
Coffee

SHOPPING LIST	HAVE READY
4 Eggs	1 Frying Pan
Celery (Small Stalks)	Tablespoons
¼ Pound Mushrooms	Salad Plates
2 Onions	Dessert Plates
4 Rolls	Sharp Knife
2 Bananas	Opener
Strawberry Jam	Silver Knife for Bananas
2 Tomatoes	Butter
Fruit Cake	Platter
½ Pint of Cream	Bowl

Light the gas oven.

Slice the tomatoes and arrange on salad plates.

Set the table, putting on the vinegar, oil, and a bowl with a small piece of ice to dress the tomatoes at the table.

The proportions for the dressing are:

Three tablespoons of oil to 1 tablespoon of vinegar with ½ teaspoon of salt. Beat until creamy. The bowl may first be rubbed with a piece of garlic cut in half, if you like it.

Heat the rolls.

Make the coffee.

Slice the bananas and cut the cake.

Put two tablespoons of butter into a frying pan to heat.

When hot slice the well-washed vegetables into it, in thin slices. Sauté 5 minutes. Dish on to the platter and put in the oven to keep warm.

Break 4 eggs into a bowl. Add 4 tablespoons of water and beat. Turn into the hot pan. As this browns, lift the edge to let the liquid run under until all is cooked and the bottom a delicate brown. The top should be creamy. This should be made rapidly and watched every minute.

Put 2 tablespoons of the vegetables from the oven between the omelet. Fold and serve immediately on the hot platter, surrounded by the vegetables.

CHAPTER XVI

COURSE DINNERS IN TWENTY MINUTES

English Mutton Chops
Steamed Potatoes
Bread and Butter   Mustard Pickles
Corn and Tomatoes
Ice Cream with Preserved Peaches
Coffee

SHOPPING LIST	HAVE READY
2 Mutton Chops, each cut 2 inches thick	Frying Pan
2 Potatoes	Saucepan
4 Slices Bacon	Sharp Knife
4 Ears of Corn	Tablespoons
4 Tomatoes	Opener
1 Onion	Bay Leaf
1 Pint of Ice Cream	Salt
Preserved Peaches	Paprika
Bread	

Place ice cream against ice in refrigerator until wanted.

Light gas oven.

Sear chops on both sides. They should broil for 20 minutes and be turned often.

Heat 2 cups of water in saucepan for potatoes.

Scrub the potatoes, but do not peel. Cut them in ¼ inch slices. Put slices into boiling water and cover closely. Cook 15 minutes.

Brown 4 slices of bacon. Remove to gas oven and keep warm for serving with the chops.

Slice the tomatoes into the bacon fat.

Cut the corn from the cob. Add to the bacon fat.

Add small piece of bay leaf, ½ teaspoon salt, ¼ teaspoon paprika. Cook until dinner is ready to serve.

Open the preserved peaches.

Set the table.

Make the coffee.

For dessert, serve the ice cream in sherbet glasses, dressed with the preserved peaches.

Melon
Steak with Cream Gravy and Waffles
Boiled Potatoes
Water Cress   Radishes
Olives
Waffles and Maple Syrup
Coffee

Shopping List	Have Ready
1 lb. Sirloin Steak	2 Frying Pans
4 Potatoes	Saucepan with Cover
Water Cress	Teaspoon
Radishes	Measuring Cup
Olives	Tablespoons
Milk	Mixing Bowl
Maple Syrup	Sharp Knife
	Eggs
	Flour
	Pepper and Salt
	Paprika
	Butter

Light gas flame.

Heat water in saucepan for potatoes.

Peel and cut potatoes into dice. Drop them into boiling water.

Melt 2 tablespoons of butter in frying pan. Dust steak with flour. When the butter is sizzling hot, put steak in the pan and turn often.

Heat second frying pan.

When the steak has cooked 7 minutes, remove it from frying pan together with some of the butter and seasoning to the second frying pan to finish cooking.

Into the butter left in the first pan, stir 2 tablespoons of flour. Add 1 pint of milk and cook 10 minutes.

Prepare vegetables.

Set the table.

Make the coffee.

If the waffles are to be made in the kitchen, next heat the waffle iron and make them, placing them in the oven to keep hot. If made at table on an electric iron, the iron should be heated for 10 minutes before they are wanted, unless it has the modern heat indicator.

The recipe for waffles follows:

Sift 1 cup of flour. Add ¾ cup of milk, 2 tablespoons melted butter. Beat in 1 egg. Add 2 teaspoons of baking powder.

Waffles with steak should be served with the cream gravy; and more waffles, with maple syrup, for dessert.

To garnish the steak, cut a lemon in slices and dust with paprika. Surround the steak with water cress and slices of lemon which are also good with the cress.

Flounder with Tartar Sauce
Sauté Tomatoes
Savory Potatoes
Strawberries and Cream
Cake
Coffee

Shopping List	Have Ready
1 lb. filet of Flounder	2 Frying Pans
Parsley	Saucepan
Small Jar Mayonnaise	2 Dessert Plates
Chives	Tablespoons
Bottle of Capers	Poultry Seasoning
2 Tomatoes	Bowl
4 Potatoes	Sharp Knife
1 Lemon	Butter
1 Onion	Flour
Fresh Strawberries	Chopping Bowl
½ Pint Cream	Chopping Knife
Cake	

Heat 1 tablespoon of butter in each frying pan.

Heat water for the potatoes in saucepan.

Sprinkle the flounder with flour, salt and pepper. Brown in the butter.

Slice the tomatoes. Sprinkle with flour, salt and pepper. Sauté them in butter.

Peel a small onion.

Peel 4 potatoes.

Chop potatoes and onion together, add to the boiling water and cook in saucepan.

Prepare Tartar sauce as follows:

Mince chives and parsley.

In the mixing bowl squeeze ½ lemon. Add small bottle of mayonnaise; 1 tablespoon of minced parsley; 1 tablespoon minced chives; 1 tablespoon of capers. Beat together.

Stem the strawberries.

Cut the cake.

Set the table.

Make the coffee.

Drain the potatoes and add to them 1 tablespoon of butter and ¼ teaspoon of poultry seasoning or sage. Salt to taste and heat and serve.

Serve the fish garnished with parsley and sliced lemon.

COURSE DINNERS—TWENTY MINUTES

Creamed Dried Beef
Boiled Potatoes
Jelly   Rolls
Radishes   Young Onions
Sweet Pickles
Cake   Cooked Fresh Apricots
Coffee

Shopping List	Have Ready
¼ lb. Dried Beef	Double Boiler
4 Potatoes	Frying Pans
1 Pint Milk	Saucepan
Parsley	Dish for Vegetables
Jelly	Tablespoons
Rolls	Sharp Knife
Radishes	Flour
Young Onions	Cracked Ice
Sweet Pickles	Salt
1 doz. Small Apricots	Pepper
Cake	1 Egg
	Butter
	Measuring Cup

Light gas flame.

Heat water for potatoes.

Peel and slice potatoes lengthwise in ¼ inch slices. Boil in water.

Make cream sauce in top of double boiler, using 1¼ measuring cup of milk, 2 tablespoons of flour blended with 1 tablespoon of butter. Stir over flame until sauce thickens. Finish cooking over hot water in bottom of double boiler.

Prepare the fresh vegetables and arrange on dish over mound of cracked ice.

Set the table.

Make the coffee.

Heat rolls in oven.

Boil in a saucepan 1 cup of water. When boiling, add the apricots stoned and cut in halves and cook covered for 5 minutes. Then add **1** measuring cup of sugar and cook 3 minutes longer.

In the frying pan, heat **1** tablespoon of butter. Sauté the dried beef until crisp.

Add **1** well beaten egg to the cream sauce.

Serve the beef on platter with cream sauce poured over.

Drain the potatoes and serve.

Onion Soup
Kidneys and Bacon on Toast
Hot French Bread
Cucumbers and Onions
Country Style
Roquefort Cheese
Currant Jelly　　　Crackers
Coffee

SHOPPING LIST	HAVE READY
6 Lambs' Kidneys, split	2 Frying Pans, 1 with cover
1 Cucumber	Measuring Cup
¼ lb. Bacon	Flour
Loaf of French Bread	Vinegar
Loaf of Bread for Toast	Salt
2 Onions	Pepper
½ Pint Cream	Tablespoon
Parmesan Cheese	2 Metal Skewers
Roquefort Cheese	Sharp Knife
Currant Jelly	1 Enamel Pan with cover
Crackers	Bowl
1 Lemon	

Peel the cucumber and onion. Slice thin.

Over these put **1** teaspoon of salt, ½ cup of water, ½ cup of vinegar and **1** teaspoon of sugar.

Set the table.

Make the coffee.

COURSE DINNERS—TWENTY MINUTES

Light the broiler.

Make the soup as follows:

Heat, but do not brown, 3 tablespoons of butter. Peel the onion and mince fine. Cook this in the butter, but do not brown. When tender, stir in 1 teaspoon of flour. Add ½ pint of thin cream and cook until thickened. Serve this with grated Parmesan cheese to be sprinkled over the soup at table.

String the kidneys and bacon alternately on the two metal skewers. (These skewers may be had at any meat market if your kitchen has none.)

Broil the skewered meat in the frying pan under the flame, for 10 minutes, turning often.

Slice the bread for toasting and trim the crusts. Toast the slices brown and butter generously and keep warm in covered pan in the oven until wanted.

Moisten the French loaf under the faucet a few seconds and heat it in the oven.

Serve the kidneys and bacon on toast with the liquid in the frying pan poured over and slices of lemon around them.

Creole Omelet
Orange Marmalade   Hot Rolls
Banana Salad
Steamed Fruit Cake with Maple Sauce
Coffee

SHOPPING LIST	HAVE READY
4 Eggs	2 Frying Pans
2 Green Peppers	Saucepan with Cover
4 Tomatoes	Colander
2 Onions	Small Saucepan
2 Bananas	Salad Plates
Orange Marmalade	Sharp Knife
6 Rolls	Tablespoons
Mayonnaise	Measuring Cup

Shopping List—Con'd	Have Ready—Con'd
Fruit Cake	Spatula
Maple Syrup	Bowl
Confectioners' Sugar	Olive Oil
Lettuce	Paprika
	Salt

Light the gas burner.

Into one frying pan put 2 tablespoons of olive oil. Heat and cut into this the onions, tomatoes and peppers. Add 1 teaspoon of salt and ½ teaspoon of paprika. Cook slowly until wanted for omelet.

Arrange lettuce on salad plates.

Peel and split the bananas, putting 2 halves on each salad plate. Cover tops with mayonnaise.

Heat water in the saucepan for the fruit cake. When it is hot, put the cake in the colander, put the colander over the saucepan and cover all closely, letting the cake steam until wanted for dessert.

Make the sauce for the cake, using ½ cup of maple syrup, ¼ cup of cream and 1 cup of confectioners' sugar and 1 teaspoon of butter. Stir together and put into bowl from which it is to be served. Set this in hot water in the small saucepan. Do not let the water boil.

Set the table.

Light the gas oven.

Heat a platter.

Heat the rolls in the oven.

Make the coffee.

In second frying pan, heat 2 tablespoons of butter. Beat 4 eggs in bowl with 4 tablespoons of water. When the butter in the frying pan is heated to a light brown, turn in the beaten eggs. As they brown, lift the edge with the spatula and let the uncooked part run under. When the omelet is brown underneath and creamy on top, fold once and slip on to a hot platter, surrounding it with the Creole sauce from the first frying pan. Send this to the table at once, as it is spoiled by waiting.

COURSE DINNERS—TWENTY MINUTES

Grapefruit
Lamb Chops Sauté   Creamed Potatoes
Alligator Pear Salad
Preserved Figs with Cream
Vanilla Wafers
Coffee

SHOPPING LIST	HAVE READY
1 lb. of Loin Lamb Chops	Frying Pan with Cover
4 Small Potatoes	Saucepan with Cover
1 Alligator Pear	Double Boiler
1 Grapefruit	Salad Plate
1 Pint of Milk	Salt
Preserved Figs	Pepper
Vanilla Wafers	Paprika
	Mustard
	Vinegar
	Butter
	Flour
	Measuring Cup
	Tablespoon
	Teaspoon

Heat 1 pint of water in a saucepan for the potatoes.

Heat 2 tablespoons of butter in the frying pan.

Remove fat and ends from the lamb chops, leaving small rounds of meat. Dust with salt, pepper and flour. Sauté on each side in the hot butter. Dust more flour over the top and cook covered closely for 15 minutes. Turn occasionally each time dusting a little flour on the top. This is to keep the juice in the chops. They should cook with the flame turned half on.

Peel potatoes. Cut into small dice and drop into the boiling water. Cook 10 minutes.

While the potatoes are cooking, make cream sauce thus:

Blend 2 tablespoons of flour with 2 tablespoons of butter. Put 1 cup of milk into top of double boiler. Add the flour and butter to this. Place over a flame. Stir constantly until thickened. Now join the two parts of the double boiler and finish cooking over the hot water.

Drain the potatoes. Add them to the cream sauce in the double boiler and heat until chops are done.

Split the alligator pear. Take out the large seed. Place the halves on 2 salad plates. Fill the cavities with the following dressing:

Blend ⅛ teaspoon mustard; ¼ teaspoon of salt; 1 teaspoon of sugar with 2 tablespoons of vinegar and 2 tablespoons of water and a dash of paprika.

Prepare grapefruit.
Open figs.
Make the coffee.
Set the table.

Clear Broth
Russian Steak
Ground Whole Wheat, Cooked
Rye Bread and Butter
Tomatoes, Onions and Anchovy Salad
Cake   Grapefruit with Grape Juice
Coffee

Shopping List	Have Ready
1 lb. of Ground Steak	Frying Pan with Cover
Loaf Rye Bread	2 Saucepans
¼ lb Mushrooms	2 Salad Plates
Package Wheatena or any Ground Whole Wheat Cereal	2 Dessert Plates
	Sharp Knife
	Tablespoon
1 Lemon	Bowl
2 Tomatoes	Olive Oil
1 Onion	Lemon
Bottle of Anchovies	Sugar
Cake	Measuring Cup
1 Grapefruit	Teaspoon
Small Bottle Grape Juice	
Sprig of Fresh Mint or Peppermint Candy	
½ pt. Cream	

COURSE DINNERS—TWENTY MINUTES

Mould the ground steak into 7 cakes. Put 1 cake aside for the broth.

Light the gas flame.

In the frying pan, heat 1 tablespoon of butter.

Dust 6 meat cakes with flour. Sauté them in the butter. Add 1 slice of onion, the mushrooms cut small, 1 teaspoon of sugar, 1 tablespoon of water. Dust the tops of the cakes with flour again.

In a saucepan, heat 2½ measuring cups of water and ½ teaspoon of salt. When boiling, add to this ½ measuring cup of Wheatena (or any ground, whole wheat cereal). Stir well. Cook 10 minutes. Dust with pepper. Stir in 1 tablespoon of butter.

Pour 1½ cups of water into second saucepan and add 1 cake of the ground steak saved for broth. Let simmer and strain. Serve with salt and pepper and a slice of lemon in each cup.

Slice the onions and tomatoes thin and arrange on salad plates. Put the anchovies on top. For this make a dressing as follows:

1 tablespoon of vinegar; 3 tablespoons of olive oil; a bit of onion; ½ teaspoon of salt and ¼ teaspoon of mustard. Beat well and pour over salad.

Cut grapefruit in 2 halves and separate fruit from membrane. Arrange on plates. Pour over each ¼ measuring cup of grape juice. Top with a sprig of mint. (If you cannot get fresh mint, sprinkle with pink and white peppermint candy, crushed fine.)

Set the table. Start the coffee.

To the meat cakes, cooking in the frying pan, add ½ cup of cream and the juice of ½ lemon. Let this come to a boil. Keep warm until wanted. Dust with salt and pepper.

Serve the broth.

Curried Fish Chowder
Apple, Cabbage and Red Pepper Salad
Whole Wheat Bread   Preserved Pineapple
Cooked Cranberries
Coffee

Shopping List	Have Ready
1 lb. of Fish Flesh, no bones	Frying Pan
Small Head Cabbage	2 Large Saucepans, with covers
1 Red Pepper	Sharp Knife
1 Red Apple	Tablespoons
1 Lemon	Teaspoons
1 Orange	Measuring Cup
1 Onion	Bay Leaf
4 Slices of Bacon	Sugar
Loaf Whole Wheat Bread	Salt
Bottle Curry Powder	Pepper
1 lb. of Cranberries	
½ lb. of Rice	
Cream	

Heat 2 cups of water in a saucepan for the cranberries.

Cut the bacon into small squares. Heat half of this amount in the frying pan with ½ teaspoon of sugar. When browned, add 1 measuring cup of uncooked rice. Stir and brown. Slice into this the onion, saving out one slice. To the rice add 2 teaspoons of curry powder. Cook and add 1 cup of water. As the water cooks into the rice add more, a little at a time, letting it cook away before each addition.

Brown the rest of the bacon and the slice of onion in a saucepan.

Cut the fish into inch cubes and add to the bacon with a small piece of bay leaf, ½ teaspoon of salt and a small bit of orange peel. Add 2 cups of water and simmer gently.

When the rice has cooked 15 minutes, combine it with the fish and cook 5 minutes longer. Add the juice of 1 orange. (Save out 1 tablespoon of orange juice for salad dressing.)

Wash the cranberries.

Put the cranberries into the water, which must be boiling very hard. Cover and cook 5 minutes. Stir in 2 cups of sugar and cook 3 minutes longer.

For the salad: Chop the apple fine. (Do not peel it.) Chop 1 measuring cup of cabbage and the red pepper from which the seeds must be removed. Dress this with ½ measuring cup of cream, ¼ teaspoon of salt, 2 rounding teaspoons of sugar, 1 tablespoon of orange juice, 2 tablespoons of lemon juice. Beat thoroughly before using.

Set the table.

Make the coffee.

Cut 2 slices of whole wheat bread in quarters and arrange on platter. Pour the curried rice and fish over these. The curry should have a very small amount of liquid. If properly cooked the liquid will be absorbed by the rice and fish.

Clear Broth
Chicken with Vegetables
Rice   Rolls
Apple Butter
Preserved Ginger   Camembert Cheese
Saltines   Ginger Snaps
Coffee

Shopping List	Have Ready
1½ lbs. Chicken or Left-over Chicken	Frying Pan
Apple Butter	2 Large Saucepans
Heart of Celery	Colander
½ lb. Rice	Tablespoons
Jar of Preserved Ginger	Teaspoon
Saltines	Small Sharp Knife
Camembert Cheese	Sugar
Ginger Snaps	Salt
	Pepper
	Measuring Cup
	Strainer

Heat 2 quarts of salted water for the rice.

Wash the rice well.

When the water is boiling, stir in 1 cup rice.

With the small, very sharp knife, remove the meat from the uncooked chicken, discarding skin and bone.

Use the skin and bone for the broth, putting them in a saucepan with 1 pint of water, 1 slice of onion and a leaf of celery. Simmer until wanted. Strain before serving.

Put a piece of chicken fat into the frying pan. Fry this and add ½ teaspoon of sugar, 1 onion sliced thin, the chicken meat and the celery, cut very thin across the stalk. Brown these and add ½ measuring cup of stock and cook covered until wanted. (Chicken left over from a previous meal will serve for this dish.) When the meat is cooked, keep hot until wanted.

Warm the rolls in the oven.

Set the table.

Make the coffee.

Drain the rice in the colander. Pour hot water through it and heat again.

Serve the soup.

CHAPTER XVII

COURSE DINNERS IN THIRTY MINUTES

Farm Sausages
Fried Apples   Mashed Potatoes
Lettuce Salad with Russian Dressing
Bread and Butter
Grapefruit with Raspberry Jam
Ginger Snaps
Coffee

Shopping List	Have Ready
1 Pound of Little Sausages	2 Frying Pans, 1 Cover
4 Small Red Apples	1 Saucepan with Cover
4 Potatoes	Colander
Head of Lettuce	Bowl
Mayonnaise, Small Jar	Measuring Cup
Bottle of Chili Sauce	Ricer
Grapefruit	Tablespoons
Raspberry Jam	Sharp Knife
Ginger Snaps	Sugar
1 pt. Milk	Butter
	Cream
	2 Dessert Plates
	2 Salad Plates

Light the gas oven.

Half fill the saucepan with water and put to heat for the potatoes.

Heat the frying pan for the sausages. Brown them. When they have cooked ten minutes, finish cooking them in the oven.

Quarter, core and slice the apples in thin slices lengthwise. Put the slices into the frying pan, adding 1 measuring cup of sugar and 3 tablespoons of butter. Cover and cook slowly 25 minutes.

Peel the potatoes, cut in small dice and put into the saucepan of boiling water.

Wash the lettuce. Discard the outer leaves using only the heart. Dry on a cloth and cut the heart in two. Arrange on salad plates.

Mix 3 tablespoons of chili sauce with 3 tablespoons of mayonnaise. Stir well and dress the salad.

Cut the grapefruit in half. Loosen the sections of pulp from the membrane so that it will be easy to eat. Put each half on a dessert plate and place a tablespoon of raspberry jam on top of each.

Set the table.

Start the coffee.

Drain the potatoes into a colander.

Into the saucepan from which the potatoes have been emptied, put 1 tablespoon of butter and 3 tablespoons of cream. Heat this. Turn off the flame, and rice the potatoes into the hot liquid. Beat a moment until creamy.

Creamed Codfish
Potatoes with Parsley
French Bread
Apple and Onion Salad
Baked Bananas and Oranges
Coffee

SHOPPING LIST	HAVE READY
½ lb. Boned Salt Codfish	Double Boiler
4 Potatoes	Large Saucepan
Loaf French Bread	Covered Saucepan
1 Quart Milk	Measuring Cup
1 Red Apple	Baking Dish
1 Small Onion	Salt
1 Egg	Pepper
Parsley	Sugar
3 Bananas	Bowl
1 Orange	Lemon

COURSE DINNERS—THIRTY MINUTES

Have Ready—Con'd

Cream, off the Milk	Sharp Knife
Flour	Tablespoon
Cinnamon	Teaspoon

Heat water in saucepan for potatoes.

Almost fill large saucepan with cold water. Put in the codfish and when hot, not boiling, drain and fill saucepan with cold water again. Bring this just to a boil. Codfish never should boil, or it will be tough. Keep the water just hot until ready for the cream sauce.

Peel the potatoes, cut into eighths and put in saucepan to boil.

Make the cream sauce for the codfish as follows:

In the top of the double boiler, blend 4 tablespoons of flour with 2 tablespoons of butter. Add 1 pint of milk. Cook over the flame, stirring constantly until thickened. Finish cooking in the double boiler.

Peel the bananas. Slice them into the baking dish. Squeeze the juice of 1 orange over them. Add ¼ measuring cup of sugar and a bit of butter. Dust with cinnamon. Bake in the oven 10 minutes. Keep warm until wanted.

Slice the apples very thin, leaving the skins on. Peel and slice the onion thin. Arrange on salad plate and dust with salt and ½ teaspoon of sugar. Make the dressing for this salad as follows:

¼ measuring cup of cream; 1 teaspoon of sugar; salt, juice of half a lemon. Beat together.

Beat the egg for the cream sauce.

Set the table.

Make the coffee.

Drain the codfish, break into small pieces and arrange in the center of serving dish.

Stir the beaten egg into the hot cream sauce and pour over the codfish. Garnish with parsley.

Drain potatoes and dress with minced parsley.

COOKING

Grapefruit
Broiled Chicken   Minced Potatoes
Egg Plant Sauté
Quince Jelly   Finger Rolls
Ice Cream
With Hot Butter Scotch Sauce
Coffee

SHOPPING LIST	HAVE READY
A Chicken Weighing About 2½ Pounds, Split for Broiling	Small Saucepan
4 Potatoes	Large Frying Pan with Cover
1 Grapefruit	Frying Pan with Cover
1 Eggplant	Sharp Knife
Quince Jelly	Tablespoons
Finger Rolls	Measuring Cup
Molasses	1 Egg
Brown Sugar	Butter
Ice Cream	1 Soup Plate
	Chopping Bowl
	Chopping Knife

Put ice cream against ice.

Light the broiler flame.

Quickly sear each side of the split chicken.

Broil chicken 20 to 25 minutes. Turn occasionally.

Light a gas flame and heat 1 tablespoon of butter in a frying pan.

Peel the potatoes and chop fine. Brown them in the butter and cook them covered, turning occasionally.

In the large frying pan, heat 2 tablespoons butter. Beat up the egg with 1 tablespoon of water on the soup plate.

Peel and slice the eggplant crosswise. Dip the slices in the beaten egg and brown in butter in the large frying pan. Finish cooking with the pan covered.

Set the table.

Heat the rolls in oven.

Make the coffee.

Prepare the hot Butter Scotch sauce as follows:

In the small saucepan, mix 1 cup of molasses, 1 cup of

COURSE DINNERS—THIRTY MINUTES

brown sugar, 1 tablespoon of butter. Let this come to a boil once. Keep warm over hot water until wanted.

Meat Loaf
Sweet Potatoes
Endive Salad with Roquefort
Cheese Dressing
Poppy-Seed Rolls
Grape Jelly
Red Apples in Syrup with Cream
Coffee

Shopping List	Have Ready
1 lb. Round Steak, Ground	1 Frying Pan and Cover
4 Small Sweet Potatoes	1 Large Saucepan and Cover
6 Poppy-seed Rolls	1 Small Saucepan
1 Egg	1 Enamel Pan
½ Pint Cream	Apple Corer
2 Red Apples	Sharp Knife
1 Glass Grape Jelly	Tablespoons
¼ lb. Endive	Teaspoon
2 oz. Roquefort Cheese	1 Bowl
	Salt, Pepper and Sugar
	Poultry Seasoning
	Olive Oil and Vinegar
	Paprika and Butter

Light the gas oven.

Light the gas under large saucepan half full of water, to which has been added 1 teaspoon of salt. Heat for potatoes.

Light gas under small saucepan containing 1 cup of water.

Add 1 poppy-seed roll, ½ teaspoon of salt, 1 teaspoon poultry seasoning. Stir until the roll is dissolved and the whole mass hot. Remove from fire. Beat into this mixture 1 egg, then stir in the ground steak. Brown 2 tablespoons of butter in the frying pan. Turn into the center of the pan the meat mixture, keeping it in a round cake, about 2 inches thick, shaping it with the back of tablespoon to make compact. Cook about 3 minutes, basting the top with the hot butter in the pan. Slip under the broiler flame for 5 minutes to sear the top of the roast. Replace on top of stove. Dust the top with flour and cover closely. Finish with flame at half heat. One minute before serving, brown the top under broiler flame.

Entire cooking time for loaf, 25 minutes. While the loaf is cooking under cover, peel 4 small sweet potatoes, cut into eighths. Drop into the boiling, salted water. Cooking time, 20 minutes.

In enamel saucepan, place 1 cup of sugar and 1 cup of water. Dissolve over flame. Core 2 red apples and cut into 1/4 inch slices, cutting across the apple. Drop these into the hot syrup and cook until transparent, about 15 minutes. Serve with cream.

Wash, dry and cut the endive into lengthwise pieces. Arrange on salad plates. Mash the Roquefort cheese in the bowl with 2 tablespoons of olive oil, 2 tablespoons of vinegar and 1/2 teaspoon of salt. Beat. Spread this over the endive and dust the tops with paprika.

Heat rolls and plates in the oven.
Start the coffee. Set the table.

Scalloped Oysters
Jelly   Parker House Rolls
Sweet Pickles
Hot Cabbage Salad
Indian Pudding with Cream
Coffee

SHOPPING LIST
1½ Dozen Oysters
Package of Saltines
Jelly

HAVE READY
Shallow Frying Pan
1 Saucepan
Measuring Cup

COURSE DINNERS—THIRTY MINUTES 117

SHOPPING LIST—Con'd
Sweet Pickles
Small Head of Cabbage
6 Parker House Rolls
2 Eggs
1 Quart Milk
Molasses
Cornmeal

HAVE READY—Con'd
Chopping Bowl
Chopping Knife
Double Boiler
Tablespoons
Teaspoons
Sharp Knife
Flour
Sugar
Cloves
Cinnamon
Ginger
Salt
Pepper

Light the oven.

Use the cream from top of the milk to serve with the pudding and for the oysters.

Heat 2 tablespoons of butter in the frying pan. Break about 24 saltines into bits and heat in the butter, stirring them so they are heated evenly. Put a thin layer of the hot crumbs into a large, shallow dish. Next lay the oysters, salting and peppering them. Over the oysters and around them lay the rest of the crackers. Pour over this 1/4 measuring cup of oyster liquor and 1/4 measuring cup of cream. Bake in the oven until wanted. Scalloped oysters should be made in a shallow dish and kept not more than an inch deep.

For the Indian pudding, heat 1 cup of milk in the top of the double boiler. Stir into the hot milk, 1/2 measuring cup of cornmeal, 1 tablespoon of butter and 1 egg. Beat well between each addition. Join the double boiler, filling the bottom with hot water. Add 1/2 measuring cup of sugar, 4 tablespoons of molasses, 1/8 teaspoon of cloves, 1/4 teaspoon of nutmeg, 1/4 teaspoon of ginger, 1/4 teaspoon of cinnamon. Cook for five minutes. Turn out the flame and let it stand over the hot water until wanted.

For hot cabbage salad, chop enough cabbage to make 1 pint. In a saucepan, heat 1 cup of milk. When hot, remove from the fire and stir into it 1 egg, well beaten, and 1 tablespoon of butter. Stir over a slow fire until it is like custard. Add ½ measuring cup of vinegar, ½ teaspoon of salt and a dash of pepper. Heat and stir in the cabbage.

Set the the table.
Make the coffee.
Heat the rolls.

Veal Pot Roast
Sweet Chopped Pickle
Browned Potatoes
Spinach
Floating Island
Coffee

Shopping List	Have Ready
1 lb. of Veal Steak	2 Large Frying Pans
4 Slices of Bacon	2 Saucepans
1 lb. of Spinach	2 Small Bowls
1 Onion	Double Boiler
Bunch Small Celery	Measuring Cup
3 Eggs	Tablespoons
Bottle Sweet Chopped Pickle	Teaspoons
1 Pint of Milk	Sugar
	Butter
	Salt, Pepper
	Dishpan
	Vanilla

Put the spinach to soak in large dishpan full of water. Light the gas oven.

Cut 2 slices of bacon into small bits.

Fry and add the onion sliced. Brown this with ½ teaspoon of sugar, and celery sliced thin.

Flour the veal.

Remove the vegetables from frying pan. Add a little butter to the fat and brown the roast.

Replace the vegetables in frying pan, lay the meat on top

COURSE DINNERS—THIRTY MINUTES

and cook covered until wanted. Finish the roast in the oven so that the top of the stove may be free for the other pans.

Heat water for the potatoes in saucepan.

Heat 1 cup of water to which is added 2 teaspoons of salt, for the spinach.

Peel the potatoes and cut into ¼ inch slices lengthwise. Put into the boiling water.

In the double boiler, heat 1 pint of milk.

Beat the yolks of 3 eggs well. Add ¼ measuring cup of sugar. Dip about ¼ measuring cup of the hot milk onto them, stirring until the sugar and egg are blended. Add this mixture to the rest of the hot milk and cook in the boiler about 5 minutes, or until slightly thickened. Flavor with vanilla.

Beat the whites of the eggs stiff. Into them beat 3 tablespoons of sugar and 1 teaspoon of vanilla. Remove the yellow custard to a shallow dish. Drop large tablespoons of beaten egg white on to the top of the hot custard. Cool by setting over a pan of cracked ice, or place in refrigerator.

Lift the spinach from the top of water, being careful not to disturb the sand which settles to bottom. Wash well of sand. Cut off roots. Plunge into the boiling, salted water. Cook 10 minutes.

When the potatoes have cooked 10 minutes, try out 2 slices of bacon in a large frying pan. Add a little butter and brown them, keeping each slice separate. Turn each slice until browned on both sides.

Set the table.

Make the coffee.

Drain the spinach and dress with salt and pepper and butter.

Fried Chicken
New Potatoes
Asparagus, with Lemon and Butter Sauce
Grape Marmalade   Finger Rolls
Strawberry Shortcake
Coffee

SHOPPING LIST	HAVE READY
3 lbs. Young Chicken Cut for Frying	Large Frying Pan with Cover
New Potatoes	2 Saucepans
Bunch of Asparagus	1 Cover
Lemon	Double Boiler
Parsley	Opener
Milk	Mixing Bowl
Finger Rolls	Pie Plate
Cream	Measuring Cup
Grape Marmalade	Teaspoon
Box of Strawberries	Tablespoon
	Sharp Knife
	Butter
	Sugar
	Flour
	Baking Powder
	Salt
	Wire Potato Masher

In the 2 saucepans heat water for the potatoes and asparagus. In large frying pan, heat 2 tablespoons of butter.

Singe the chicken. Sprinkle with flour, salt and pepper. Brown it in the butter. Add 2 tablespoons of water. Cover closely and cook. When nearly done, add 4 tablespoons of cream.

Scrape the potatoes and start them boiling.

Wash the asparagus and cut off the hard ends. Put in water to cook.

Pick over the strawberries and mash with a wire potato masher. Add to them, 1 measuring cup of sugar. Light the oven. Butter pie pan for the shortcake.

Into the mixing bowl, sift 1 cup of flour, ½ teaspoon of

salt, 1 rounding tablespoon of sugar. Blend with this, 2 tablespoons of butter. When it is like cornmeal, add 1 heaping teaspoon of baking powder. Work into this 1/3 measuring cup of milk. Do not roll this dough, but shape with a spatula into round biscuits. (This may be also made as 1 large cake or baked on a waffle iron.) Bake in oven until brown. About 10 minutes.

Make the asparagus sauce as follows:

In the double boiler put 2 tablespoons of butter and the juice of half a lemon. Melt and stir until blended. Add salt and pepper.

Drain the asparagus and dress with sauce when the rest of the meal is ready.

Set the table. Heat the rolls.

Remove chicken from pan to oven and keep warm. Make gravy in the pan: 2 tablespoons of flour stirred into 2 tablespoons fat. Add 1 cup of water, 1/2 teaspoon of salt and pepper. Cook until thickened. Stir well.

Split the biscuits and put together with crushed berries between and on top. The shortcake may be assembled when removing the first course.

Casserole of Chops
Boiled Potatoes
Sweet Chopped Pickle
French Rolls
Date Conserve with Cream
Coffee

SHOPPING LIST	HAVE READY
1 lb. of Chops	Large Covered Casserole
Eggplant	Frying Pan
2 Onions	2 Saucepans
Small Cabbage	1 Cover
4 Potatoes	Measuring Cup

SHOPPING LIST—Con'd
½ Pint Cream
Bottle Sweet Chopped Pickle
French Rolls
½ lb. Dates
2 Apples
Small Bottle Grape Juice

HAVE READY—Con'd
Tablespoon
Sharp Knife
Flour Sifter
Opener
Flour
Sugar
Salt
Pepper

Light the oven.
Put the casserole to heat in the oven.
In a saucepan, heat salted water for the potatoes.
Peel the eggplant and cut into dice.
Shred about 1 cup of cabbage.
Sauté the onions, eggplant and cabbage in frying pan in 2 tablespoons butter, remove to casserole. Salt and pepper and dust lightly with flour.
Flour the chops and brown them in frying pan.
Remove the chops to casserole laying them on top of vegetables. Dust on a little flour and salt and pepper.
Into the frying pan pour 1 cup of water. Heat this and pour it around vegetables in the casserole. It should not rise as high as the chops. Cover closely and finish cooking in the oven, 25 minutes.
Peel the potatoes, cut into eighths and boil in salted water.
In the second saucepan, boil 1 cup of water.
Peel, core and quarter the apples. Put them to boil in the saucepan. Cook 8 minutes.
To the apples, add ½ lb. stoned dates, 1 cup of sugar, ½ measuring cup of grape juice. Cook 5 minutes. Serve the conserve warm, with cream.
Set the table.
Make the coffee.
Drain the potatoes, adding more salt and pepper.
Remove the casserole cover and brown the chops for a minute under the broiler flame.

COURSE DINNERS—THIRTY MINUTES

Pork Chops, Floured
Scalloped Sweet Potatoes
Apple Sauce
India Relish
Drop Biscuits
Honey
Coffee

Shopping List	Have Ready
1 lb. Loin Pork Chops	Frying Pan with Cover
4 Sweet Potatoes	Shallow Enamel Pan
6 Greening Apples	Saucepan with Cover
India Relish	Colander
Honey	Pie Plate
1 Pint Milk	Wire Masher
	Mixing Bowl
	Measuring Cup
	Teaspoon
	Tablespoons
	Sharp Knife
	Butter
	Pepper, Salt
	Flour
	½ Cup Cream
	¼ Cup Milk
	Baking Powder

Light the gas flame.

Into the frying pan put 2 tablespoons of butter.

Heat water in shallow saucepan for potatoes.

Dust the chops with flour. Salt and pepper them.

Brown the chops in butter and dust over them more flour. Cook at half heat for 25 minutes. Prepared in this way, pork chops taste like chicken.

Light the oven.

Peel the sweet potatoes and cut them into dice. Drop them in the boiling water in shallow enamel pan.

Into the saucepan put 1 pint of water and boil for the apples.

Peel, core and quarter the apples and drop into saucepan when the water is boiling hard. Cook 8 minutes. Mash with the wire masher. Add to them, ¾ of a cup of sugar and cook 2 minutes longer. Remove to dish for serving and dust with cinnamon.

Drain the potatoes in the colander and replace them in the enamel pan. Dust them with pepper and salt. Add 1 tablespoon of butter and ½ cup of cream and finish cooking in the oven.

Set the table.

Make the coffee.

Make the drop biscuit as follows:

Place 1 tablespoon of butter in the pie plate and melt it in the oven. Sift 1 measuring cup of flour into the mixing bowl. Add ½ teaspoon of salt, about ⅓ measuring cup of milk, the melted butter and 3 teaspoons of baking powder. Drop this batter from a tablespoon on to the pie plate and bake for about 10 minutes. These may bake as dinner is being eaten.

Roast Steak
Fried Onions   Scalloped Potatoes
Yorkshire Pudding
Horseradish
Bread and Butter
French Pastry
Coffee

Shopping List	Have Ready
Porterhouse Steak, 2½ Inches Thick	2 Frying Pans with Covers
6 Onions	Mixing Bowl
4 Potatoes	Measuring Cup
1 Quart Milk	Tablespoons
Bread	Sharp Knife
French Pastry	Butter
Bottle Horseradish	Flour
2 Eggs	Salt and Pepper
	Teaspoon

Light the broiler.

Sear the steak quickly. Broil 25 minutes, turning it every 5 minutes.

Heat in a frying pan, 2 tablespoons of butter.

Peel the onions and slice into the frying pan with the melted butter. Salt and pepper them. Brown and cook covered until wanted.

In the second frying pan, heat 1 tablespoon of butter.

Peel the potatoes, cut into small pieces and place in second frying pan. Add 1 cup of milk. Cover the pan and cook. The milk will cook into the potatoes. Add more milk in small amounts, from time to time. Mince the potatoes with a knife as they cook. When done, they will be covered with a light brown, creamy sauce. Dust them with salt and pepper.

When the steak has broiled about 10 minutes, make the Yorkshire pudding as follows:

In the bowl, mix 1 cup of milk, 2 eggs, 1 cup of sifted flour. Beat with a Dover egg beater for 2 minutes. Remove broiler and steak from the oven and place it over gas flame on top of stove. When the broiler is sizzling hot, pour in the pudding batter into the broiler drip pan, being sure that it covers all of the pan bottom. Replace the steak and broiler in the gas oven. The cooking steak will drip onto the pudding. If the pudding is not sufficiently brown when the steak is done, it may be browned close to the flame after the steak has been removed for serving.

(In this recipe, the steak takes the place of the usual roast of beef. If there is some steak left, it may be used instead of chops in the Casserole of Chops recipe printed on another page.)

Set the table.

Make the coffee.

Cut the Yorkshire pudding in squares and serve around the steak.

Pork Chops with Dressing
Sweet Potatoes in Honey
Egg Rolls
Cabbage Salad
Apple and Raisin Conserve
With Cream
Coffee

Shopping List	Have Ready
1 lb. Loin Pork Chops	Small Saucepan
4 Sweet Potatoes	Saucepan
1 Onion	Frying Pan with Cover
Small Head of Cabbage	Casserole or Glass
4 Apples	Baking Dish
1 Orange	Chopping Knife
Small Jar of Honey	Chopping Bowl
Package of Raisins	Poultry Seasoning
½ Pint Cream	Teaspoon
Egg Rolls	Tablespoon
	Vinegar
	Pepper
	Salt
	Sugar
	Sharp Knife
	Measuring Cup
	Paprika

Heat water in large saucepan for the potatoes.

Place casserole in lighted oven to warm.

Heat 1 cup of water in small saucepan. Into this put 4 slices of bread, ½ teaspoon of poultry seasoning, 1 tablespoon of bacon fat or butter, ¼ teaspoon of salt. Beat this well. Beat in 1 egg.

Sauté the pork chops in 2 tablespoons of melted butter. When they are browned, heap the top of each chop with the dressing. Cover the pan and finish cooking.

Peel the potatoes. Cut them in ¼ inch slices lengthwise. Boil them 15 minutes. Drain. Add the jar of honey, the juice of ½ orange, salt and pepper. Finish cooking in the oven.

Chop the cabbage fine. Dress with the following:

¼ cup of vinegar; ¼ cup of water; ½ teaspoon of salt; 1 teaspoon of sugar. Dust the salad with paprika.
Set the table.
Make the coffee.
In the saucepan heat 1 cup water.
Peel and core the 4 apples and cut into eighths. Cook in the hot water until nearly done, about 8 minutes.
Add to the apples, the juice of ½ orange, a slice of orange peel, ½ cup of raisins and ¾ cup of sugar. Dust with cinnamon and sugar and cook a few minutes longer.

Roast Pork Tenderloin with Gravy
Creamed Carrots   Mashed Sweet Potatoes
Bread and Butter   Currant Jelly
Oranges with Coconut
Cake
Coffee

SHOPPING LIST
1 Whole Pork Tenderloin Split
1 Bunch Carrots
4 Sweet Potatoes
1 Pint of Milk
1 Glass of Currant Jelly
2 Oranges
Shredded Coconut
Cake

HAVE READY
1 Frying Pan with Cover
1 Saucepan with Cover
1 Shallow Pan
Colander
Measuring Cup
Dessert Plates
Potato Ricer
Opener
Salt
Pepper
Flour
Tablespoons
Sharp Knife
Teaspoon

In the saucepan, heat the water for the sweet potatoes.
Heat 2 tablespoons of butter in the frying pan.
Salt, pepper and flour the split tenderloin. Brown it in the

pan. Add 4 tablespoons of water, dust the top with flour and cover closely. Cook with the flame at half heat for 28 minutes.

Into the shallow pan put 1 pint of water to heat for the carrots. Peel the sweet potatoes, cut into small pieces and add to the boiling water.

Peel the carrots, cut into small pieces and add to the boiling water. Cook rapidly. When these have cooked for 10 minutes the water should be about half cooked away. Add 2 tablespoons of butter. Cook two or three minutes and add 1 cup of rich milk. As they cook, mince them with a knife until they are quite fine. Cook for 8 minutes longer. When finished there should be very little liquid left. The water, butter and milk will be cooked into the carrots.

Set the table.

Slice the oranges. Dust with sugar. Sprinkle with coconut.

Cut the cake.

Make the coffee.

Drain the potatoes in the colander. Heat in their saucepan 3 tablespoons of cream and 1 tablespoon of butter. Rice the potatoes into this and beat a moment.

CHAPTER XVIII

ADDITIONAL TIMED RECIPES

Meat and Fish

Ham and Potatoes—10 Minutes

Use a slice of boiled ham, ½ inch thick.

Heat ½ cup of milk with ⅛ teaspoon of dry mustard in a frying pan.

Put in the ham and cook, turning it often.

Add more milk if it cooks away. The sauce should be thick and creamy.

Cook sliced potatoes 8 minutes.

Remove the ham from frying pan and stir the potatoes into the sauce, letting them heat for serving.

Calves Liver and Bacon—15 Minutes

Pour boiling water over 1 pound of calves liver.

Brown ¼ pound of bacon.

Remove the bacon to a warm place. Add a little butter to the bacon fat in the frying pan.

Salt and pepper the calves liver and cover with flour. Sauté the meat in the fat, dusting over more flour as it is turned.

Make a sauce to pour over the liver from 1 tablespoon of flour, stirred into fat in pan and ½ cup of water. Stir until smooth.

Smoked Sturgeon With Egg Sauce—15 Minutes

One pound of smoked sturgeon in one solid piece.
Put the fish in a frying pan with cup of hot water and heat covered for 15 minutes.
Prepare the sauce as follows:
In the top of the double boiler, heat ¾ of a cup of milk. Remove from the fire. Stir into the milk, yolks 2 eggs, well beaten, with the juice of 1 lemon. Cook in the double boiler until it thickens. Add minced parsley, 3 drops of onion juice and 1 teaspoon of butter.

Pork Tenderloin Frenched—25 Minutes

Have the butcher French the tenderloin.
Flour the meat and sauté in 2 tablespoons of butter.
Add ½ cup cream and cook covered.
Salt and pepper well.

Baked Chicken With Mushrooms—30 Minutes

Heat the gas oven.
Warm a casserole in the oven.
In a frying pan, brown 1 tablespoon butter; 1 pint of cooked chicken meat, cut in small pieces; ¼ pound of mushrooms, cut fine.
Remove to the uncovered baking dish and place in moderate oven. (350° F.)
Make gravy in the frying pan of 1 tablespoon of flour browned in the chicken and mushroom liquor. When the flour is browned, add 1 cup of water, salt and pepper. Let this boil and pour over the chicken and mushrooms.
Bake 25 minutes.

Potatoes and Rice

Mashed Potatoes Sauté—10 Minutes

When mashed potatoes are on the menu, cook enough for the following day.

Sauté the mashed potatoes in hot butter, in a frying pan. Brown them well.

Potato Soup—10 Minutes

Heat 1 cup of water in a saucepan.
Peel 1 small potato. Cut in very small slices.
Peel and slice 1 small onion.
Cook together rapidly for 8 minutes. The liquid should be partially cooked away.
Add 1 cup of rich milk and a lump of butter. Salt and pepper and heat.
For a French peasant soup, add 1 cup of soup stock and powdered mint and celery leaves, instead of the milk.

Lyonnaise Potatoes—20 Minutes

Heat 2 tablespoons of butter in the frying pan.
Peel and slice into the butter, 4 uncooked potatoes and 1 onion. As they cook, hash them with a knife.

Creamed Rice—20 Minutes

Boil a large saucepan of salted water.
When this is boiling, add 1 cup of well washed rice.
When the rice has cooked 10 minutes, drain it and pour hot water over it. Drain again and return to the saucepan.
Add 1 cup of milk.
Cook 10 minutes.
Salt and pepper and add 1 tablespoon of butter.

Potatoes O'Brien—20 Minutes

Peel 4 potatoes and 1 onion.
Remove the seeds from 1 green pepper.
Cut all these vegetables fine and sauté in a shallow enamel pan, using 2 tablespoons of butter. Sauté for 5 minutes.
Add 1 cup of milk and cook for 15 minutes. Mince with a knife while cooking. Add more milk as it cooks away. When finished, this should be a rich, creamy mass.
Salt and pepper.
Stir in ½ cup of grated cheese. Put the pan under the broiler flame and brown the top.

Candied Sweet Potatoes—20 Minutes

Peel 4 sweet potatoes.
Cut in dice and boil in boiling water for 10 minutes.
Remove to a shallow, enamel pan.
Add ½ cup of brown sugar, bits of butter, salt and pepper and ½ cup of water. Squeeze in 1 teaspoon of lemon juice. Add a little lemon rind and a sprinkling of mace.
Cook for 10 minutes longer.

Vegetables

Cauliflower—15 Minutes

Cut cauliflower in small pieces and cook in boiling water 15 minutes.
Make a Hollandaise sauce as follows:
Blend 2 tablespoons of butter with 1 tablespoon of flour. Add a bit of bay leaf and a small bit of onion. Cook over hot water until thickened slightly.
To this add the juice of ½ lemon and ½ teaspoon of salt. Heat again.

Remove from the hot water and beat in the yolks of 2 eggs.

Let stand over hot water a moment. Serve over drained cauliflower.

Creamed Celery—20 Minutes

Heat 1 cup of water in a shallow pan.

Wash hearts of celery. Slice very thin, across the stalk.

When the water is boiling, add the celery. Cook fast for 10 minutes. The water should be partially cooked away by this time.

Add 1 tablespoon of butter and cook 2 minutes.

Add 1 cup of rich milk and cook 8 minutes.

When done, the liquid is almost cooked away.

Scalloped Onions—20 Minutes

Heat 2 quarts of water.

Peel 4 onions. Slice them thin.

When the water is boiling, boil the onions for 5 minutes. Drain them.

In a shallow pan, heat 3/4 of a cup of milk with 1 tablespoon of butter.

Put the onions in the shallow pan with the milk and cook for 15 minutes. Do not let them burn.

When finished, add salt and pepper.

Creamed Cabbage—20 Minutes

Cut into small pieces enough cabbage to make 1 quart.

Sauté in frying pan with 2 tablespoons of hot butter.

Add 1 cup of milk. Turn occasionally.

When the milk has cooked away and the cabbage browned, add more milk, a little at a time.

As the cabbage cooks, mince it with a knife.

When finished, the cabbage is a brown, creamy mass with very little liquor.

Summer Squash—20 Minutes

Heat 2 cups of water in a saucepan.
Peel a summer squash and cut small. Add to the water and cook rapidly 20 minutes. The water should have cooked away.
Add a lump of butter and 2 tablespoons of cream.
Salt and pepper well.
Cucumbers are excellent cooked in this same way.

Desserts

Vanilla Soufflé—3 Minutes

Light the gas oven and get it very hot.
Vanilla soufflé must cook rapidly and should be brown on top and creamy in the center. Bake it in the dish from which it is to be eaten and serve instantly after it is finished.
Beat 3 egg whites.
Add 1/8 teaspoon of Cream of Tartar, 2 tablespoons of sugar and beat until very dry. Flavor with vanilla.
Arrange the mixture in the baking dishes. Dust the top of each portion with sugar.
Bake in the hot oven for 1 minute.
Now put each portion directly under the gas flame where they should brown very quickly. Be careful lest they burn. Serve instantly.
For chocolate soufflé, add 1 tablespoon cocoa to the egg mixture.
The yolks of the eggs are useful for date custard or chocolate pudding.

Blueberry Pancakes—5 Minutes

Sift 1 cup of flour into a bowl. Stir into this ½ cup of milk and 1 well beaten egg.

Add ½ cup of blueberries and 3 teaspoons of baking powder.

Heat 1 tablespoon of butter in a frying pan.

Make the cakes about 6 inches in diameter. Brown on each side in the hot butter. Dust with powdered sugar and eat hot.

It is a good idea, when serving these for dessert, to use two frying pans, making 2 cakes at once.

Scones—5 Minutes

Sift 1 cup of flour into a bowl and add ⅓ cup of milk, 3 teaspoons of baking powder and beat into this 1 egg and 1 tablespoon of sugar.

Drop in tablespoonfuls on a hot griddle.

These may be cooked at the table on an electric stove of the disc type.

Serve with jam, honey or maple syrup.

Jumbles—10 Minutes

Light gas oven.

Cream ¾ of a cup of butter with ¾ of a cup of powdered sugar. Add 1 well beaten egg. Add alternately, 1½ cups of flour which has been sifted together with 1 rounding teaspoon of baking powder and 4 tablespoons of cream. First a little flour, then a little cream until all is used.

Beat between each addition.

Add 1 teaspoon of vanilla. Drop in teaspoonfuls on a greased, floured baking pan.

Bake 10 minutes in a moderate oven (350° F.).

These should be frosted while hot. For the frosting use

1 cup of confectioners' sugar mixed with 4 tablespoons of cream and 1 teaspoon of vanilla.

For chocolate jumbles, substitute ½ cup of cocoa for ½ cup of flour.

Hot Frosted Gingerbread—10 Minutes

Light the gas oven.

Melt ¼ measuring cup of butter with ¼ cup of strong, hot coffee. Beat 1 egg and stir into it ¼ cup of sugar and ¼ cup of molasses. Cool slightly.

Combine this with the warm mixture. Sift in 2 cups flour to make a soft drop batter. Stir in 2 teaspoons of baking powder, ½ teaspoon nutmeg and ½ teaspoon ginger. Beat.

Grease and flour a pan, size about 9 x 12 inches. Spread the batter about ½ inch thick.

Bake 10 minutes in a moderate oven (350° F.).

While hot, frost this with 1 cup of confectioners' sugar stirred with 4 tablespoons of cream, flavored with 1 teaspoon vanilla.

Date Custard—10 Minutes

In the top of the double boiler, blend 3 tablespoons of butter, 6 tablespoons of flour. Add 1 pint of milk.

Heat, stirring constantly until thickened.

Add ½ cup of sugar and 3 beaten egg yolks. Join the boiler and cook over hot water 10 minutes. Flavor with vanilla. As it is nearing completion, stir in 1 teaspoon of butter to make it smooth.

Stone 1 measuring cup of dates. Cut into small pieces and put in a dish. Pour the custard over them.

The pudding may be served in sherbet glasses by placing a portion of dates in each and pouring the custard over. This should be served either hot or cold, with cream.

For chocolate pudding, substitute ⅓ cup of cocoa instead of 3 tablespoons of the flour.

Berry Pudding—20 Minutes

Into a deep kettle put 1 quart of berries, 1 cup of sugar and ½ cup water. When the mixture is bubbling over the flame, drop the following batter on top:

Beat 1 egg. Add 3 tablespoons melted butter. Beat. Add ½ cup milk, ½ cup sugar, 1 cup of sifted flour. Beat between each addition. Add 3 teaspoons baking powder. Beat.

After the batter is added, cover the kettle closely. Cook gently for 20 minutes. Take care that it does not burn.

CHAPTER XIX

PLATE DINNERS FOR THE BUSY WOMAN

Everything Ready at the Right Moment

That time saving is one of the vital problems of this age nobody can deny. Countless articles on the subject have appeared in current magazines. Efficiency experts in all kinds of business are receiving large salaries for working out shorter methods of getting tasks done.

Whether a woman uses the time saved for business or for the betterment and advancement of the community—a task for which her sex is so well fitted—or employs it for the cultivation of her own charm and intelligence, surely the world will reap the benefit. It will be a pleasanter place to live in because she has saved time from routine labor.

Doctors and scientists agree that some leisure for the development of the individual is necessary. The woman who saves time for this task is wise. Her family and friends will find her a better companion because she has time for interests outside of the ancient daily tasks.

Born in an age when housekeeping, particularly cooking was a passion and the long, elaborate details of it consumed hours, it was difficult for me to believe that there was any other way to do woman's work. Perhaps I never would have been convinced if it had not been for a circumstance that forced me to change my old-fashioned method of preparing meals for an easier one without sacrificing the charm of my table that had always been my pride. I believed that appetizing, well cooked foods attractively served were an æsthetic necessity; that to sit down to such a meal made for the health, happiness and well-being of myself, my husband and the friends we asked to share it.

I had been interested in modeling for some time. I designed some small, sculptured figures and took them to a gift shop wholesale house. When the orders began to pour in I found myself swamped with business overnight.

I was confronted with the necessity of choosing between three things: Either I must give up my home or my business or make a nervous wreck of myself. I found a way to keep my home and my business and also my health.

It was obvious that a certain number of hours must be spent on my business. A certain number I determined to spend in companionship with my husband and friends. What time was left I would use for the cooking and dishwashing—and the dishwashing took the most time of all.

My chief concern was to keep the same atmosphere of pleasant living which I had always loved and without which I knew I would be unhappy. I wanted to avoid any bleakness due to saving time from domestic tasks.

Plate dinners, step by step cooking and the choice of menus that would fit into the time which I could spare to prepare meals made up the solution of my problem.

Serving all of the main course of dinner on large individual dinner plates saved washing many dishes. This eliminated the use of serving dishes for vegetables, the platter, the salad plates and individual vegetable dishes. Bread and butter plates were used to hold rolls or bread and saved the washing of the large dish usually used.

Not only was the saving in dishes tremendous, but the beauty of my table was enhanced also. The various colors of the food on individual plates was a delight to the eye. Colorful food, attractively served plays a large part in pleasant dining. If the sense of sight is pleased the desire for food is accentuated and the appetite created aids digestion. "Making the mouth water," is a culinary secret which every woman who would be a successful cook should adopt.

Most women have a natural sense of the artistic, a desire to create beauty. The world is in need of more beauty. If women use their gift to beautify their tables they will develop a talent of untold value to themselves and those whose lives they touch.

Another advantage I found in the plate dinner is that it saves space on the dining table. If the table is small this is particularly appreciated. A clutter of dishes, an overloaded table makes a confusion in dining which is annoying. A sense of space, leisure and quiet should be a part of every meal so that those who partake of it may have the feeling of well being which follows that most delightful of occasions—A GOOD DINNER—a delight to the eye, the taste, the soul. May you enjoy many of them!

If you have a tea wagon use it at the dinner table. Placed at your right hand it will hold the dessert, coffee and anything else needed during the meal that you do not wish to place on the table. A small table may be used in place of a tea wagon. Either will save needless jumping up during dinner, a practice which mars the most perfectly cooked meal.

The tea wagon may be used in the kitchen when preparing a meal. The whole dinner can be wheeled to the table in one trip, a saving of countless journeys between kitchen and table. Or a large tray may be used instead of a tea wagon.

The restaurant started the vogue for plate dinners. Since they have become popular, china and glass makers have placed on the market attractive plates for household use with sections marked off to hold various portions. Gay flowers scattered on a creamy background, dull blue and white china, and glass plates colored in green or rose are some of the loveliest designs. A plain, large dinner plate will answer the purpose, if you do not care to invest in special china.

After perfecting the plate dinner method of serving I became interested in the others described in this section as means to cut down pan washing and provide variety. Platter dinners are those which arrange the different foods on one large serving platter. They are particularly good when entertaining guests as they save arranging many individual plates. Plank dinners are baked all on one wooden plank. At hotels and restaurants they are usually the finest dinners that can be had. A hardwood plank suited to this purpose may be bought wherever household utensils are sold. A large earthen casserole with a cover, or a glass baking dish may be used for the casserole meals. Covered baking dishes are attractive to use, retain all the flavor of the food and save many pans.

The systems presented in these chapters have served me well. That they may fill the need of the many busy women in the world is the sincere hope of one of them.

Step-by-Step Cooking

In conserving time I found it important to know the exact number of minutes it would take to prepare a meal or a dish.

Everything I cooked was timed and noted upon the recipe.

I recommend this procedure to all cooks. To start a dish that will take thirty minutes when you have but fifteen to give to it, causes one of the many petty annoyances that the inexperienced cook often encounters.

It is because of these avoidable mistakes that so many women dislike cooking. The purpose of the following chapters is to eliminate them so that cooking may become the delight it should be.

The difficulty of most amateur cooks in preparing a meal is to have everything ready at the proper moment. If the potatoes, which require from twenty minutes to half an hour, are started after the spinach, which needs ten minutes, a great deal of time will be wasted. If the dinner is all cooked and will spoil through waiting for the table to be laid this mismanagement will ruin the menu.

I have arranged the cooking directions given so that each step in the preparing of a dinner will fit into its proper place and the whole process will go forward in an orderly manner, with ease and with a saving of time and effort.

In describing plate dinners the menu is given first. To have it before your eyes saves time. If you are not following these menus it will save trouble to write out your menu and avoid carrying details in your mind.

The menus given are properly balanced and designed to please the eye as well as the palate. In making other menus it should be borne in mind that a well balanced dinner must contain a balanced portion of starchy food such as bread and potatoes and desserts with flour; protein, such as meat, fish, eggs and cheese; a green vegetable such as spinach, lettuce or tomatoes; some liquid; something tart for an appetizer and a sweet for the finish. A variety of color in the food served is also necessary. A dinner that is all white or brown or red is unappetizing to look at and unpleasant to eat.

In the left hand column of the page appears a shopping list so that nothing will be forgotten. Try to avoid the annoyance of dropping work in the middle of preparing dinner in order to go after a forgotten article.

By arranging cooking directions in their actual step-by-step order the writer believes that anybody, whether they have cooked or not, can open the book at the menu they desire and by following directions cook a perfect dinner.

Each separate step in preparing the dinners has been described in a single sentence for the convenience of the reader.

The recipes given here have all been prepared in my own kitchen. A three burner gas stove with built-in oven was used. I realize that varying degrees of skill in various cooks may affect the speed with which the dinners are prepared. The actual cooking time, however, is correct for a gas range and may be relied on implicitly.

Desserts mentioned in the menus are not included in describing the preparation of the meal, but appear in a separate chapter on Desserts. They may either be prepared while getting the dinner or beforehand.

CHAPTER XX

PLATE DINNER MENUS

A Twenty-Minute Dinner

Shad Roe with Bacon
Toast Triangles
Potatoes with Egg Sauce   Alligator Pear Salad
Olives   Celery
Apple Compote
Coffee

Shopping List
2 Shad Roe
4 Potatoes
1 Alligator Pear
1 Bunch Celery
1 Bottle Olives
Mint
2 Red Apples
Cream
Milk
¼ lb. Bacon

Have Ready
Bowl
Toaster
2 Frying Pans
Double Boiler
Sharp Knife
Tablespoon
Measuring Cup
Opener
Percolator
2 Dinner Plates
Saucepan

Preparation (Time: 20 minutes)

Pour boiling water over shad roe. Let stand 5 minutes.
Peel potatoes. Cut in very small dice.
Cook potatoes 10 minutes in boiling water.
Heat 1 tablespoon butter in frying pan for shad roe.
Brown, turning often, for 15 minutes.
Wash celery. Cut in thin strips. Soak in ice water.
Cook the bacon 10 minutes in a frying pan.

Cut the alligator pear in half and fill the cavity with French dressing.

For the dressing use 3 tablespoons olive oil, 1 tablespoon vinegar, ½ teaspoon salt, ½ teaspoon paprika and 1 tablespoon mint cut fine.

To make a cream sauce for the potatoes:
In the top of double boiler put 1 cup of milk.
Blend 2 tablespoons flour with 2 tablespoons butter.
Add to the milk with ½ teaspoon salt and pepper.
Cook over hot water 10 minutes. Drain the potatoes. Add 1 well beaten egg to the cream sauce and heat the potatoes in the sauce.
Set the table.
Make the coffee.
Make the toast. Cut in triangles and butter it.

Serving

Arrange alligator pears on the plates.
Next the olives and celery.
Then a mound of potatoes.
Put the shad roe on the toast triangles.
Place the bacon around it.
Serve immediately.

Twenty-Five-Minute Dinners

Broiled Steak
Noodles in Cream   Onions Sauté
Beet Salad
Parker House Rolls
Peaches in Honey
Macaroons
Coffee

PLATE DINNER MENUS

Shopping List	Have Ready
1 lb. Porterhouse Steak	Broiler
1 Package Noodles	Saucepan
4 Onions	Frying Pan
1 Can Whole Beets	Tablespoon
1 Cucumber	Sharp Knife
6 Parker House Rolls	Can opener
4 Peaches	Percolator
1 Jar Honey	2 Dinner Plates
Macaroons	Bowl
Lemon	
Parsley	
Cream	

Preparation (Time: 25 minutes)

Light broiler flame. Heat broiler.

Heat water for noodles. Add ½ package of noodles and ½ teaspoon salt.

Boil 15 minutes.

Heat 1 tablespoon butter in frying pan.

Peel the onions and cut very fine.

Cook in butter 15 minutes, turning occasionally.

Sear the steak on each side. Broil 10 minutes.

Turn steak every 3 minutes.

Peel cucumber. Open can of beets.

Scoop centers from 4 beets and mince the part that has been removed.

Mince an equal amount of cucumber.

Combine minced beet and cucumber.

Dress with 2 tablespoons olive oil, 1 tablespoon vinegar, ¼ teaspoon salt and pepper.

Pile into the beet cups.

Heat the rolls.

Set the table.

Make the coffee.

Cut 2 slices of lemon and dust with paprika and minced parsley.

Dress the noodles with 4 tablespoons cream. Keep warm.

Serving

Arrange the salad on the plates.
Then a mound of noodles.
Next the onion sauté.
Cut the steak in strips. Decorate with lemon which is to be used as a dressing for steak at table.
Serve immediately.

Broiled Lamb Steak
Browned Rice Tiny Beets
Quince Jelly
Parker House Rolls
Apricot Skillet Cake
Coffee

Shopping List	Have Ready
1 lb. Lamb Steak	1 Broiler
1 Package Rice	1 Frying Pan
1 Can Tiny Beets	1 Saucepan
Quince Jelly	Tablespoon
Parker House Rolls	Teaspoon
1 Can Apricots	Measuring Cup
Cream	Percolator
Onion	2 Dinner Plates
Mint	Can Opener
Parsley	

Preparation (Time: 25 minutes)

Light the gas oven and heat the broiler.
Heat 2 tablespoons butter in the frying pan for the rice.
Add 1 cup of rice and 1 sliced onion. Brown them in the butter.
Add 1 teaspoon salt, pepper and ½ teaspoon curry powder and 1 cup water. Cook 20 minutes, stirring occasionally.

Sear the steak under the gas flame. Add bits of butter. Broil 15 minutes.

Open the can of beets. Put 1 cup of beet juice into the saucepan.

Add the beets and 1 teaspoon salt, 2 teaspoons sugar, 2 tablespoons vinegar and 1 tablespoon butter blended with 1 tablespoon flour.

Cook until the sauce is thick and transparent.

Mince 1 tablespoon mint for the beets. Add just before serving.

Heat the rolls.
Set the table.
Make the coffee.

Serving

Arrange a mound of beets on each plate.
Next the rice and quince jelly.
Cut the steak in strips, decorate with parsley.
Serve immediately.

Spitted Steak with Oysters
Leeks on Toast   Hominy
Chili Sauce
Hot French Rolls
Cream Sponge Pudding
Coffee

Shopping List	Have Ready
½ lb. Top Sirloin Steak	2 Metal Skewers
¼ lb. Bacon	Broiler
1 Bunch of Leeks	2 Saucepans
Chili Sauce	Tablespoon
1 Pint of Cooked Hominy	Teaspoon
1 Dozen Oysters	Sharp Knife

SHOPPING LIST—Con'd
Cream
Lemon
Water Cress
French Rolls

HAVE READY—Con'd
Toaster
Percolator
2 Dinner Plates
Measuring Cup

Preparation (Time: 25 minutes)

Heat water in a saucepan for the leeks. Wash the leeks, remove the root and a part of the green top, leaving stalks 4 inches long.

Put the leeks into the boiling water. Add ½ teaspoon salt. Cook 20 minutes.

Light the broiler flame. Heat the broiler.

Cut the steak into strips about 1½ inches by 1 inch in size. Cut the bacon the same size.

Place a piece of steak on each of the skewers, then a piece of bacon, then an oyster, alternating until all are used.

Broil for 10 minutes. Turning every 3 minutes.

Heat the hominy in the saucepan in 2 tablespoons butter. Drain the leeks, saving ½ cup of the juice. Return this to the saucepan with 1 tablespoon butter. Heat well.

Set the table.

Make the coffee.

Toast 2 slices of bread.

Heat the rolls.

Serving

Place mounds of hominy on the plates.

Next slices of toast. Pour the juice from the leeks over the toast and lay the leeks on them.

Then the portions of Chili sauce and the spitted steak.

Decorate with water cress.

Serve immediately.

PLATE DINNER MENUS

Meat Balls with Mushrooms
Scalloped Sweet Potatoes   Stuffed Celery
India Relish   Plum Jelly
Rye Bread
Peach and Cherry Compote
Coffee

SHOPPING LIST
1 lb. Round Steak Ground
½ lb. Mushrooms
4 Sweet Potatoes
1 Bunch Celery
1 Package Snappy Cheese
1 Glass Plum Jelly
India Relish
Rye Bread
Milk
Cream
2 Peaches
½ lb. Cherries

HAVE READY
2 Frying Pans
Sharp Knife
Tablespoon
Teaspoon
Measuring Cup
Bowl
Percolator
2 Dinner Plates

Preparation (Time: 25 minutes)

Peel the sweet potatoes and cut them into dice.

Heat 2 tablespoons butter in a frying pan. Cook the potatoes in this for 5 minutes. Add 1 cup of milk and finish cooking, turning occasionally. Dust with salt and pepper.

Mould the meat into cakes. Brown them in the frying pan in 2 tablespoons of butter. Dust with salt and pepper.

Wash and slice the mushrooms. Cook them in the pan with the steak.

Wash the celery. Cut into pieces 4 inches long.

Mash the cheese with 4 tablespoons cream. Fill the celery stalks with the cheese and dust the top with paprika.

Set the table.

Make the coffee.

Serving

Arrange the stuffed celery on the plates.

Then the India relish and the plum jelly.
Next a mound of sweet potatoes.
Then the meat balls with the mushrooms over them.
Serve immediately.

Thirty-Minute Dinners

Veal Chops Breaded
Corn Soufflé   Lyonnaise Potatoes
Endive Salad
Cranberry Jelly
Charlotte Russe
Coffee

Shopping List	Have Ready
1 lb. Veal Chops	Baking Dish
1 Can of Corn	2 Frying Pans
4 Potatoes	Bowl
1 Onion	Sharp Knife
2 Stalks of Endive	Measuring Cup
1 Jar Cranberry Jelly	Bottle Opener
Lady Fingers	Tablespoon
Jam	Fork
Cream	Percolator
Mayonnaise	2 Dinner Plates
Cracker Crumbs	
Chili Sauce	

Preparation (Time: 30 minutes)

Light gas oven. Heat 1 tablespoon butter in baking dish. Beat 2 eggs and mix with corn. Add butter to the mixture. Bake 25 minutes.

Heat 1 tablespoon butter in frying pan for chops. Beat 1 egg with 1 tablespoon water. Dip the chops into this.

Then cover them with cracker crumbs.

Brown in the hot butter. Cook 20 minutes.
Heat 1 tablespoon butter in frying pan for potatoes.
Peel onion and potatoes and cut fine. Brown in butter and finish cooking more slowly.
Wash and dry the endive. Split each piece in half.
Spread with Russian Dressing made with 2 tablespoons mayonnaise and 2 tablespoons Chili sauce.
Set the table.
Make the coffee.

Serving

Arrange the salad on the plates.
Next a helping of corn soufflé and potatoes.
Then the breaded veal chops and a spoonful of cranberry jelly.
Serve immediately.

Braised Liver
French Fried Potatoes   Baked Tomatoes
Hot Buttered Rolls
Onion and Cucumber Salad
Jelly Roll
Coffee

Shopping List	Have Ready
1 lb. Calves Liver	Dripping Pan
4 Small Potatoes	Frying Kettle
2 Tomatoes	Sharp Knife
1 Small Onion	Bowl
1 Cucumber	Measuring Cup
Jelly	2 Dinner Plates
6 Finger Rolls	Tablespoon
Cream	Teaspoon

Preparation (Time: 30 minutes)

Light the gas oven.
Put 2 lbs. of lard to heat for potatoes.
Pour boiling water over liver. Drain and flour.
Sprinkle with salt and pepper.
Heat 2 tablespoons butter in dripping pan.
Brown the liver on each side. Turn gas half off in oven.
Cook slowly 25 minutes in the oven.
Cut the tomatoes in slices and cook in pan with liver.
Peel potatoes, wash and cut in thin slices.
Dry on a towel.
Fry 1 cupful at a time in hot fat.
Keep temperature 380 degrees.
Remove potatoes from fat when brown. Drain on soft paper.
Keep warm in the oven until all are fried.
Split and butter the rolls. Heat in the oven.
Peel the cucumber and onion. Slice thin.
Dress with 1/4 cup water, 1/4 cup vinegar, 1/2 teaspoon salt and pepper.
Let the salad stand until ready to serve. Then drain free from liquid.
Set the table.
Make the coffee.

Serving

Arrange mounds of drained cucumber and onion on each plate.
Next the tomatoes.
Then the French fried potatoes.
Last the braised liver.
Serve immediately.

PLATE DINNER MENUS

Steak with Tomato Sauce
Corn Dodgers   Brussels Sprouts
Poppy Seed Rolls
Maple Sugar Custard
Coffee

Shopping List	Have Ready
1 lb. Sirloin Steak	Baking Pan
1 Package Cornmeal	2 Saucepans
1 lb. Brussels Sprouts	Frying Pan
6 Poppy Seed Rolls	Measuring Cup
1 Bottle of Chili Sauce	Tablespoon
1 Green Pepper	Sharp Knife
1 Small Onion	2 Dinner Plates
Maple Sugar	Teaspoon
Cream	

Preparation (Time: 30 minutes)

Light the gas oven.
Heat 1½ cups water for the cornmeal.
Heat 1 pint of water for the Brussels sprouts.
Wash and trim the outside leaves from the sprouts.
Put them into boiling water with 1 teaspoon salt.
Cook 25 minutes.
Place the steak in hot buttered baking pan. Mince the onions and pepper.
Sprinkle over the steak. Add salt and pepper. Cover steak with one cup of tomato catsup.
Bake in a hot oven 20 minutes.
Sprinkle into boiling water ½ cup cornmeal.
Stir until smooth.
When slightly thickened, remove from the fire.
Beat into this ¼ cup flour and 1 egg.
Heat 2 tablespoons butter in the frying pan.
Drop spoonfuls of the cornmeal into this.
Brown well on each side.
Set the table.

Make the coffee.
Heat the rolls.
Drain Brussels sprouts, dress with 1 tablespoon butter.

Serving

Remove the steak from oven. Cut into strips.
Place a portion on each plate.
Next the corn dodgers.
Then a mound of Brussels sprouts dusted with paprika.
Serve immediately.

English Mutton Chops
Mint Dressing
Fried Potatoes   Buttered Toast
Creamed Celery and Minced Red Pepper
Cranberry Tart
Coffee

Shopping List	Have Ready
2 English Mutton Chops cut 2 inches thick	Broiler
1 Bunch Mint	Frying Pan
4 Small Potatoes	Bowl
Bread	Saucepan
1 Bunch Celery	Chopping Bowl
1 Sweet Red Pepper	Chopping Knife
1 Jar of Cranberry Sauce	Sharp Knife
Cream	Tablespoon
Lemon	Measuring Cup

Preparation (Time: 30 minutes)

Light broiler flame and heat broiler.
Heat 1½ cups of water for the celery.
Clean celery and cut the hearts in thin slices.

PLATE DINNER MENUS

Cook rapidly in boiling water for 20 minutes.
Peel potatoes. Slice thin. Brown in butter.
Turn often and cook 25 minutes.
Broil the chops 20 minutes. Turn every 5 minutes.
Clean mint. Chop enough leaves to make 4 tablespoons.
Cream 2 tablespoons butter and 1 tablespoon lemon juice. Add mint.
Set aside until the chops are broiled.
Mince very fine 2 tablespoons red pepper.
Cut the bread. Toast at the table on electric toaster.
Set the table.
Make the coffee.
Drain celery. Dress with salt, 1 tablespoon butter and 2 tablespoons cream. Keep warm.

Serving

Arrange mounds of celery on the plates.
Sprinkle each with the minced red pepper.
Next the potatoes.
Last the mutton chops spread with the mint butter and dusted with paprika.
Serve immediately.

Ham Creole
Buttered Potatoes   Celery and Olives
Green Pepper and Cottage Cheese Salad
Baked Red Bananas
Coffee

SHOPPING LIST
1 Slice of Ham
Chili Sauce
Small Onion
Celery

HAVE READY
Baking Dish with Cover
Baking Pan
Sharp Knife
Tablespoon

SHOPPING LIST—Con'd
Olives
2 Green Peppers
½ lb. Cottage Cheese
4 Potatoes
Parsley
Mayonnaise

HAVE READY—Con'd
Teaspoon
Measuring Cup
Percolator
2 Dinner Plates

Preparation (Time: 30 minutes)

Light the gas oven. Put ½ cup of water in the baking pan. Place the pan in the oven.

Spread the ham with 1 cup of Chili sauce. Cut the onion fine and lay over the Chili sauce. Mince 1 teaspoon celery leaves, sprinkle over the top. Add bits of butter.

Place in the pan; baste occasionally with the liquid around the meat. Add more water if it cooks away.

Peel and slice the potatoes thin. Put a layer of potatoes in the baking dish.

Add bits of butter, salt and pepper. Repeat until all the potatoes are used. Cover and bake 20 minutes.

Wash the celery. Cut into small pieces. Lay on ice until wanted.

Cut the tops from the peppers. Remove the seeds. Fill the peppers with cottage cheese. Pack it well into them. Slice in thin slices with a very sharp knife across the pepper.

Set the table.
Make the coffee.

Serving

Arrange the rings of peppers in overlapping slices. Dress with mayonnaise.

Next the celery and olives.
Then a mound of potatoes.
Next slices of ham Creole.
Decorate with parsley and serve immediately.

PLATE DINNER MENUS

Baked Halibut
Oyster Dressing
Buttered Rice   Tomatoes Sauté
Mixed Pickles
French Rolls
Date Pudding with Cream
Coffee

Shopping List	Have Ready
1 Center Slice of Halibut	Small Baking Pan
12 Small Oysters	Saucepan
1 Package of Rice	Frying Pan
3 Tomatoes	Bowl
Mixed Pickles	Sharp Knife
1 Package of Dates	Measuring Cup
Cream	Tablespoon
4 French Rolls	Teaspoon
Curry Powder	Percolator
	2 Dinner Plates

Preparation (Time: 30 minutes)

Light the gas oven. Put 2 tablespoons butter in the baking pan to heat for the halibut.

Mix 2 cups soft bread crumbs with ½ cup oyster juice.

Add the oysters, ¼ teaspoon salt, pepper and the hot butter from the pan.

Cover the slice of halibut with the dressing. Put in the hot pan. Bake 25 minutes in a moderate oven.

Heat 1 quart of water for the rice. When boiling add 1 cup rice and 1 teaspoon salt. Boil 20 minutes.

Heat 1 tablespoon butter in the frying pan for the tomatoes.

Slice the tomatoes. Dust with salt and pepper and dip in flour.

Sauté 15 minutes, turning often.

Drain the rice. Dress with 1 tablespoon butter, ½ teaspoon curry powder. Keep the rice warm.

Heat the rolls.

Set the table.
Make the coffee.

Serving

Arrange a mound of rice on each plate.
Next the tomatoes sauté and the mixed pickles.
Divide the halibut in half with a sharp knife.
Serve a portion on each plate.
Serve immediately.

Hearts of Lamb Chops
Stuffed Green Peppers   Creamed Potatoes
Sliced Tomatoes with Mint
French Bread
Baked Custard
Coffee

Shopping List	Have Ready
1 lb. Loin Lamb Chops	Large Baking Pan
4 Green Peppers	Saucepan
4 Potatoes	Double Boiler
2 Tomatoes	Bowl
French Bread	Measuring Cup
Mint	Tablespoon
Cream	Teaspoon
Milk	Sharp Knife
	Percolator
	2 Dinner Plates

Preparation (Time: 30 minutes)

Light the gas oven for the chops.
Heat 1 tablespoon butter in the pan, on top of the stove.
Remove the bone and fat from the chops, leaving the hearts.

Dust the meat with flour, salt and pepper. Brown in butter. Finish cooking in the oven.

Remove seeds and tops from the peppers.

Stuff them with a dressing made from 2 cups of bread crumbs, 1 sprig of mint, ¼ teaspoon salt, 1 egg beaten with 3 tablespoons cream and ⅛ teaspoon sage.

Put them in the pan with the meat. Bake 20 minutes.

Peel the potatoes and cut into small dice. Boil 10 minutes. Make cream sauce in the double boiler for the potatoes.

Use 1 cup of milk, 2 tablespoons butter blended with 2 tablespoons flour. Add ½ teaspoon salt. When the cream sauce is thick drain the potatoes and cook over hot water until wanted.

Slice the tomatoes. Dust with salt, pepper and minced mint. Set the table.

Make the coffee.

Serving

Arrange a mound of creamed potatoes on the plates. Dust with paprika.

Next the sliced tomatoes.

Then the lamb chops and green peppers. Decorate with sprigs of mint.

Serve immediately.

Pork Chops with Apple Rings
Browned Sweet Potatoes   Asparagus
Mustard Pickles
Bavarian Cream
Coffee

SHOPPING LIST
1 lb. Pork Chops
2 Red Apples

HAVE READY
Large Baking Pan
2 Saucepans

Shopping List—Con'd
4 Sweet Potatoes
1 Bunch Asparagus
Mustard Pickles
Cream

Have Ready—Con'd
Sharp Knife
Percolator
2 Dinner Plates
Tablespoon
Teaspoon

Preparation (Time: 30 minutes)

Light the gas oven.

Put water to heat in the saucepans for asparagus and sweet potatoes.

Brown the chops in the baking pan on top of stove with 1 tablespoon butter.

Core the apples. Slice in ¼ inch rings. Lay them around the chops.

Put in the oven. Bake 25 minutes.

Peel the potatoes. Boil 10 minutes.

Drain and lay them in the pan with the chops and apples.

Wash the asparagus and cut off hard ends. Cook 20 minutes.

Set the table.

Make the coffee.

Drain the asparagus. Dress with 1 tablespoon butter. Keep warm.

Serving

Arrange the pork chops on the plates.

Surround them with the apples.

Next the sweet potatoes and a spoonful of mustard pickle.

Then the stalks of asparagus. Dust asparagus with paprika.

Veal Steak with Vegetables
Browned Potatoes   Stuffed Tomato Salad
Dill Pickles
Honeydew Melon with Ice Cream
Coffee

Shopping List	Have Ready
1 lb. Veal Steak	Baking Pan
4 Potatoes	Saucepan
2 Tomatoes	Bowl
Mayonnaise	Chopping Bowl
Celery	Chopping Knife
Walnuts	Sharp Knife
Dill Pickles	Tablespoon
Honeydew Melon	Teaspoon
Ice Cream	Measuring Cup
1 Onion	Percolator
Sweet Red Pepper	2 Dinner Plates

Preparation (Time: 30 minutes)

Light the gas oven for the veal steak.

Prepare the vegetables. Chop fine 1 onion, 1 red sweet pepper, 3 pieces of celery and 1 tablespoon walnuts.

Heat 2 tablespoons butter in the baking pan and brown the vegetables 5 minutes.

Remove the vegetables and brown the steak which has been floured.

Cover the steak with the vegetables. Dust with salt, pepper and curry powder. Add ½ cup hot water.

Bake 20 minutes in a moderate oven.

Slice the peeled potatoes into a saucepan of boiling water. Cook 10 minutes.

Remove the potatoes to the pan, placing them around the meat. They should brown in 10 minutes.

Remove the centers from the tomatoes, cut the pieces fine.

Mix this with an equal amount of finely cut celery and 2 tablespoons mayonnaise. Heap in the tomato cups.

Slice the dill pickles, lengthwise.

Set the table.
Make the coffee.

Serving

Arrange the tomatoes on the dinner plates.
Next the potatoes and slices of dill pickles.
Cut the steak into portions.
Serve immediately.

Ham Baked

Potatoes O'Brien   Pineapple Salad
   French Rolls   Young Onions   Grape Jelly
          Chocolate Jumbles
              Coffee

SHOPPING LIST	HAVE READY
1 Slice Ham ½ inch thick	Baking Pan
Brown Sugar	Frying Pan
French Mustard	Chopping Bowl
Milk	Chopping Knife
Lettuce	Sharp Knife
Small Can Sliced Pineapple	Tablespoon
Mayonnaise	Teaspoon
Grated Cheese	Measuring Cup
4 Potatoes	Percolator
French Rolls	2 Dinner Plates
Young Onions 1 Bunch	2 Bread and Butter
1 Green Pepper	Plates
Parsley	

Preparation (Time: 30 minutes)

Light the gas oven for the ham.
Put 1 cup of milk in the baking pan. Heat in the oven.
Spread the slice of ham with French mustard. Cover this with ½ inch of brown sugar.

Place the ham in the baking pan. Bake 25 minutes in a moderate oven.

Peel the potatoes and 3 young onions and remove the seeds from the pepper.

Chop together in the chopping bowl.

Heat 1 tablespoon butter in the frying pan. Cook the vegetables 5 minutes in the butter. Add 1 cup of milk. Turn occasionally. Cook 15 minutes. Add more milk if it cooks away.

Wash and dry the lettuce. Spread each slice of pineapple with mayonnaise, sprinkle with grated cheese and dust with paprika.

Arrange the pineapple on the lettuce. Put in the refrigerator until wanted.

Set the table.

Make the coffee.

Heat the rolls.

Serving

Serve the rolls, jelly and butter on the bread and butter plates.

Arrange the salads on the dinner plates.

Next the potatoes O'Brien and the young onions.

Cut the ham into strips. Decorate with parsley.

Serve immediately.

Pork Tenderloin
Mashed Sweet Potatoes   Summer Squash
Radish Roses
Mixed Pickles
Raspberry Compote
Coffee

Shopping List	Have Ready
1 lb. Pork Tenderloin Cut in Portions	Frying Pan and Cover
4 Sweet Potatoes	2 Saucepans
1 Bunch Radishes	Bowl
Mixed Pickles	Tablespoon
1 Orange	Teaspoon
Cream	Measuring Cup
Raspberries	Percolator
Currants	2 Dinner Plates
1 Summer Squash	

Preparation (Time: 30 minutes)

Put the water to heat in the saucepans for the potatoes and the summer squash.

Put 2 tablespoons butter to heat for the meat. Dust the meat with salt, pepper and flour.

Brown each side of the meat. Cook covered, slowly, 25 minutes.

Turn the meat occasionally. Add 4 tablespoons cream when it is partly cooked.

Peel the potatoes and summer squash. Cook 20 minutes in boiling water.

Wash the radishes. With a sharp knife peel thin strips of the red skin of the radish half way down to imitate a rose. Put on ice until wanted.

Cut the orange in two and squeeze it. The juice is used for the potatoes.

Drain and mash the potatoes. Add the juice of the orange, 2 tablespoons cream, salt and pepper. Heat thoroughly.

Drain the squash and dress with 4 tablespoons cream, 1 tablespoon butter, salt and pepper.

Set the table.

Make the coffee.

Serving

Arrange the radishes and mixed pickles on the plates.
Next the mashed sweet potatoes.
Then a mound of summer squash dusted with paprika.
Last the pork tenderloin.
Serve immediately.

Broiled Pork Chops
Pineapple   Pimento Salad
New Potatoes in Cream
Celery
Floating Island
Coffee

Shopping List	Have Ready
1 lb. Small Pork Chops	Baking Pan
1 Can Pineapple	Saucepan
1 Can Pimentos	2 Bowls
Celery	Sharp Knife
1 Tomato	Tablespoon
Walnuts	Teaspoon
Mayonnaise	Percolator
6 New Potatoes	2 Dinner Plates
Cream	Can Opener

Preparation (Time: 30 minutes)

Light the gas oven and heat the pan for the chops.

Remove the fat from the chops. Lay them in the pan. Broil 25 minutes. Turn every five minutes.

Heat the water for the potatoes. Scrape them and cook 20 minutes.

Wash the celery and cut it into small pieces. Let stand in a bowl of ice water.

Open the pimentos and fill 2 of the pimento cups with

salad. For the salad cut the tomato fine. Add an equal amount of celery cut fine and 1 tablespoon broken walnut meats. Mix with 4 tablespoons mayonnaise mixed with 2 tablespoons cream. Fill the cups.

Open the pineapple. Place the slices in the pan with the chops.

Cook 10 minutes.

Set the table.

Make the coffee.

Drain the potatoes and heat with 4 tablespoons cream. Dust with salt and pepper.

Serving

Arrange the pimento salad on the plates.
Next the potatoes.
Then the pork chops and pineapple rings.
Decorate with the celery.
Serve immediately.

Baked Flounder
Potato Balls   Alligator Pear Salad
Pickled Onions
Toasted Finger Rolls
Blueberry Pudding
Coffee

SHOPPING LIST	HAVE READY
1 lb. Filet of Flounder	Baking Dish
4 Potatoes	Saucepan
Alligator Pear	Vegetable Ball Cutter
Small Can of Shrimps	Sharp Knife
Pickled Onions	Tablespoon
Finger Rolls	Teaspoon
Blueberries	Measuring Cup

PLATE DINNER MENUS

Shopping List—Con'd	Have Ready—Con'd
Parsley	Percolator
Cream	2 Dinner Plates
Mayonnaise	2 Bowls
Orange	
Lemon	

Preparation (Time: 30 minutes)

Light the gas oven for the fish.
Squeeze the juice of the orange into the baking dish.
Add 1 tablespoon minced parsley and a slice of onion.
Cut the flounder into strips, dust with salt and pepper.
Lay the fish in the baking pan. Cook 25 minutes.
Baste occasionally with the liquid in the dish.
Heat the water for the potatoes. Peel the potatoes. Cut balls from them with the vegetable cutter. Cook 20 minutes.
Cut the alligator pear in half. Peel it and cut into crosswise slices.
Mix 4 tablespoons mayonnaise with 2 tablespoons cream, add ½ teaspoon paprika.
Open the shrimps and wash them.
Cut lemon into slices.
Set the table.
Make the coffee.
Split the rolls and toast them at the table.
Drain the potatoes. Dress with 1 tablespoon butter and minced parsley.

Serving

Arrange the alligator pear slices in circles on the dinner plates.
Cover with dressing and decorate with shrimps.
Place next a portion of pickled onions.
Then the potato balls.

Last the strips of flounder decorated with parsley and sliced lemon.
Serve immediately.

Broiled Duck
Young Onions Boiled Broiled Sweet Potatoes
Water Cress Currant Jelly
Hot Rolls
Caramel Tapioca
Coffee

Shopping List	Have Ready
Young Duck Split for Broiling	Baking Pan
2 Bunches Young Onions	2 Saucepans
4 Sweet Potatoes	Bowl
Rolls	Measuring Cup
Water Cress	Tablespoon
Currant Jelly	Teaspoon
Tapioca	Sharp Knife
Cream	Percolator
Parsley	2 Dinner Plates

Preparation (Time: 30 minutes)

Light the gas oven and heat the baking pan.
Dust the duck with salt and pepper. Brown well 5 minutes.
Move the broiler to the center of the oven. Broil with the skin side up for 20 minutes.
Heat the water for the onions and sweet potatoes.
Use the white part of the onion. Boil 15 minutes.
Peel the sweet potatoes and cut lengthwise in ½ inch slices.
Boil 8 minutes. Drain the potatoes. Dot with butter, place around the duck and brown them on each side.
Wash and dry water cress.
Toss the water cress in 3 tablespoons olive oil, 1 tablespoon vinegar and ½ teaspoon salt beaten together.

Drain the cress free from liquid.
Heat the rolls.
Drain the onions and dress with 2 tablespoons cream, salt and pepper. Keep hot.
Set the table.
Make the coffee.

Serving

Arrange the onions on the plates.
Next the water cress and broiled sweet potatoes.
Next the duck and the currant jelly.
Decorate with parsley.
Serve immediately.

Forty-Minute Dinners

Broiled Salmon, Sauce Tartare
New Potatoes with Peas   Apple and Onion Salad
Sweet Pickles
Whole Wheat Bread Toasted
Crushed Strawberries
Hard Sauce
Coffee

Shopping List	Have Ready
1 Center Slice Salmon	Frying Pan
Mayonnaise	2 Saucepans
1 Bottle Capers	2 Bowls
Sweet Pickles	Egg Beater
6 New Potatoes	Tablespoon
1 lb. Peas	Teaspoon
2 Small Apples	Measuring Cup
Young Onions	Toaster
Whole Wheat Bread	Percolator
1 Box Strawberries	Sharp Knife

Shopping List—Con'd
Cream
Lemon
Parsley

Have Ready—Con'd
2 Dinner Plates

Preparation (Time: 40 minutes)

Light the broiler flame for the salmon.
Spread the salmon on each side with 1 tablespoon butter. Put in the frying pan. Broil 30 minutes.
Shell the peas and scrape the potatoes.
Put the potatoes into boiling water.
Boil 20 minutes.
Put the peas into a saucepan using 2 cups boiling water. Boil 20 minutes.
Remove the cores from the apples, leaving them whole. Scoop the centers out to form apple cups.
Slice 2 young onions thin and cut the centers of the apples into small pieces.
Mix the onion and apple with 1/3 cup of cream, whipped, 1 teaspoon sugar, 1/8 teaspoon salt, 1/2 teaspoon paprika and juice of half a lemon.
Heap the salad in the apple cups.
For the sauce *Tartare* use 4 tablespoons mayonnaise mixed with 1 teaspoon capers, 1 sweet pickle minced, 1 teaspoon parsley minced.
Drain the potatoes and peas. Combine them.
Dress with 4 tablespoons cream and 1 tablespoon butter. Heat them and keep warm.
Set the table.
Make the coffee.
Make the toast at the table.

Serving

Arrange the apple salads on the plates.
Then a mound of potatoes and peas.

Next the sweet pickles.

Cut the salmon in half and place the sauce *Tartare* beside it. Decorate with sprigs of parsley.

Broiled Chicken
New Potatoes   Broiled Egg Plant
Cabbage and Apple Salad
Strawberry Short Cake
Finger Rolls   Quince Jelly
Coffee

SHOPPING LIST	HAVE READY
1 Chicken Weighing 2½ lbs. split for Broiling	Saucepan with Cover Frying Pan
6 New Potatoes	Chopping Bowl
1 Small Egg Plant	Chopping Knife
1 Small Head of Cabbage	Sharp Knife
1 Apple	Tablespoon
1 Box of Strawberries	Measuring Cup
½ Pint of Cream	Large Bowl
1 Small Jar of Mayonnaise	Coffee Pot
Quince Jelly	Salt and Pepper
Finger Rolls	2 Dinner Plates
Lemon	2 Bread and Butter
Parsley	Plates

Preparation (Time: 40 minutes)

Put water to heat for potatoes.
Peel potatoes and put to cook.
Cook 30 minutes.
Light broiler flame.
Quickly sear each side of the split chicken.
Move broiler to the lower part of oven.
Broil 25 minutes with the skin side up.
Chop ½ head of cabbage with cored, unpeeled apple.

Add jar of mayonnaise, ⅓ cup cream, juice of ½ lemon, 1 teaspoon paprika, and 1 teaspoon sugar.

Blend with the cabbage and arrange in 2 cabbage leaves.

Heat 1 rounding tablespoon butter in frying pan.

Peel eggplant, slice ½ inch thick, sauté 2 minutes in butter.

Place eggplant under broiler flame beside the chicken.

Turn occasionally. Broil 10 minutes.

Drain potatoes. Dress with 1 tablespoon butter. Keep warm.

Set the table.

Make the coffee.

Heat rolls.

Serving

Arrange the rolls, butter, and a spoonful of jelly on bread and butter plates.

Place cabbage salad on each plate.

Next the eggplant, then the potatoes.

Last the broiled chicken and sprays of parsley.

Serve immediately.

Roast Loin of Lamb
Browned Potatoes   Combination Salad
Mint Jelly
Rice Pudding with Cream
Coffee

Shopping List	Have Ready
2 lbs. Loin of Lamb in one piece	Roasting Pan
	Tablespoon
4 Potatoes	Teaspoon
2 Tomatoes	Bowl
1 Cucumber	Sharp Knife
1 Head of Lettuce	Percolator

SHOPPING LIST—Con'd
 Mint Jelly
 Rice
 Cream
 Parsley

HAVE READY—Con'd
 2 Dinner Plates
 Opener

Preparation (Time: 40 minutes)

Light the broiler flame. Dust the lamb well with salt and pepper.

Brown the meat well under the flame for 10 minutes.

Light the oven flame and finish baking, keeping the temperature at 400° F.

Scrub the potatoes. Cut into lengthwise slices ½ inch thick.

Place the potatoes around the meat. Turn occasionally so that they will brown evenly.

Wash and dry the lettuce. Form salad cups out of the tenderest lettuce leaves.

Slice the tomatoes. Peel and slice the cucumber.

Arrange the cucumber and tomatoes in the salad cups.

Rub a bowl with cut garlic for the salad dressing.

Put a piece of ice in the bowl. Add 5 tablespoons olive oil, 1 tablespoon vinegar, ½ teaspoon salt and ½ teaspoon paprika. Beat until creamy and thick.

Set the table.

Make the coffee.

Open the mint jelly.

Serving

Arrange the salad on the dinner plates. Beat the dressing again and pour over the tomatoes and cucumbers.

Next the potato slices and a mound of mint jelly.

Carve the meat by cutting between the bones.

Lay on the plates and decorate with parsley.

Serve immediately.

A Seventy-Minute Dinner

Roast Beef
Horseradish
Browned Potatoes   String Beans
Stuffed Pimentos
Celery Hearts
Chocolate Cake
Coffee

Shopping List	Have Ready
3 lbs. Rolled Beef	Roasting Pan
6 Small Potatoes	Saucepan
1 lb. String Beans	Steamer
1 Can Pimentos	2 Bowls
1 Bottle Horseradish	Measuring Cup
1 Bunch Celery	Tablespoon
Parsley	Teaspoon
Cream	Sharp Knife
	Percolator
	2 Dinner Plates

Preparation (Time: 70 minutes)

Light gas oven. Heat to 500° F.
While the oven is heating, prepare vegetables.
Cook beans in boiling salted water 45 minutes.
Put the roast in the oven. Brown it.
When it is brown on each side reduce heat to 450° F.
Roast 55 minutes from the time the roast goes into the oven.
Place the peeled potatoes in the pan around the roast.
Bake 45 minutes.
Stuff the pimento cups with the following dressing:
Mix 2 cups bread crumbs with ½ cup water.
Add 1 egg, 1 teaspoon minced celery leaves, 1 teaspoon minced parsley, salt and pepper. Steam pimentos over hot water.
Mix ¼ cup horseradish with ¼ cup cream.

Soak the celery hearts in ice water. Dry before using.

Drain the beans. Dress with 1 tablespoon butter and 2 tablespoons cream. Keep warm.

Set the table.

Make the coffee.

Serving

Put 2 pimentos on each dinner plate.

Next the hearts of celery.

Then the potatoes, a mound of beans, and a spoonful of horseradish.

Carve slices of roast beef across the top of roast.

Lay them on the plates and decorate with parsley.

Serve immediately.

CHAPTER XXI

PLATTER DINNERS

Thirty-Five-Minute Dinners

Rib Lamb Chops

Mashed Potatoes   French Peas
Endive   Water Cress
Spiced Pimentos

Shopping List	Have Ready
6 Rib Lamb Chops	Broiler
1 Can of French Peas	2 Saucepans
1 lb. of Endive	Sharp Knife
6 Potatoes	Small Saucepan
Bunch of Water Cress	Small Casserole with Cover
1 Small Can of Pimentos	Measuring Cup
Whole Cloves	Tablespoon
Whole Cinnamon	Teaspoon
Cream	Potato Ricer
	Can Opener
	Platter

Preparation (Time: 35 minutes)

Heat the water for the potatoes. Peel the potatoes, cut into dice. Cook in boiling water 25 minutes.

Heat water for the endive. Wash the endive. Cut it in half lengthwise. Put ½ teaspoon salt in the water. Boil rapidly.

Light the gas oven. Open the peas. Put the drained peas into the casserole with 1 tablespoon butter. Cover and heat.

Wash and dry the water cress.

In the small saucepan, heat ½ cup of water, ½ cup of

vinegar, 2 tablespoons sugar, ½ stick of cinnamon and 6 cloves.

Open the can of pimentos, drain them, add them to the hot liquid. Remove from the fire and let stand until wanted.

Light the broiler flame. Heat the broiler. Broil the lamb chops 10 minutes.

Drain the potatoes. Put them through the ricer. Add ½ cup of hot cream, ½ teaspoon of salt and dust with pepper. Beat until creamy.

Keep warm.

Drain the endive. Dress it with 4 tablespoons cream, salt and paprika. Heat and keep warm.

Serving

Place the mashed potatoes in a cone shaped mound in the center of a large platter.

Stand the lamb chops on end. Press them half way into the mound at regular intervals to look like a crown roast.

The meat side should be toward the potatoes.

Place alternate mounds of endive and peas around the crown.

Decorate with spiced pimentos and water cress.

Serve immediately.

Braised Chicken
Baked Cucumbers   Minced Beets
Mashed Potatoes
Pears with Cream Cheese and Currant Jelly

Shopping List	Have Ready
2½ lb. Chicken cut in pieces	Frying Pan with Cover
2 Cucumbers	2 Small Baking Dishes
1 Can of Beets	Saucepan
	Tablespoon

Shopping List—Con'd	Have Ready—Con'd
6 Potatoes	Teaspoon
1 Can of Pears	Sharp Knife
1 Cream Cheese	Potato Ricer
Currant Jelly	Can Opener
Cream	Colander
Parsley	Platter
Milk	

Preparation (Time: 35 minutes)

Light the gas oven for the vegetables.

Heat 2 tablespoons butter in the frying pan for the chicken.

Dust the chicken with flour, salt and pepper. Brown it in the butter. Add ½ cup of water and cook closely covered for 30 minutes over a low flame.

Heat the water for the potatoes. Peel them and cut into dice. Put into boiling water and add 1 teaspoon salt.

Put 2 tablespoons butter into a baking dish for the cucumbers.

Heat it in the oven. Peel the cucumbers and cut into small dice. Stir into the hot butter, add salt and pepper. Bake 20 minutes covered (350° F.).

Open the beets. Drain them saving ⅓ cup of liquid.

Put the beets into the baking dish. Mince them. Stir into them 1 tablespoon of flour. Add 1 tablespoon sugar, ⅓ cup of beet juice, ½ cup of cream, ½ teaspoon salt and sprinkle with pepper. Mix well and bake in the oven; stir them occasionally.

Open the can of pears. Into each half put in the center 1 tablespoon of cream cheese. On top of the cheese place 1 teaspoon currant jelly.

Drain the potatoes in the colander. Put ½ cup of milk into the saucepan with 1 tablespoon of butter. Heat.

Rice the potatoes into the hot liquid. Remove from the fire and beat until creamy and white.

Serving

Place the chicken in the center of a large platter. At one end of the platter put the cucumbers. At the opposite end the beets.

Place the mashed potatoes at each side.
Arrange the pears between the vegetables.
Decorate with parsley.
Serve immediately.

A Forty-Five-Minute Dinner

Whole Pork Tenderloin with Dressing
Sliced Tomatoes   India Relish   Diced Potatoes
Tiny Lima Beans with Mushrooms
Lettuce

Shopping List	Have Ready
1 Whole Pork Tenderloin Split	Small Roasting Pan
2 Tomatoes	Small Baking Pan
4 Potatoes	Saucepan
1 Can Tiny Lima Beans	Sharp Knife
½ lb. Mushrooms	Can Opener
1 Head of Lettuce	Tablespoon
India Relish	Bowl
1 Apple	Teaspoon
Shelled Walnuts	Measuring Cup
Whole Wheat Bread	Platter
Cream	

Preparation (Time: 45 minutes)

Light the gas oven.

Put 2 tablespoons butter in the roasting pan. Brown the pork tenderloin in it on top of the stove.

Put 4 slices of whole wheat bread into the bowl. Pour 1

cup of hot water over it. Add 1 tablespoon of butter. Stir well. Add to this mixture, 1 slice of apple minced, 1 tablespoon of broken walnut meats, ½ teaspoon salt and ½ teaspoon sage.

Spread on the pork tenderloin. Bake 35 minutes in a moderate oven at 350° F.

Add ½ cup of water when the meat has been in the oven 10 minutes.

Heat water for the potatoes. Peel and dice them. Add to the boiling water with ½ teaspoon of salt.

Wash and slice the mushrooms. Open the lima beans and mix them with the mushrooms. Put in the baking pan with ½ cup of cream, ¼ teaspoon of salt, and dust with pepper. Bake in the oven. Stir them occasionally.

Wash and dry the lettuce. Cut the head in half and shred one-half of the head with the sharp knife.

Slice the tomatoes. Dust with salt and pepper and put a spoonful of India relish in the center of each.

Drain the potatoes. Add 1 tablespoon butter, salt and pepper.

Serving

Remove the meat from the oven. Place it in the center of a large platter.

Place alternate mounds of potatoes and lima beans and mushrooms around the meat.

Around the edge of the platter arrange the shredded lettuce. Lay the tomatoes on it.

Serve immediately.

A Sixty-Minute Dinner

Roast Duck
Cauliflower   Swiss Chard
Baked Sweet Potatoes
Slices of Orange and Apple
Mint

Shopping List	Have Ready
2½ lb. Duck	Roasting Pan
Head of Cauliflower	2 Saucepans
1 lb. Swiss Chard	Sharp Knife
6 Sweet Potatoes	Tablespoon
1 Orange	Teaspoon
1 Apple	Platter
Cream	Skewers
Bunch of Mint	Trussing Needle
	Twine

Preparation (Time 60 minutes)

Light the broiler flame for the duck. Fasten wings of the duck close to the body with skewers.

Thread the trussing needle with twine. Fasten the legs together at the ends. Run the trussing needle through tail and fasten legs to tail.

Dust with salt and pepper and brown under the broiler flame.

Turn out the broiler flame and light the oven. Roast 40 minutes at 400° F.

Scrub the sweet potatoes and put them in the oven to bake.

Heat water in the saucepans for the cauliflower and Swiss chard.

Wash the chard, cut it into pieces, add 1 teaspoon salt to the water. Put it into the saucepan of boiling water. Cook 30 minutes.

Cut the cauliflower into flowerets. Drop them into boiling water. Add 1 teaspoon salt.

Cut the orange and apple into thin slices. Do not peel.

Mince 2 tablespoons mint, sprinkle the apple and orange rings with it.

Drain the cauliflower. Dress it with 2 tablespoons butter, the juice of ½ lemon, salt and pepper. Heat and keep warm.

Drain the Swiss chard. Mince it with a knife. Dress with 4 tablespoons cream, ¼ teaspoon salt and dust with pepper. Heat and keep warm.

Remove the potatoes from the oven, make a slit in one side. Insert 1 teaspoon butter in each one. Sprinkle with paprika.

Remove the skewers and string from the duck.

Serving

Place the duck in the center of the platter.
Put the cauliflower at one end of the platter.
Arrange the Swiss chard at the opposite end.
Put the potatoes at each side of the duck.
Decorate with slices of orange and apple.
Use the sprigs of mint around the platter.

CHAPTER XXII

PLANK DINNERS

Thirty-Five-Minute Dinners

Planked Steak
String Beans in Pimento Cups
Potato Balls Cucumbers
Pickled Onions Radishes

SHOPPING LIST
1½ lbs. Porterhouse Steak
4 Potatoes
Small Can of Pimentos
Can of Wax Beans
Pickled Onions
Bunch of Radishes
Cucumber
Cream

HAVE READY
Plank
Broiler
Saucepan
Sharp Knife
Bowl
Vegetable Cutter
Tablespoon
Teaspoon
Can Opener

Preparation (Time: 35 minutes)

Light the gas oven and heat the plank.

Heat water for the potatoes. Peel the potatoes and cut balls from them with the vegetable cutter. Boil 15 minutes.

Open the pimentos and beans. Fill the pimento cups with the beans. Add 2 tablespoons cream to each portion. Dust with salt and pepper.

Wash the radishes and remove the tops.

Peel and slice the cucumber. Cover with ¼ cup of vinegar, ¼ cup of water and ½ teaspoon salt.

Drain the potatoes and stir them in 1 tablespoon butter.

Sear the steak on the broiler directly under the flame.

Remove the hot plank from the oven. Place the steak in the center of the plank.

Around the steak put alternate mounds of potato balls and pimento cups.

Place the plank in the oven for 15 minutes.

Drain the dressing from the cucumbers.

Remove the plank from the oven. Decorate with pickled onions, cucumbers and radishes.

Send the plank immediately to the table.

Corned Beef Hash and Eggs
Purée of Lima Beans   Water Cress
Tomatoes
Lemon Slices with Parsley

Shopping List	Have Ready
6 Potatoes	Plank
½ lb. Cooked Corn Beef	Saucepan
1 Can Lima Beans	Measuring Cup
Water Cress	Sharp Knife
2 Tomatoes	Tablespoon
Lemon	Teaspoon
Parsley	Purée Sieve
Cream	Chopping Knife
4 eggs	Chopping Bowl

Preparation (Time: 35 minutes)

Light the gas oven and heat the plank.

Put water on for the potatoes. Peel and cut them into small pieces.

Cook the potatoes 15 minutes.

Chop the corned beef. Put the lima beans through the sieve.

Mash the potatoes and beat into them 4 tablespoons cream, 1 tablespoon butter and the chopped corned beef.

Spread the hash in the center of the plank. Make a border around it with the beans.

With a spoon press 4 hollows in the hash and break into each an egg.

Put the plank into the oven and bake 15 minutes until the eggs are set.

Slice the tomatoes. Cut the lemon into slices and sprinkle with chopped parsley. Wash and dry the water cress.

Remove the plank from the oven and decorate with water cress, tomatoes and lemon.

Send the plank at once to the table.

Planked Crab Meat

Mushrooms   Spinach

Eggplant

Lemon Slices with Paprika

Shopping List	Have Ready
1 Pint of Crab Meat	Plank
½ lb. of Mushrooms	2 Saucepans
2 lbs. Spinach	Sharp Knife
Small Eggplant	Measuring Cup
Lemon	Tablespoon
Parsley	Teaspoon
Milk	
1 Package Snappy Cheese	
2 Eggs	

Preparation (Time: 35 minutes)

Light the gas oven. Heat the plank.

Put 1 pint of water and 1 teaspoon of salt to heat for the spinach.

Clean the spinach thoroughly. Cook 10 minutes.

While the spinach is cooking wash the mushrooms. Peel the egg plant, slice it and cut the slices into quarters.

Put the crab meat into the saucepan. Stir into it 2 heaping tablespoons flour and 2 tablespoons butter. Mix well and add ½ teaspoon salt, pepper, 1½ cups of milk, 1 cup bread crumbs and the snappy cheese broken into pieces. Cook, stirring constantly until it is well blended. Beat into this mixture 2 whole eggs.

Arrange the crab meat in center of plank in an oval.

Around this place the egg plant and mushrooms alternately. Dot with bits of butter.

Drain the spinach. Dress with 1 tablespoon butter, salt and pepper. Make a border around the edge of the plank.

Bake 20 minutes in the oven.

Cut the lemon into slices, dust with paprika.

Remove the plank from the oven. Decorate with the slices of lemon and bunches of parsley. Send immediately to the table.

Forty-Minute Dinners

Planked Hamburg Steak

Tomatoes   Onions

Sweet Potatoes

Celery   Green Peppers

Shopping List	Have Ready
1 lb. Chopped Steak	Plank
2 Bunches Young Onions	Saucepan
Celery	Sharp Knife
3 Tomatoes	Tablespoon
2 Green Peppers	Teaspoon
Tomato Catsup	Chopping Bowl
Parsley	Measuring Cup
4 Sweet Potatoes	Chopping Knife

Preparation (Time: 40 minutes)

Light the gas oven. Put the water to heat for the sweet potatoes. Heat the plank.

Cut the tomatoes in half. Cut the tops from the onions, using only the white balls.

Remove the seeds from the peppers. Clean the celery.

Chop the celery and peppers together, using an equal amount of each.

Place the meat in the center of the plank in an oval, smoothing the top. Dust with salt and pepper.

Arrange the tomatoes, onions and chopped vegetables alternately around the edge; dot with bits of butter. Spread 1 cup tomato catsup over the meat.

Bake 30 minutes.

Peel the sweet potatoes. Cut in slices and boil 10 minutes.

Drain the potatoes. Arrange them on the plank. Finish cooking in the oven.

Remove the plank from the oven. Decorate with parsley. Send at once to the table.

Planked Filet of Beef
New Potatoes   Asparagus
Bacon with Stuffed Olives   String Beans
Radishes

SHOPPING LIST	HAVE READY
1 Filet Cut in 4 Portions	Plank
6 New Potatoes	Frying Pan
1 Bunch of Asparagus	2 Saucepans
1 Can Stringless Beans	Tablespoon
1 Bottle Stuffed Olives	Teaspoon
¼ lb. Sliced Bacon	Measuring Cup
1 Bunch of Radishes	Can Opener
Parsley	Sharp Knife
	Tooth Picks

Preparation (Time: 40 minutes)

Light the gas oven. Heat the plank.
Heat water for the potatoes and asparagus.
Scrape the potatoes and boil 20 minutes.
Cut the hard end from the asparagus using only the green part.
Heat 1 tablespoon butter in the frying pan. Brown the filets in it for 8 minutes.
Put the asparagus to cook.
Arrange the filets in the center of the plank.
Open the beans. Drain the potatoes.
Wrap small pieces of bacon around each olive and fasten with a toothpick.
Arrange the potatoes, beans and olives around the filets.
Put the plank in the oven. Cook 20 minutes.
Wash the radishes and save to decorate the plank.
Drain the asparagus and dress with 1 tablespoon butter.
Remove the plank from the oven. Lay the asparagus around the edge. Decorate with radishes.
Send to the table at once.

CHAPTER XXIII

CASSEROLE DINNERS

Forty-Minute Dinners

Lamb Steak Chopped
Eggplant　　　　　Tomatoes
Onions　　　　　　Rice

SHOPPING LIST
1 lb. Lamb Steak Ground
1 Small Eggplant
1 Onion
2 Tomatoes
½ lb. Rice
Parsley

HAVE READY
Casserole with Cover
Large Bowl
Saucepan
Chopping Bowl
Chopping Knife
Sharp Knife
Measuring Cup
Tablespoon
Teaspoon

Preparation (Time: 40 minutes)

Heat 1 quart of water with 1 teaspoon salt in the saucepan for the rice. Light the gas oven. Put 1½ cups water in the casserole and heat it in the oven.

While the water is heating peel and chop the eggplant.

Peel and chop the onion. Cut the tomatoes into small pieces.

Mix the chopped vegetables in the bowl. Add the meat, 1 teaspoon of salt, ⅛ teaspoon pepper. Stir the ingredients together.

Put into the casserole. Cover and bake 30 minutes.

Stir the rice into the boiling water. Boil 20 minutes.

Drain the rice. Stir into it 1 tablespoon butter. Spread the rice over the meat in the casserole. Cover and finish baking.

Mince 1 tablespoon parsley.

Remove the casserole from the oven. Sprinkle the parsley over the rice. Cover and send at once to the table.

Steak
Mushrooms   Potatoes
Hearts of Lettuce
Roquefort Cheese Dressing

Shopping List	Have Ready
1 lb. Top Sirloin	Casserole with Cover
1 lb. Mushrooms	Bowl
4 Potatoes	Measuring Cup
1 Head Lettuce	Tablespoon
¼ lb. Roquefort Cheese	Teaspoon
Worcestershire Sauce	Sharp Knife
Garlic	Frying Pan
	2 Salad Plates

Preparation (Time: 40 minutes)

Light the gas oven. Put 1 cup of water into the casserole. Heat in the oven.

Peel the potatoes. Slice them very thin. Lay them in the casserole. Dust with salt and pepper. Dot with butter. Cover them so they will begin to cook.

Cut the steak in portions. Dust them with flour, salt and pepper.

Heat 2 tablespoons of butter in the frying pan. Brown the meat in it and lay it on top of the potatoes.

Wash the mushrooms. Cut them into pieces and brown them in the frying pan. Put the mushrooms over the meat. Cover the casserole and finish baking.

Wash the lettuce for the salad. Remove the outer leaves.

CASSEROLE DINNERS

Cut the lettuce in two. Lay the hearts on the salad plates. For the dressing rub the bowl with a cut bud of garlic.

Put a small piece of ice in the bowl. Add 5 tablespoons olive oil, 2 tablespoons vinegar, ½ teaspoon salt and 1 tablespoon Worcestershire sauce. Beat together until thick.

Mash the Roquefort cheese into the dressing. Pour over the salads on the plates.

Remove the casserole from the oven and send covered to the table.

Forty-Five-Minute Dinners

Chicken
Carrots   Onions
Summer Squash
Dumplings

Shopping List	Have Ready
2½ lb. Roasting Chicken cut in pieces	Casserole with Cover
6 Small Carrots	Frying Pan
2 Onions	Bowl
Summer Squash	Tablespoon
Milk	Teaspoon
	Measuring Cup
	Sharp Knife
	Chopping Bowl
	Chopping Knife

Preparation (Time: 45 minutes)

Light the gas oven. Heat the casserole.

Peel the summer squash, onions and carrots. Cut into pieces.

Chop each separately in the chopping bowl.

Heat 2 tablespoons butter in the frying pan. Cook the carrots 3 minutes and remove to the casserole.

Next cook the summer squash 3 minutes and put into the casserole. Then cook the onions 3 minutes and put into the casserole. Add 2 tablespoons butter to the pan. Brown the chicken in it.

Lay the chicken on top of the vegetables in the center of the casserole. Dust with flour, salt and pepper.

Pour 2 cups of water into the frying pan. When it is hot put it into the casserole. Cover and bake in a moderate oven 30 minutes.

Ten minutes before the dish is finished, drop dumplings around the chicken. They should come in contact with the liquid. Add hot water if necessary.

The dumplings are made with 1½ cups of flour sifted with 2 teaspoons of baking powder. Stir into this ½ cup milk. Beat in 2 eggs, drop spoonfuls into the hot liquid. Cover and bake 10 minutes.

Remove from the oven. Send immediately to the table.

Thin Slices of Ham
Macaroni and Cheese   Spinach
Stuffed Olives   Tomatoes

Shopping List	Have Ready
½ lb. Cooked Ham sliced thin	Casserole with Cover
1 Package of Macaroni	(Not glass)
Small Bottle of Stuffed Olives	Saucepan
½ lb. Grated Cheese	Sharp Knife
1 lb. Spinach	Tablespoon
2 Tomatoes	Teaspoon
Milk	Measuring Cup
	Chopping Bowl
	Chopping Knife

Preparation (Time: 45 minutes)

Heat water for the macaroni. Break ½ package of macaroni into pieces and drop into boiling water. Boil 20 minutes.

Light the gas oven. Put 1 cup of water into the casserole. Heat it in the oven.

Wash the spinach, discard the roots and chop it in the chopping bowl. Put the spinach in the bottom of the casserole.

Drain the macaroni. Add 1 cup of milk, the grated cheese, ½ teaspoon salt and pepper. Heat until the cheese is melted.

Cover the spinach with the macaroni and cheese.

Cut the tomatoes in half. Arrange them around the edge.

Place the ham in the center. Decorate with the stuffed olives.

Bake 20 minutes.

Remove the cover. Brown the ham under the broiler flame.

Cover and send at once to the table.

CHAPTER XXIV

DINNERS PREPARED AHEAD OF TIME

The fore-handed dinner is a convenient method of cooking a dinner before it is needed, so that less time must be spent in the kitchen at the dinner hour.

If you must be away from home in the afternoon this is a convenient method to follow. Vegetables may be prepared and cooked, salad greens washed and put against the ice, salad dressings made, desserts and even meats prepared in advance.

Casserole cooking may be used to advantage in the fore-handed dinner. The casserole dish is prepared and baked and simply heated at dinner time.

In the summer jellied meats or salads, cold roasts, deviled eggs, jellied soups, frozen desserts should all be ready in advance. If you have an electric refrigerator time may be saved by shopping twice a week for the vegetables. Cook them all at one time, store the vegetables in the refrigerator for future use. They may be made into creamed dishes, salads or soups.

The oven dinner lends itself admirably to fore-handed cooking. Small baking dishes are used. The different foods are prepared for the oven in their respective dishes, stored in the refrigerator and all baked at one time in the oven. If you use a glass or china baking dish warm it in hot water before placing it in the oven. Left-overs and previously cooked foods are the best ones to use for this kind of dinner.

The utilization of previously cooked foods is a study in itself. To concoct an interesting dinner out of the contents of the refrigerator taxes the ingenuity. But the art makes for variety and economy in cooking.

Supposing your refrigerator contained part of a roast, gravy, carrots, peas, string beans, mashed potatoes, asparagus and lettuce. The menu prepared might be:

Shepherd's Pie
Baked Carrots and Peas   String Beans au Gratin
Asparagus Salad

Chop the meat for the Shepherd's pie. Moisten it with gravy. Put it into a baking dish. Spread the mashed potatoes evenly over the top. Dot with bits of butter, sprinkle with salt and pepper. Store in the refrigerator until dinner time. Put the string beans into a baking dish. Moisten them with cream sauce. Sprinkle buttered crumbs over the top. Put into the refrigerator until wanted. The carrots and peas are mixed together and moistened with cream and placed in a baking dish. Bake the dinner in a moderate oven, 350° F., for 25 minutes. Dress the asparagus and lettuce with French dressing.

Menus that adopt themselves to fore-handed dinners follow.

Moulded Jellied Chicken
Cold Sliced Ham   Deviled Eggs
String Beans, Beet and Carrot Salad
Cranberry Jelly   Sweet Pickles

Sliced Veal Loaf
Mashed Potatoes Sauté   Creamed Wax Beans
Cauliflower and Pimento Salad
Spiced Peaches   Radishes

Chicken Curry
Rice Baked   Buttered Asparagus
East Indian Chutney   Celery
Rye Bread

SECTION FOUR
ENTERTAINING

CHAPTER XXV

COCKTAILS

There are two ways to serve fruit juice or vegetable cocktail as an appetizer for a first course. One is to serve it at the table in cocktail glasses placed on a service plate. The other way is to pass cocktails in glasses to the guests assembled in the living room before sitting down to the table. The latter method has grown in favor lately.

Serve hors d'œuvres or canapés or both with the cocktail, particularly if it is served in the living room. These should be small and the type that may be eaten from the fingers. Tiny cocktail napkins should accompany them. There are gay paper cocktail napkins with modern and amusing designs or they may be of linen.

The vogue for these fruit or vegetable cocktails has been responsible for a large number of bottled and canned varieties. These may be served as they are, chilled, but some individual touch of your own may be added. It is the wise hostess who always leads her guests to expect a little surprise in the foods she offers them.

Here are some of the most recent cocktail concoctions to interest your guests:

White Grape Juice

These cocktails are mixed as they are served. Arrange a

tray with iced white grape juice, cocktail glasses, ice cubes and carbonated water. Half fill the cocktail glasses with grape juice. Add ice. Fill with carbonated water. A white seedless grape of the canned variety may be added to each glass.

Grapefruit and Prune

Squeeze enough grapefruit to make 2 cups. Add 1 cup of prune juice. Add 1 to 2 tablespoons of honey depending on the sweetness of the grapefruit. Shake in a cocktail shaker with ice until the shaker is frosty. Serve immediately. A green minted cherry adds to the attractiveness of this cocktail. Makes 8 cocktails.

Cranberry Cocktail

Add 4 cups of cranberries to 4 cups of boiling water together with 4 whole cloves and a thin slice of lemon peel. Cook slowly 15 minutes crushing the berries as they cook. Add ¾ cup of sugar. Cook 5 minutes. Strain through a fine meshed wire sieve. Cool and keep in the refrigerator. When serving shake in a cocktail shaker with ice. For variety the white of an unbeaten egg may be added to 1 pint of the cranberry juice. Shake with ice in a cocktail shaker. This cocktail when poured into the glasses will have white foam decorating the top of the red liquid.

Grape Juice Cocktail

Two cups of grape juice, 1 cup of orange juice, 1 tablespoon lemon juice, 2 whole cloves, 1 thin slice of lemon peel. Shake in a cocktail shaker with ice. Serve in cocktail glasses. Decorate with a maraschino cherry. Makes 8 cocktails.

Loganberry Juice

Half fill cocktail glasses containing crushed ice with loganberry juice. Fill glasses with ginger ale. Decorate with green cherry.

Lime Cocktail

Juice of 2 limes mixed with 2 tablespoons of honey and 2 cups of orange juice. Add 1 whole egg white. Shake in cocktail shaker with ice for 2 minutes. Half fill cocktail glasses. Fill up the glasses with iced ginger ale.

Pineapple Crème de Menthe

Mix 1 pint of pineapple juice with 2 tablespoons of crème de menthe syrup. Shake in a cocktail shaker with crushed ice. Serve with a green or red cherry in each glass. Makes 6 cocktails.

Currant and Raspberry

Mix 1 cup of currant juice with 1 cup of raspberry juice. Shake in cocktail shaker with ice. Pour into glasses with a triangle of candied orange peel in each glass. Makes 6 cocktails.

Sauerkraut Juice

One pint of sauerkraut juice, 1 teaspoon lemon juice, $\frac{1}{8}$ teaspoon paprika, $\frac{1}{8}$ teaspoon of salt. Shake with ice in a cocktail shaker. Serve immediately. A pickled onion or a stuffed olive may be added to each glass when served. Makes 6 cocktails.

Tomato Juice Cocktail

One pint of tomato juice, $\frac{1}{2}$ teaspoon of salt, 1 tablespoon of lemon juice, 1 teaspoon minced onion, 1 teaspoon minced celery or a few grains of celery salt, thin slice of lemon peel. Cover and let stand in the refrigerator until ice cold. Strain. When serving shake in a cocktail shaker with ice. Serve with a pickled onion or large green olive in each glass for variety. Makes 6 cocktails.

Clam Juice

One pint of clam juice, thin shaving of lemon peel, $\frac{1}{8}$ teaspoon of salt, 1 tablespoon lemon juice, dash of pepper. Shake in a cocktail shaker with ice. Serve with a thin sliver-like paring of lemon peel in each glass. Makes 6 cocktails.

Clam Juice and Tomato

One cup of clam juice, 1 cup of tomato juice, 1 tablespoon lemon juice, lemon peel, $\frac{1}{8}$ teaspoon salt, dash of paprika. Shake in a cocktail shaker with ice. Serve a stuffed ripe or green olive in each glass for variety. Makes 6 cocktails.

CHAPTER XXVI

HORS D'ŒUVRES AND CANAPÉS

Hors d'œuvres and canapés, those smart morsels which are served with the cocktail before dinner, luncheon, or in the evening, lend an air of sophistication to any entertainment. They make an occasion out of a gathering that might otherwise be just another party. They are coming more and more into favor.

Of course, since the cocktails and the foods which accompany them are all appetizers they should be light enough not to take the appetite for the main dishes to follow.

The purpose of the appetizer is twofold. Its piquancy stimulates the appetite; it appeals to the eye as well. It should always be bright and colorful.

The hors d'œuvres are usually salty, crisp or tart. The canapé may be all of these things but its difference is that it is served on a foundation of lightly toasted bread. The bread may be sautéd in place of toasting. Crackers, the thin light type in various shapes are used as well as specially manufactured foundations. These last come in assorted shapes in each package and have a rim to enclose the filling to hold it in place.

In arranging either the hors d'œuvre plate or the canapé plate select those that make an interesting contrast of color on the central dish.

Antipasto

An arrangement of hors d'œuvres on one central dish is interesting. These should be grouped in mounds so that it is easy to select what one wishes. Some of the appetizers which might be used are: chopped beets with chopped cabbage mixed with French dressing, chilled and drained; stuffed eggs trimmed with strips of pimentos; curls of celery which are made by soaking thin strips of celery in ice water; sardines; spiced pimentos; olives; sweet pickles, anchovies; hearts of artichokes; highly seasoned sausage; smoked fish; radish roses; tiny tomatoes, peeled and chilled.

Stuffed Tomatoes

Peel tiny tomatoes of either the red or yellow variety. Remove the center. Chop fine and mix with an equal quantity of cottage cheese. Stuff the tomatoes and place a bit of caviare that has been mixed with lemon juice on the top of each one.

Stuffed Eggs

Boil 6 eggs until they are hard, for 20 minutes. Pour cold water over them. Remove the shells and cut the eggs in half lengthwise. Remove the centers and soak the white in pickled beet juice for several hours until they are deep red in color. Mash the yolks. Mix with 2 tablespoons of vinegar, 2 tablespoons of cream, 1 teaspoon of French mustard, 1 teaspoon minced parsley, ½ teaspoon of salt and a dash of celery salt. Fill the egg cups with this mixture. Place a bit of mayonnaise on the top of each and decorate with pickled capers. The egg cups may be left uncolored if you prefer. Makes 12 portions.

Salami or Smoked Salmon

Make a filling of 2 tablespoons of Roquefort cheese mashed with 4 tablespoons of cream cheese and 4 tablespoons of cream. Add 1 tablespoon of dill pickle minced and 2 radishes with the peel left on, minced fine. Place 2 teaspoons of this in the center of a slice of salami sausage or a thin slice of smoked salmon. Make into cornucopias, securing each with a toothpick. Makes 12 portions.

Potato Chips with Pimento Cheese

Spread crisp potato chips with pimento cheese. Serve plain or with a thin slice of pickle in the center of each.

Stuffed Pickled Beets

Soak 1 can tiny cooked beets in a mixture made from ½ cup of vinegar, ½ cup of water, 1 tablespoon of sugar cooked with 2 whole cloves and ½ teaspoon of salt. Remove the centers from the beets. Mince them and add 1 tablespoon minced celery, 1 tablespoon minced cucumber, 1 teaspoon anchovy paste, 1 tablespoon cottage cheese and 2 tablespoons of mayonnaise. Stuff the beets with this mixture. Decorate with a sprig of parsley.

Cucumber

Peel 1 cucumber. Score the outside with a fork. Cut into ¾ inch slices. Remove the centers leaving a ¼ inch shell. Soak in ice water until crisp. Drain and dry in a towel. Mix ½ cup of cottage cheese with 1 tablespoon of chopped chives and 1 tablespoon mayonnaise. Heap in the drained cucumber shells. Sprinkle with paprika.

Stuffed Radishes

Cut the bottoms from radishes so that they will stand erect. Cut to within ¼ inch of the bottom crosswise of the radishes with a sharp knife in ⅛ inch slices in opposite directions so that you have tiny squares. Peel back the red portion to simulate a rose. Soak in ice water. When crisp, remove the center portion of the radishes. Mince fine. Mix with an equal quantity of chopped hard boiled egg and caviare. Moisten with mayonnaise. Stuff the radishes.

Tiny Sausage Rissoles

Make a puff paste. (See directions in recipe under Pastry.) Roll the paste ⅛ inch thick. Cut into rounds with a cutter. Moisten edges with water. Place a tiny cooked sausage in the center. Fold pastry over it. Press edges together with the tines of a fork or a pastry marker. Prick top. Brush the tops lightly with a mixture made from 1 egg yolk beaten with 1 teaspoon cold water. Use a pastry brush for this. Bake in a hot oven (450° F.) for 10 minutes. A small sardine placed in the center makes another variety of rissole.

Sausage and Almond

Into each end of a tiny sausage place a blanched almond. Broil until the sausages are crisp. Serve with a toothpick stuck into the sausage to serve as a handle to eat it.

Dried Beef Hors D'Œuvres

Mash 1 cream cheese. Mix with it 1 teaspoon of minced sweet pickle. Place 2 teaspoons of this mixture in the center of a square of dried beef. Make into a cornucopia and secure with a toothpick. 12 portions.

Celery Stuffed with Shrimp

Shred 1 cup of shrimp. Mix with ¼ cup of minced celery. Add 2 tablespoons of mayonnaise. Stuff stalks of celery with the mixture. One end of the celery may be cut in fine strips, soaked in ice water, drained and the remaining portion stuffed. The ice water causes the strips to curl. 12 portions.

Celery Stuffed with Chicken

Chop 1 cup of chicken fine. Mix with 2 tablespoons minced celery and 2 tablespoons minced cucumber. Moisten with 2 tablespoons mayonnaise. Stuff pieces of celery.

Celery Stuffed with Avocado

Scrape deep stocks of celery. Cut into 3 inch lengths. Throw into ice water with lemon juice in the water. The celery may be placed in a covered jar in an iceless refrigerator until crisp if you prefer. Mash enough avocado pear to make 1 cup. Add salt and pepper and ½ tablespoon of lemon juice. Just barely moisten with mayonnaise. Fill the celery. Level the mixture on top and decorate with bits of pimento.

Canapés

Caviare Canapé

Cut the bread in diamond-shaped pieces. Sauté in butter or toast lightly. Spread with a thin layer of caviare. Decorate the edges with 1 finely minced hard boiled egg, and the center with chopped pickled beets. Eight canapés.

Asparagus Tip Canapé

Dip asparagus tips in mayonnaise. Roll each asparagus tip in a thin slice of bread from which the crust has been removed. Fasten the bread with toothpicks. Toast lightly.

Cheese and Onion Canapé

Cut slices of bread ¼ inch thick. Cut into rounds with a cutter. Lightly toast 1 side of the bread. Spread the opposite side with snappy cheese. Place a few tiny pickled onions in the center of each. Broil under the gas flame until the cheese and onions are hot. The onions used for these canapés come in bottles and are about the size of tapioca.

Peanut Butter and Bacon

Toast ½ inch slices of bread lightly on one side. Spread the untoasted side with peanut butter. Cut into small squares. Place a small square of bacon in the center of each. Broil until the bacon is crisp. Decorate with a slice of stuffed olive.

Sardine Canapés

Spread saltines with butter and dust with paprika. Heat in the oven. Mix ⅓ cup of butter with 1 tablespoon of French mustard. When it is creamed add 1 tablespoon of chopped parsley. Spread the crackers with this. Mince sardines with enough tomato catsup to moisten. Put 1 teaspoon on each cracker and decorate with pickled walnut cut in slices. 12 crackers.

Avocado Canapés

Cut slices of bread, ¼ inch thick. Shape with a crescent cutter. Toast lightly on one side. Spread the other side with thin slices of avocado pear. Place a tiny bit of Chutney in the center, decorate with thin strips of pimento and heat in the oven.

Anchovy Canapés

Mash 1 ounch of Roquefort cheese with 1 tablespoon of

Worcestershire sauce. Heat potato chips in the oven. Spread the chips with the cheese. Place a rolled anchovy in the center of each. Decorate with finely minced sweet pickles.

Surprise Canapé

Spread rounds of lightly toasted bread with sardine paste. Place a slice of hard boiled egg in the center. Make a border around the edge with cream cheese which has been colored with a small amount of beet juice.

Prunes and Bacon

Steam prunes until tender. Remove the pit. Fill the cavity with a stuffed olive. Wrap in small thin slices of bacon just big enough to cover the prune. Secure with a toothpick. Broil until the bacon is crisp. Pitted prunes may be purchased in jars for this purpose.

Apple and Cheese

Core a red apple. Do not peel. Quarter and cut into thin slices. Spread with a mixture of 4 tablespoons Roquefort cheese mashed with 2 tablespoons of orange juice or 2 tablespoons of cooking wine. Camembert cheese may be used instead of Roquefort and the juice omitted.

Cheese and Mustard Butter Canapés

Place slices of American cheese on saltines. Spread the cheese with mustard butter. Toast until the cheese is melted. The butter is made by creaming one tablespoon of butter with 1 teaspoon of French mustard and ½ teaspoon of horse-radish.

Stuffed Olives and Bacon

Wrap a stuffed olive in a thin strip of bacon. Fasten the bacon to the olive with a toothpick. Broil until the bacon is crisp and brown. These delicious morsels are eaten in the fingers, the toothpick serving as a handle.

Mushroom Canapé

Cut slices of bread with a round cutter with a hole in the center. Lightly toast one side of the bread. Lay a large flat mushroom cap on the untoasted side. Dot with bits of butter and broil under a flame for 3 minutes.

Lobster Canapés

Heat together 1 cup of minced lobster meat, 2 tablespoons of cream, 2 tablespoons of butter and 1 tablespoon of walnut catsup. Spread on lightly toasted bread cut in rounds. Decorate the center with a small star cut from a pimento. 12 canapés.

Pickled Mussels

Spread rounds of bread cut ¼ inch thick with softened butter. Sprinkle with minced parsley. Heat in the oven. Heat pickled mussels. Lay on the rounds of bread, dust with paprika. Decorate with a thin slice of pickle and strips of pimento. 8 canapés.

Water Cress and Shrimp

Cream 2 tablespoons of butter. Mix with it 2 tablespoons of finely minced water cress. Spread rounds of lightly toasted bread with this mixture. Mash ½ cup of shrimps with 1 teaspoon of lemon juice. Place in the center of the canape so that there is a border of the green water cress showing. Put a tiny bit of mayonnaise and a sprig of parsley in the center. This may be spread on light, round crackers instead of the toast. 12 canapés.

Blini

Make a pancake batter from the recipe under hot breads. Make into pancakes about 2 inches across. Cover them with caviare that is just moistened with sour cream and a little lemon juice. Whip ½ cup of thick sour cream with 1 teaspoon lemon juice and a few grains of salt. Heap a spoonful of sour cream in the center. The pancakes should be hot. Another way to make the blini is to use the recipe for French pancakes given under hot breads. Make the cakes 2 inches across. Spread with the caviare mixture, mask with cream, roll up each cake and secure with a toothpick. Place a small amount of sour cream mixture on each one. A small can of caviare will make 6 canapes.

What kind of COFFEE?

Boiled? Then you'll want a regular coffee pot, in enamel, like the one shown B.

Perked? On the stove, in one of aluminum like illustrations, E and G. Or at the table, in an electric percolator, shown F.

Drip? In drip coffee makers like the French type of enamel and pottery shown A and H. Or if you like to make very clear coffee, use the special glass equipment illustrated C, or the china pot with an aluminum drip, shown in D.

For FRYING and BROILING

PROPER UTENSILS

Illustrated are skillets of iron and aluminum which come in various sizes and with covers if you want them. Also an omelet pan, and a combination griddle and broiler.

For BOILING

Illustrated is one saucepan of a set of three; a four quart sauce pot with cover; a one quart stainless steel double boiler; and a jolly little copper tea kettle.

For ROASTING

Illustrated are an oblong roaster in aluminum, an aluminum baking pan and a Dutch oven in iron.

If you have all of these in your cupboard you are ready for any sort of cooking.

The gentle art of
TABLE COOKERY

is a comparatively new one with this generation. We have learned how to make things a little easier for ourselves, with electricity as an important help, of course.

Illustrated

A—This small and compact electric grill can boil, fry, and toast, and its amazingly versatile performance is no more surprising than the fact that all this goes on in such a little space.

B—The electric percolator is a very important member of the trio. It makes good coffee, too.

C—This broiler and hot plate is ample for the small family in a city apartment where space is limited. It has an ingenious broiling compartment. It works with speed and excellent results.

CLEANING ACCESSORIES

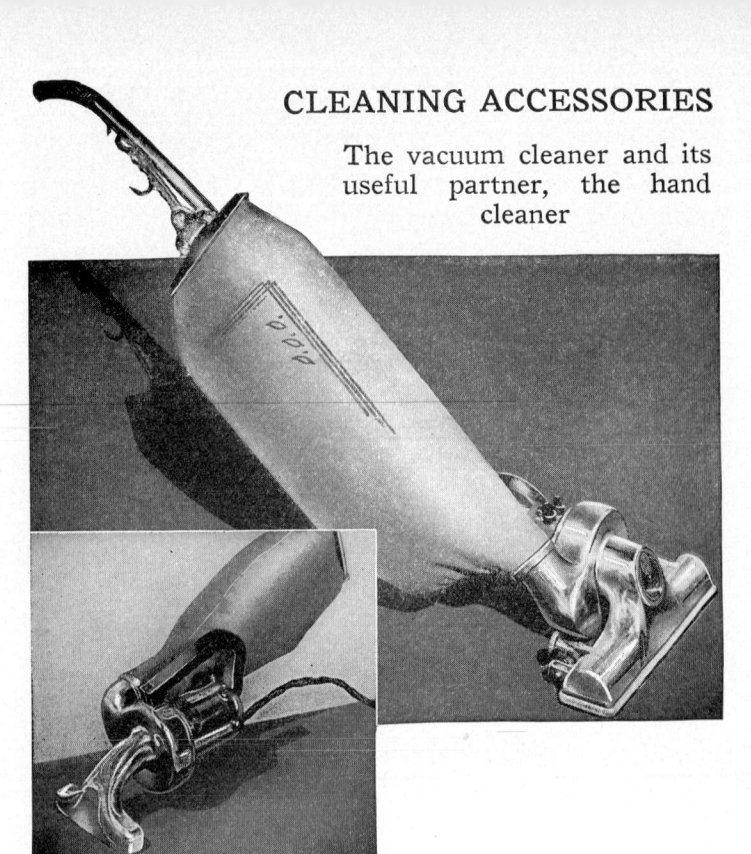

The vacuum cleaner and its useful partner, the hand cleaner

With the three machines shown here, any home can be kept immaculate as far as floors, furniture, draperies, mattresses, rugs, radiators and screens are concerned.

Top—the vacuum cleaner for all general work. Center—the hand cleaner for smaller surfaces, for cushions, etc. Left—the electric waxer and polisher which gives your freshly washed floor a soft lasting brilliance.

Here's real Help for HOUSE CLEANING

Do a thorough job—have ready all the special helps that make your work lighter and pleasanter—your cupboard should hold special polish for silver, for pewter, for furniture, for floors. And special cleansers for tile, for painted surfaces, for fabrics.

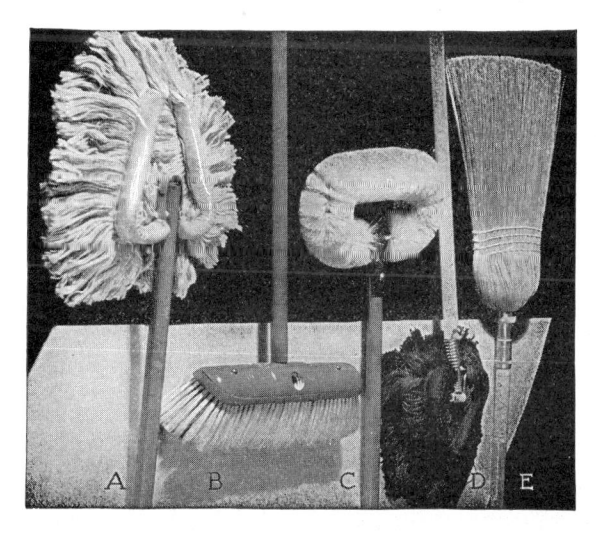

Special MOPS too—

A—Dust mop

B—Push broom

C—Wall brush

D—Polish mop

E—Sweeping broom

213

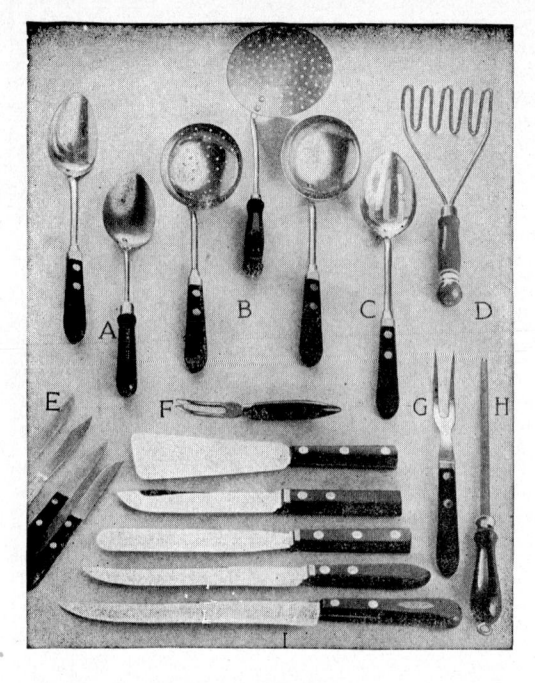

Good CUTLERY is essential for good COOKERY

You should have all of these:

A—Spoons for basting, mixing, stirring.
B—Ladles for skimming, serving.
C—Spoon for straining juice from vegetables.
D—Potato masher of strong wire and wood.
E—Paring knives of various shapes.
F—Grapefruit knife for extracting seeds.
G—Meat fork with short strong prongs.
H—Knife sharpener of butcher steel.
I—Slicing knives and spatulas, various sizes.

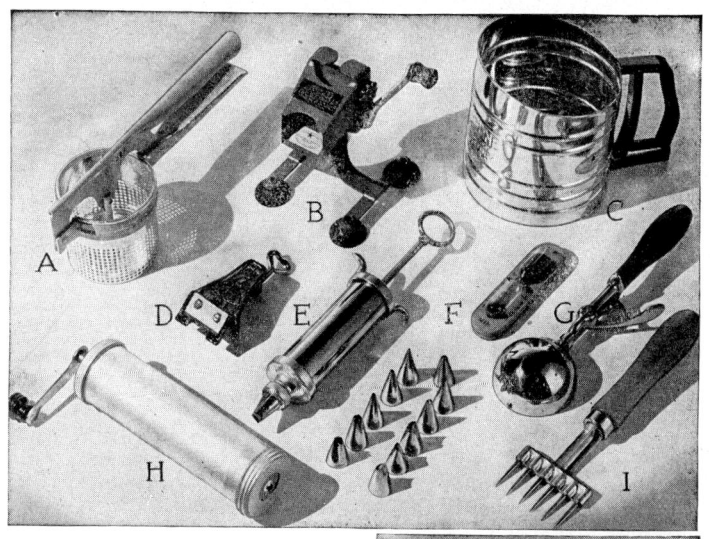

Special TOOLS to speed work

A—Potato ricer or press.
B—Mechanical pea sheller.
C—One-hand flour sifter.
D—Table bean stringer.
E—Cake decorating set.
F—This egg timer will prevent over-boiling.
G—Scoop for ice cream or mashed potatoes.
H—A cookie press for fancy little cakes.
I—Many-pointed ice pick works faster.
J—Meat grinder which cuts raw meat efficiently.
K—Food chopper for vegetables, nuts, crackers.
L—If you like really fresh coffee use a grinder.

If you want to MOULD puddings, or ice cream, or custard

A—For steaming Boston brown bread, or puddings. With or without center tube.
B—Individual jelly moulds are pretty.
C—Ice box cookie moulds are amusing.
D—For making a very special, fancy mousse.
E—For making ice cream in a melon mould. Cuts nicely.
F—For making Neapolitan ice cream bricks.
G—For pretty cakes, use the checkerboard cake pan.
H—Pans like this for corn cake, muffins, or popovers.
I—This is for angel cake or sponge cake-making.

Are you a GOOD MIXER?

You can be if you have the proper implements.

A—Special mixing bowl with spatter-proof edge and knobs to hold it by. Of strong glass, with lip for pouring.
B—Measuring spoons are indispensable.
C—Mixing spoons and ladles of aluminum or enamel.
D—Mixing bowls of crockery in sets.
E—Some cunning cups for custard or cakes.
F—Some cooks prefer wooden mixing spoons.
G—An egg beater of stainless steel.
H—Bread mixers come in various sizes.
I—Cake mixers make your work easier and they do a thorough job of mixing ingredients.

If there is a baby—or an invalid to cook for—you'll need some SPECIAL EQUIPMENT

A—Beef juice extracted by turn of handle.
B—A fruit juice extractor, easy to use.
C—Sieve for making purée of cooked vegetables.
D—Double boiler for cereals, puddings, and baby's formula.
E—Steamer for cooking vegetables and cereal at once.
F—Top stove oven for baking potatoes, custards, vegetables.
G—To remove fibrous matter from vegetables, tendons from meat, seeds and skin from fruits.

When you start to make A SALAD—
have these ready...

A—Nice glass bowls with good, wide edge.
B—A chopping set if you're using nuts.
C—A parsley mincer is a handy thing.
D—A quirler does decorative things to vegetables.
E—No tomato can escape this sharp knife.
F—The egg slicer is indispensable.
G—For slicing and grating vegetables.
H—The expert chooses wooden forks and spoons.
I—For beating eggs, mayonnaise or cream, easily.

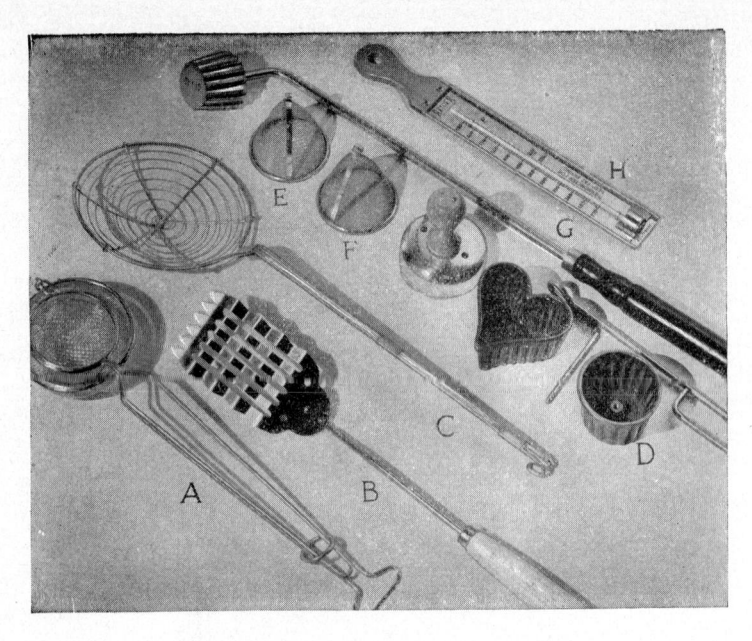

When you're getting ready for
DEEP FAT FRYING
be prepared with proper tools

A—Fryer for making birds' nests.
B—A frying fork with rippled tines.
C—A wire skimmer is useful.
D—Cast iron moulds for patties.
E—Croquette moulds of wire.
F—Wood-handled doughnut cutter.
G—This long-handled implement makes timbales.
H—You will need a deep-fat thermometer.

This BUSINESS of "Waterless Cooking"

Waterless cooking is really a misnomer for this cooking method is really accomplished by low pressure steam. The proper equipment is a variety of cast aluminum utensils as shown above, and in these vessels, little or no water is used.

This is a Pressure Cooker

It saves about a third of the time usually consumed in boiling or roasting foods, and it conserves about 2/3 of the fuel usually consumed in preparing a meal. All you need is one burner, turned low. This method improves the flavor of meats, and allows you to use less expensive cuts.

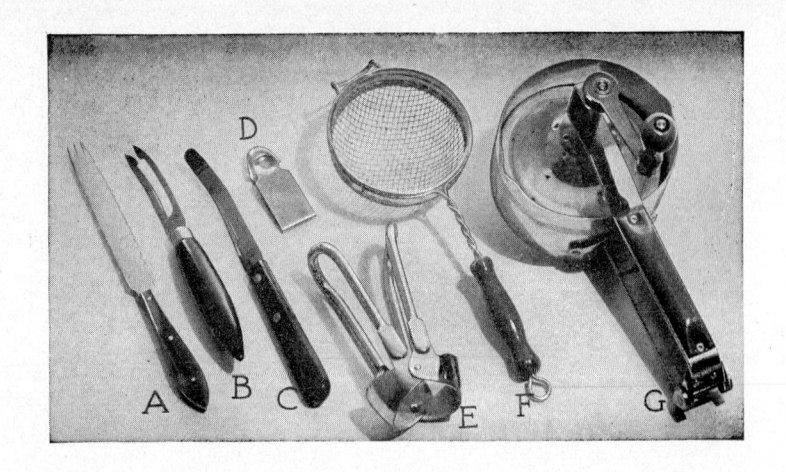

TOOLS for fixing FRUITS

A—Tomato slicer with a serrated edge.
B—Grapefruit knife for removing seeds and fruit.
C—Grapefruit knife with a sharp curved blade.
D—For hulling strawberries and picking chickens.
E—Sturdy grapefruit corer, easy to use.
F—Coarse mesh strainer for orange juice.
G—Rotary juicer for oranges; there's a larger one for grapefruit.
H—Glass reamer with strainer top and pitcher.
I—One or two strokes of the lever — and out pours the juice of limes, lemons, oranges or small grapefruit.
J—A good, big man-sized reamer of opaque glass.

CAN OPENERS, ETC.

These small tools are a great help in keeping cool, calm and collected when you're trying to cook in a hurry. It pays to have them handy, and in good condition always.

A—Nutcracker for extracting meats whole.
B—A fork for potatoes or any hot foods.
C—A high-powered, especially good corkscrew
D—A grand can opener; comes in several sizes.
E—Bottle opener with colored handle.
F—A strong, efficient nut cracker.
G—Skewers for roasts and meats en brochette
H—Makes beautiful curls of butter.
I—For making balls of potato, fruit, etc.
J—The tried and true version of canopener.
K—Corkscrew with a keen, sharp thread.
L—Quick, clean jobs done by this table model can opener.

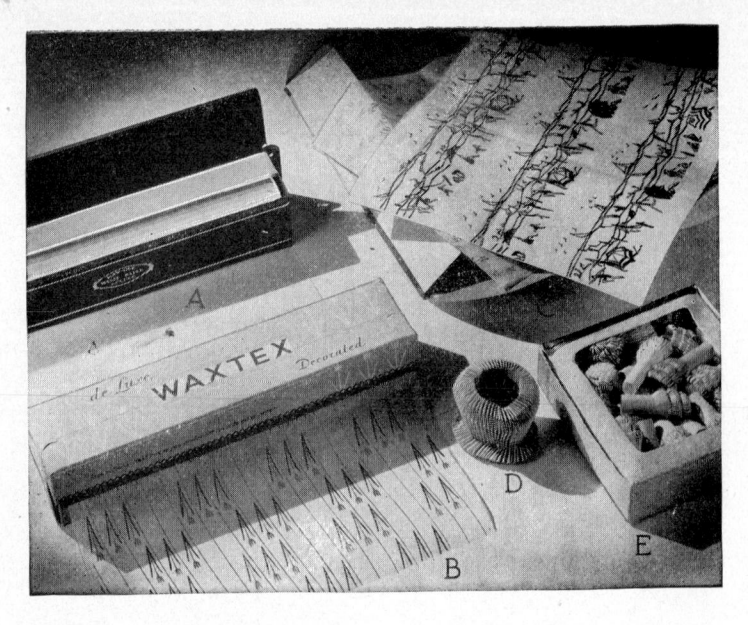

PAPER is part of the plan in a well-run kitchen.

Reduce your laundry bills—Make your work easier

A—A painted tin container with a roll of waxed paper kept clean and easily detachable.

B—This cardboard container has a sharp edge along which you can neatly detach the pretty printed paper it holds.

C—For other uses, you may find individual sheets more convenient. These are printed in gay colors and lively designs.

D—This tightly pleated paper expands to form a jolly colored collar for your pies, giving them quite a professional finish.

E—These are frills for lamb chops, ham or squab—they are inexpensive and give the table a festive air.

CHAPTER XXVII

FANCY SANDWICHES AND COOL DRINKS FOR PARTIES

With cool drinks clinking in frosted glasses, with gay sandwiches that tickle the eye and the palate, the hostess need not lack for variety in her refreshments. There are so many colorful, dainty sandwiches and such numberless cool drinks to offer her guests that she will hardly know which to choose.

It is a good plan to make several varieties of sandwiches. They are no harder to make than the same number of one kind. Then the guests can have the fun of choosing the kind that is their particular weakness, or of sampling them all. The little open faced sandwiches are the most interesting. You can use your ingenuity to make delicious and colorful ones. A few suggestions will be enough to start your mind working out other combinations, adding your own individual touch, which is the thing that makes cooking such a fascinating art.

For special occasions there are countless ways to get color into sandwich decorations. First of all there are the little vegetable coloring tablets or jars of paste. A tiny bit dissolved in water is used to color mayonnaise or whipped cream. Some of the foods that may be used for decoration are stuffed olives, sliced or minced, pimentos, paprika, hard boiled eggs, parsley, chives, and for sweet sandwiches, candied cherries. Another form of decoration is achieved by the use of small fancy shaped vegetable cutters. These are used to cut thinly sliced cooked vegetables. They are a great asset in developing attractive decoration. Some of the vegetables used are cooked beets, carrots or pimentos.

The set of fancy shaped cutters sold in department stores is inexpensive and adds greatly to the attractiveness of the finished sandwich. It can also be used in making canapés. Lacking these a sharp knife may be used to cut the bread into triangles, oblongs and squares. Mayonnaise or whipped cream can be added in fancy patterns by using a decorating set.

A tray of sweet condiments and nuts might accompany the food and iced drinks. Candied cherries, candied orange peel, candied violets, salted and spiced nuts or small colored candies, arranged attractively, add greatly to the refreshments.

The bread used for the sandwiches should be fine grained and twenty four hours old. Cut it into thin slices lengthwise of the loaf, removing the crusts. Spread with butter which has been softened and stirred until creamy. If the sandwiches are the open faced variety and they are made beforehand they may be put in the refrigerator to keep them fresh until wanted. The closed sandwiches may be arranged on a platter and covered with a damp napkin.

Here are some of the open faced sandwiches which are always favorites:

Anchovy Sandwiches

Anchovy Paste
Hard Boiled Eggs
Cream

Package Snappy Cheese
Paprika

Slice the bread thin. Spread with softened butter. Remove the crusts. Cut into small rounds with a cutter. Spread them with anchovy paste. In the center of each place a slice of hard boiled egg. Mash the snappy cheese, add enough cream to make it the consistency of softened butter. Beat into this 1 teaspoon of paprika. With the tip of a knife make a border of cheese around the edge of the sandwich. A pastry tube may be used, if you like, to decorate the edge with the cheese mixture.

Pâté de Fois Gras Sandwiches

| Jar of Pâté de Fois Gras | 2 Hard Boiled Eggs |
| Pimentos | Mayonnaise |

Slice the bread thin. Cut into an oval shape with an oval cutter. Spread with pâté de fois gras. Chop the eggs fine and mix with 2 tablespoons mayonnaise. Make a border of this around the edge with the tip of a knife. Decorate the center with a strip of pimento. Makes 12 sandwiches.

Avocado Sandwich

| 1 Small Avocado | Softened Butter |
| Grapefruit Juice | Chutney |

Slice the bread thin. Butter it. Remove the crust. Cut into fancy shapes. Peel the avocado. Remove the pulp. Mash it. Moisten it with grapefruit juice so that it will be the consistency of soft butter. Spread on the bread. Decorate the top with a bit of chutney placed in the center. This sandwich is particularly attractive because of its lovely green color.

Cheese and Ginger Sandwich

1 Cream Cheese
1 Tablespoon Preserved Ginger
2 Tablespoons Cream
Softened Butter
Candied Cherries
1 Teaspoon Lemon Juice
Angelica

Slice the bread thin. Remove the crusts. Butter it. Cut into fancy shapes. Mash the cream cheese. Combine with the cream and lemon juice. Add 1 tablespoon chopped ginger. Spread on the bread. Decorate the center with sliced cherries and tiny bits of angelica. Makes 12 sandwiches.

Pimento Cheese and Nut Sandwich

1 Pimento Cheese
¼ Cup Brazil Nuts
Softened Butter
Whole Wheat Bread
Parsley

Slice the bread thin. Butter it. Cut into rounds. Chop the Brazil nuts. Mix with the mashed cheese. Spread on the bread. Decorate the center of each with a small sprig of parsley. Makes 12 sandwiches.

Lobster Sandwich

1 Cup Lobster
3 Tablespoons Mayonnaise
Sweet Pickle
Softened Butter

Slice the bread thin. Cut into heart shaped pieces. Spread with softened butter. Mash the lobster. Moisten with the mayonnaise. Cover the bread. Serve open. Decorate with minced sweet pickles. Makes 12 sandwiches.

Chicken Sandwiches

1 Cup Chicken
⅓ Cup Cucumber
Celery Seed

3 Tablespoons Cream
1 Teaspoonful Lemon Juice
Stuffed Olives

Break the chicken into small pieces with a fork. Add the cucumber minced and a tiny bit of celery seed. Moisten with the cream. Dust with salt and pepper. Add the lemon juice. Blend. Spread thin slices of bread with softened butter, then with the chicken mixture. Lay thinly sliced stuffed olives on top. Cover with a second slice. Press together in pairs. Remove the crusts. This filling may be spread on split, buttered finger rolls. Serve these open. Decorate the top with sliced stuffed olives. Makes 12 sandwiches.

Sweet Red Pepper Sandwich

3 Sweet Red Peppers
1 Tablespoon Capers
  3 Tablespoons Mayonnaise

2 Tablespoons Whipped Cream
Softened Butter

Slice the bread thin. Butter it. Remove the crusts. Cut into fancy shapes. Remove the seeds from the sweet peppers. Mince them fine. Add the capers. Moisten with 3 tablespoons mayonnaise combined with 2 tablespoons whipped cream. Spread on the bread. Makes 12 sandwiches.

Cream Pistachio Sandwich

½ Cup Whipped Cream
1 Tablespoon Chopped Pistachio Nuts
1 Tablespoon Powdered Sugar
Softened Butter
Candied Cherries
Green Vegetable Tablet

Slice the bread thin. Remove the crusts. Butter it. Cut into fancy shapes. Color the sweetened whipped cream with a few drops of green coloring made by dissolving a bit of the vegetable tablet in water. Add nuts chopped. Have the whipped cream the palest green to contrast with the chopped pistachio meats. Decorate the center with a slice of cherry. Makes 8 sandwiches.

Summer Club Sandwich

Sandwich Bread
Creamed Butter
Sliced Tomatoes
Sliced Baked Ham
Sliced Chicken
Lettuce
Dill Pickles
Mayonnaise
Celery Curls
Radish Roses

For each person to be served allow three slices of buttered bread. Place a leaf of lettuce on the bottom slice. Spread it with mayonnaise. Add slices of chicken. Dust with salt and pepper. Lay the second slice over this. Cover with a leaf of lettuce. Spread with mayonnaise, add slices of ham and lay a slice of tomato on the ham. Spread with mayonnaise. Cover this with the remaining slice of bread. Remove the crusts with a sharp knife. Cut corner wise to form two triangles. Serve on individual plate with lettuce, celery curls, dill pickles and radish roses. The celery curls are made by cutting celery into fine strips and soaking in ice water. The radish roses are made by cutting back thin strips of the red part to imitate roses.

Deviled Ham Sandwiches

1 Can of Deviled Ham
1 Teaspoon India Relish
Softened Butter
¼ Cup Minced Celery
Rye Bread
3 Tablespoons Cream

Moisten the deviled ham with the cream. Add the teaspoon of India relish and the minced celery. Blend well and spread on thin slices of buttered rye bread. Put two slices together. Remove the crusts and cut into fancy shapes. Makes 12 sandwiches.

Bar-Le-Duc and Cream Cheese

1 Jar of Bar-le-Duc Jelly
1 Cream Cheese
Softened Butter
Whole Wheat Bread

Spread thinly sliced bread with butter. Cover half of the slices with creamed cheese and the other half with Bar-le-Duc Jelly. Currant jam may be substituted for the jelly. Put two slices together and cut with a large round cutter.

Cool Drinks

Decorative Ice Cubes

If you have an iceless refrigerator there are countless ways to use the ice cubes for decoration and added flavor in your cool drinks. Thin slices of quartered lemon or orange may be frozen in individual cubes. Freeze the water with the pan about ⅓ full. Lay the sliced fruit on the ice. Fill the pan ¾ full and finish freezing. Lemon juice may be added to the water frozen and the slice of lemon or orange added. These cubes give additional flavor to fruit drinks and iced tea. Other attractive ice cubes are made with a maraschino cherry or a sprig of mint frozen in them. Ginger Ale may be frozen and decorated or not as you choose. Delicate color may be introduced in the ice by coloring the water with vegetable tablets or paste. Be careful to use a small amount of color so that the cubes will not be very deep in tone. Decorative ice cubes using candied fruits will give you a chance to exercise your artistic ability. Candied cherries, green plums, oranges, citron, grapefruit or pineapple may be cut in thin shaped slices and arranged to simulate flowers and leaves or conventional designs.

Loganberry Punch

To the juice of 4 lemons add 2 cups of strong tea, 2 cups of loganberry juice and cracked ice. Add to this an equal amount of ginger ale. Serve at once. Sprigs of mint should dress the top of each glass. Serves 12.

Grape Juice and White Rock

Fill a glass half full of grape juice. Add an equal amount of White Rock. Dress the glass with sprigs of mint. Cut slices of orange in half. Decorate with cloves stuck into them. Cut a small gash in one side and fit on the edge of the glass.

Grenadine Delight

This should be served in cocktail glasses. The juice of 3 grapefruits, ½ cup of water, ½ cup of grenadine syrup or raspberry syrup, 3 egg whites unbeaten. Shake in a cocktail shaker with cracked ice until foamy. Serve in cocktail glasses with a maraschino cherry in each. If you have no cocktail shaker beat with a rotary egg beater.

Stonewall Jackson

Place ice cream in the bottom of tall glasses. Fill the glasses with sarsaparilla or root beer.

Raspberry Soda

Two cups of raspberry juice, 4 tablespoons pineapple juice, 8 tablespoons powdered sugar. Heat until well dissolved. Chill. Add an equal quantity of rich milk. Shake in a cocktail shaker with cracked ice until chilled. Half fill glasses with this mixture and fill up with charged water. Ice cream may be added. Any other fruit juice may be used or chocolate syrup substituted for the raspberry. Serves 8.

Golden Glow

Partly fill glasses with ice. Pour over this the juice of grapefruit and orange mixed in equal quantity. Dress the tops of the glasses with sprigs of mint and a maraschino cherry. Cut slices of orange in half, cut a gash in one side and place on the edge of the glass.

Iced Chocolate

One quart of milk, 1 pint of black coffee, ½ cake of bitter chocolate. Cook in a double boiler. Sweeten to taste and flavor with vanilla. Cool and serve in tall glasses filled with ice. Sweetened whipped cream flavored with vanilla is used to decorate the top. Serves 6.

Iced Tea

The tea should be made very strong for iced tea. Serve in tall glasses with cracked ice. Decorate with sliced orange with whole cloves stuck into the slices, maraschino cherries and mint.

CHAPTER XXVIII

SUMMER TIME SUPPERS

The best summer time supper depends upon its appetizer, its salad and a good dessert, and of course a cool drink. Hot bread just seems to go with this sort of supper. If you do not want to make the hot breads, finger rolls may be split and toasted on the electric toaster. Another kind of bread that is delicious with these suppers is a plate of thinly sliced bread spread with softened butter. Wrap in a damp napkin and allow to get quite cold in the refrigerator.

Appetizers

Tomato Cocktail

Peel and chill 4 tomatoes. Cut them into dice. Peel and cut one cucumber into dice. Mince one piece of celery, combine and chill in cocktail glasses. Cover with French dressing. Serves 8.

French Dressing

Peel an onion and cut it into quarters. Put it into a glass jar. Add one cup of olive oil, ⅓ cup of vinegar, 1 teaspoon of salt, 2 teaspoons of sugar, one tablespoon of pineapple juice and 1 teaspoon of paprika. Cover and keep in the refrigerator. When you wish to use it shake until creamy.

Pear and Pineapple Cocktail

Cut balls with a vegetable cutter from 4 fresh pears which have been peeled. Add an equal amount of diced pineapple. Put into cocktail glasses and cover with white grape juice. Decorate the tops with maraschino cherries. Add a small amount of maraschino juice to each glass. Chill well. Serves 8.

Shrimp Cocktail

Wash 2 cups shelled shrimps. Drain them and put into a bowl. Add Russian dressing, just enough to coat each shrimp. Chill in cocktail glasses. When serving add one teaspoon of Chili sauce to each glass and decorate with stuffed olives. For the Russian dressing add two tablespoons of Chili sauce to one cup of mayonnaise. Serves 8.

SALADS

Moulded Potato Salad

Chop 6 boiled potatoes fine. Chop 3 tablespoons of onion fine. Chop ½ cucumber fine. Mix together and dress with boiled dressing, just enough to moisten slightly. Boil 2 eggs 20 minutes. Slice them. Slice 3 radishes unpeeled, in thin round slices. Mix 1 package of lemon jelly powder with 1½ cups of boiling water. Cool it. Decorate the bottom of an oblong bread pan with the sliced radishes and eggs. When the gelatine is cool just cover the eggs and radishes with it. Place it on ice and when it has hardened put the potato salad on top of it. Pour the rest of the lemon gelatine over this and put on ice for several hours to harden. You may mould the salad in individual moulds if you like. When serving, unmould the salad in the center of a large platter. Surround with slices of tongue and baked ham. Decorate with crisp lettuce, pickled beets and ripe olives. Serve hot baking powder biscuit with this. For dessert serve peach and cherry compote. The salad serves 8.

Stuffed Pimento Salad

Chop ½ cup of green pepper, ½ cup of pineapple, ½ cup of blanched almonds and 1 cup of cabbage. Moisten the combination with French dressing. Fill whole pimentos, the canned variety, with the salad. Place each cup in a nest of lettuce. Decorate the top with mayonnaise. This salad is delicious with cold fried chicken. East Indian Chutney should accompany the chicken. Popovers are the hot bread. Angel parfait is the dessert recommended. Salad serves 8.

Moulded Ham and Chicken Mousse

Mix together 1 cup of finely ground ham and one cup of chicken ground fine. Add 1 teaspoon of French mustard. Dissolve 1 bouillon cube in one cup of hot water. Add 1 tablespoon of gelatine that has been softened in 3 tablespoons cold water. Mix with the meat. Put in the refrigerator and when cold, but not jellied, add ¾ of a cup of cream beaten stiff. Chill for several hours in a ring mould. When serving unmould the mousse in the center of a round chop plate. Fill the center with a mixture of 1 cup of mayonnaise combined with ¼ cup of cream whipped, 1 tablespoon of horseradish and 6 chopped olives. Decorate with alternating clusters of water cress and asparagus tips and small, chilled, peeled tomatoes that have been slashed in 6 sections to simulate a flower. Hot muffins should accompany this. Serve pickled peaches with the salad. Honeydew melon with ice cream for dessert. The mousse serves 8.

Alligator Pear Salad

Cut an alligator pear in half. Remove the hard shell. Slice the pear in thin crescents. Arrange these in a border on a round chop plate. In the center put 2 cups of cooked, diced carrots. Dress with French dressing. Serves 4.

Moulded Cucumber Salad

Heat 1½ cups of pineapple juice. Dissolve 1 package of lemon jelly powder in this. Stir until dissolved. Cool and when it is just beginning to set add 1 small cucumber chopped fine. Cool in individual moulds. Serve in nests of lettuce. Decorate with sprigs of mint. Serve with mayonnaise. Moulded cucumbers are delicious with any cold meat. Serves 8.

The recipes for popovers, muffins and baking powder biscuit will be found in the section dealing with hot breads. The recipes for Honeydew Melon with Ice Cream, Peach and Cherry Compote and Angel parfait are in the Dessert section.

CHAPTER XXIX

HOT WEATHER ENTERTAINING

For porch or indoor entertainment on hot nights the following menus are suggested:

Menu No. I

Fruit Cocktail
Guava Jelly   Sweet Pickles
Cream Cheese Sandwich Loaf
Radishes
Raspberry Sherbet
Sugared Nuts   Mints
Iced Chocolate

Fruit Cocktail

Slice in very thin slices: one pear, one peach, one grapefruit and one orange. Pour over this 1 cup of fresh strawberry juice sweetened with 2 tablespoons of powdered sugar. Add ½ cup of fresh strawberries and ½ cup of blackberries cut into thin slices. Chill thoroughly. Serves 8.

Cheese Sandwich Loaf

This should be made on the platter from which it is served. Remove the crust from a loaf of bread. Cut it into 4 lengthwise slices. Spread them with softened butter. Spread 1 layer with pimento cheese, one with equal portions of chopped hard boiled eggs and celery moistened with mayonnaise and one slice with chopped olives moistened with mayonnaise. Put the remaining slice on top. Cover the whole loaf with cream cheese moistened with cream. Decorate the top with sliced stuffed olives, sweet pickles sliced and bits of pimento. Chill. Slice the loaf at the table when serving it. Serves 8.

Iced Chocolate

Cook in the double boiler 1 quart of milk, 1 pint of water and ½ cake of bitter chocolate. Sweeten with 2 tablespoons of sugar and flavor with 1 teaspoon of vanilla. Chill and serve with sweetened flavored whipped cream on top. A new combination is iced tea and chocolate mixed together in equal quantities and served with whipped cream. Serves 8.

Menu No. II

Chicken Almond Sandwiches
Sandwich Delight   Savory Sandwich
Lime Rickey   Iced Coffee
Peach Ice Cream

Chicken Almond Sandwich

Chop 1 cup of chicken fine. Chop ¼ cup of salted almonds fine. Dust with salt, pepper and celery salt and mix with 3 tablespoons of cream. Cut bread in thin slices, spread with softened butter and the chicken mixture. Decorate with thinly sliced green and red pepper.

Sandwich Delight

Chop together ½ bottle of stuffed olives, 1 cup of raisins, ½ cup of walnut meats and 1 sweet red pepper. Moisten with mayonnaise and spread on thinly sliced bread buttered with softened butter. Cut into fancy shapes and press a walnut meat into the center of each.

Lime Rickey

Mix ¼ cup of lime juice, 1 quart of white grape juice and 8 teaspoons of powdered sugar. Shake in a cocktail shaker with crushed ice. Fill tall glasses with crushed ice. Pour the fruit mixture into the glasses ¾ full. Add white rock or charged water. Decorate with a slice of curled cucumber, maraschino cherries and a bouquet of fresh mint. Serves 8.

Menu No. III

Sweetbread and Cucumber Salad
Clover Leaf Rolls   Pimento Cups
Watermelon Pickles
Currant Cup   Iced Tea
Orange Ice, Crushed Peppermint Candy
Candied Fruit   Salted Almonds

Sweetbread and Cucumber Salad

Cover 2 sweetbreads with boiling water. Add 1 slice of lemon, 1 slice of onion, a small piece of bay leaf. Cook gently 15 minutes. Drain, cover with cold water. Let stand 5 minutes. Drain, and cool. Remove the skin and cut into cubes. Mince 1 cucumber fine. Combine the sweetbreads and cucumber with 1 tablespoon of lemon juice. Mix ⅔ cup of mayonnaise with ⅓ cup of cream whipped. Fill pimento cups with salad and serve in nests of lettuce. Sprinkle the top with paprika and minced parsley. Serves 8.

Currant Cup

Two glasses of currant juice, 2 glasses of raspberry juice, 4 glasses of tea, 4 tablespoons of syrup from preserved ginger. Shake in a cocktail shaker and pour into glasses filled with crushed ice. Cut slices of orange in half, cut a gash in 1 side and slip over the rim of the glass. Decorate with green cherries and sprigs of mint. Serves 8.

The orange ice in this menu should be piled in sherbet glasses. Decorate the top with whipped cream. The cream has 1 tablespoon of orange marmalade beaten into it. Sprinkle the cream with peppermint candy. The kind that is crisp and light in texture can be crushed in a food chopper. 1 quart of orange ice serves 8.

Menu No. IV

Frozen Tomato Salad
Cheese Balls   Tiny Bran Muffins
Spiced Pears   Hearts of Celery
Vanilla Ice Cream, Preserved Ginger
Iced Coffee

Frozen Tomato Salad

Soften 2 teaspoons of gelatine in ½ cup of cold water. Melt over hot water and add it to 2 cans of tomato soup. Whip ½ pint of cream stiff and add to the tomato soup. Pack in a mould with a cover. Heavy waxed paper should cover the top of the mould and extend over the edge. The cover is fitted over this. Bury the mould in 2 parts of crushed ice and 1 part of salt for 3 hours. Of course if you have an iceless refrigerator you simply put the salad in the icing unit to freeze. Stir occasionally. Remove the salad from the mould when ready to serve and cut into slices and serve on shredded endive or lettuce. Decorate with tiny cheese balls rolled in minced parsley.

Tiny Bran Muffins

Sift 1 cup of white flour with 3 teaspoons of baking powder. Add 2 tablespoons of brown sugar and 1 cup of bran. Beat 2 eggs and add 2 tablespoons of honey and 1 cup of milk. Beat this into the flour mixture and add 2 tablespoons of melted butter. Bake in tiny muffin pans. Before putting into the oven decorate the tops with slices of candied cherries and bits of angelica or citron cut to represent leaves.

CHAPTER XXX

HALLOWE'EN PARTIES

The colors of Harvest time make Hallowe'en party decorations the gayest of all the year. Color and the mystery of benevolent witchcraft are a great help to the gayety of such a party and should set the pace.

One of the most successful decorations for a Hallowe'en party I ever used was a large copper tray loaded with fruit. The tray was oval. In the center was a small pumpkin surrounded with apples, oranges, pears and clusters of green and purple grapes. The grapes trailed gracefully over the sides. A decoration of this sort arranged on a table or sideboard and flanked by 8 or 10 candles of orange color suggests the opulence of Harvest.

Candle light is so appropriate for Hallowe'en it is a good idea to have the rooms lighted entirely in that way with orange candles in sticks everywhere.

Another attractive lighting arrangement is orange colored paper lanterns. Paint Jack O'Lantern faces on the lanterns with black India Ink. A large pumpkin with eyes, nose and mouth cut out and burning a candle should occupy a prominent place in the room.

Of course, witches, black cats and skeletons should be purchased and hung about the room.

A successful table decoration is made from oranges. Cut the tops from the oranges, scoop out the pulp with a teaspoon. Cut Jack O'Lantern faces in them. Place a tiny candle holder and candle in the lanterns. The holders and tapers used for birthday cakes are excellent.

Marigolds or orange and yellow button chrysanthemums

are the flowers to use for the supper table. Sprays of orange Japanese Lantern flowers are beautiful and just the color for a Hallowe'en party.

Now for the menus. There is as much orange in the menus as possible, so that the Hallowe'en color scheme may be carried out.

Menu No. I

Glorified Club Sandwiches
Spiced Pears   Olives
Mince or Pumpkin Pie
Coffee
Sugared Nuts   Hallowe'en Candies

Glorified Club Sandwich

For every sandwich you wish to serve, toast 3 slices of bread lightly. Butter them, cut into triangles, cover and keep warm. Have ready sliced chicken, sliced tomatoes, strips of browned bacon, and lettuce. Make a Welsh rarebit sauce. For the sauce heat 1 pint of milk in the top of the double boiler. When the milk is hot, stir into it 2 pounds of American cheese. Cook over hot water, stirring occasionally, until the cheese is blended with the milk. Add 1 tablespoon of French mustard, 1 teaspoon salt, ½ teaspoon paprika, and 1 tablespoon Worcestershire sauce. Stir into this 2 well beaten eggs. Cook about 1 minute, stirring well, until the eggs are blended with the sauce. To serve, place lettuce leaves on individual plates. Lay 2 triangles of toast on the plates. Cover the toast with rarebit sauce. Lay strips of hot bacon on top. Cover the bacon with triangles of toast and lay sliced chicken, tomatoes and a leaf of lettuce on top. Cover with the remaining 2 pieces of toast. Put the sauce over them. Decorate with bacon, and stuffed olives.

Menu No. II

Shrimp Wiggle
Celery Curls   Sweet Mixed Pickles
Orange Cream in Orange Baskets
Assorted Frosted Cakes
Coffee
Nuts and Cluster Raisins   Hallowe'en Candies

Shrimp Wiggle

Beat 6 egg yolks until light. Add 6 tablespoons of orange juice or 6 tablespoons of cooking sherry. Add 3 cups of thin cream or milk. Add ½ teaspoon of salt and dust with pepper. Cook over hot water, stirring often. When the liquid is hot add 1 pint of shelled shrimps and 4 hard boiled eggs, shelled and cut into pieces. Cook until the liquid is like heavy cream and the shrimps are thoroughly heated. Serve on triangles of toast or heated saltines. Serves 8.

Orange Cream in Orange Baskets

To make the orange baskets select large thick skinned oranges. Mark a line about the middle similar to the equator in a globe. In the center of the top half draw 2 parallel lines ¾ of an inch apart. The skin between is the basket handle. Remove the skin and pulp on each side of the handle with a sharp knife. Cut across the orange to the handle. Scoop the pulp from the basket with a teaspoon. Fill the baskets with orange cream, made as follows: Melt 4 tablespoons of butter in the double boiler and stir in the following ingredients: The grated rind of 2 oranges, juice of 1 lemon, ½ teaspoon of salt, 1 cup of sugar mixed with ½ cup of cornstarch. Add 2 cups of orange juice. Stir constantly and bring to the boiling point. Cook 10 minutes over hot water. Whip ½ pint of cream. When the orange mixture is cold add the whipped cream. Heap the mixture in orange cups and chill. The top of the cream may be decorated with bits of candied orange peel, candied cherries and green candied angelica. The pulp taken from the oranges should be put in a vegetable press and the juice pressed out is used for the cream. This dessert might be served in sherbet glasses if you do not wish to use the orange baskets. Serves 8.

Menu No. III

Chicken or Oyster Patties
Sweet Pickled Gherkins   Cranberry Jelly
Ice Cream
Hallowe'en Orange Cake
Salted Almonds   Candied Ginger   Candies
Coffee

Chicken or Oyster Patties

The sauce for the chicken or oyster patties is the same. Add 3 cups of chicken meat to the sauce for chicken patties or 3 cups drained oysters to the sauce for oyster patties. To make the sauce beat 3 eggs. Add 1 pint of thin cream or milk to the eggs and cook 10 minutes over hot water, stirring often. Add 1 tablespoon of minced parsley, ½ teaspoon of salt and the meat. Dust with pepper. When the meat is hot add 1 tablespoon of butter and 1 tablespoon of lemon juice. The sauce should be like heavy cream when done. Serve in heated patty shells. These may be ordered from your baker. Serves 8.

Hallowe'en Orange Cake

Have ready 2 bowls. In one sift the dry ingredients, in the other beat the wet ingredients. Sift into a large mixing bowl, 2½ cups of sifted flour, 2½ teaspoons of baking powder, and 1½ cups of sugar. In the other bowl beat 2 eggs, add 1 cup of milk and beat, add ½ cup of melted butter. Beat the liquid ingredients into the dry ingredients. After they are blended beat for 1 minute with a large wooden spoon. Add 1 teaspoon of vanilla. Bake in layers in a moderate oven. Whip ½ pint of cream. Add ½ teaspoon vanilla, ½ cup chopped blanched almonds and 4 tablespoons sugar. Put between the layers. Frost the cake with orange frosting on the top and sides. Serves 16.

Orange Frosting

Mix the grated rind of 1 orange with ¼ cup of orange juice. Let stand 10 minutes. Strain and add 2 well beaten egg yolks. Add enough confectioners' sugar to thicken so that it will spread on the cake. (About 1 pound of sifted sugar.) Ice the sides and top of the cake.

Decoration for Hallowe'en Cake

To decorate the cake melt ½ a cake of chocolate over hot water. Use for a pattern a black cat, a witch or any other appropriate Halloween symbol, cut out of paper. After the frosting is thoroughly set, lay the pattern on the cake and mark around it with the point of a sharp knife. Remove the pattern and follow the outline marked with the melted chocolate. A teaspoon may be used to do this, dipping a small amount of the chocolate with it and following the design. Small tokens such as are used in wedding cakes may be baked in the cake or inserted after it is baked. A horseshoe or a black cat brings luck to the one getting it.

Menu No. IV

Chicken Bouillon with Whipped Cream
Cheese Crackers
Crab Salad
Hot Buttered Rolls
Dill Pickles
Orange Sherbet
Assorted Frosted Cakes
Candy   Coffee   Nuts

Decoration for Chicken Bouillon

Serve hot chicken bouillon in bouillon cups. Just before serving put a tablespoon of whipped cream on each cup. The cream has been colored orange with an orange vegetable coloring tablet.

Crab Salad

Combine 1 pint of crab meat with 1 minced cucumber, 1 cup of minced celery, 4 minced sweet pickles and 4 hard boiled eggs cut fine. Sprinkle with salt, paprika and the juice of 1 lemon. Mix well and chill. Arrange lettuce leaves on a large platter or on individual plates. Place the crab salad in the center and mask with mayonnaise. Decorate with parsley, capers, stuffed olives cut in half and strips of pimentos. Serves 8.

CHAPTER XXXI

HOLIDAY ENTERTAINING

Christmas to New Year is the most strenuous time of all the year for accepting and dispensing hospitality. I can never make up my mind whether it is more fun to plan a party or to go to one. But, to me, the thing that is even more pleasant than either of these, is to offer hospitality when friends drop in. There is something so thrilling about an unplanned, unexpected party.

So I wonder if you wouldn't like to be prepared at the Holiday season for that most delightful kind of entertaining —the casual kind. Just then the baker's shops and the grocer stores are filled with all kinds of fancy, fluffy extras—things we don't really need to have but that make it seem like Holiday time to have about the house. We can take advantage of this to lay in a supply of them. Or if we get really ambitious we can make our own little extras. Perhaps it is a holdover from the days when holiday baking consumed days and cookie jars and cake boxes were bursting with good things that makes us like to fuss in the kitchen and have something really home made to offer our guests. I am going to give you some recipes for making these things, along with some of those that may be prepared from the stock the shops carry.

For the casual kind of entertaining when friends drop in, there are many things that can be kept on the emergency shelf for just such occasions.

Make a list of the things that you think you will need and shop for them now. Of course you'll have your own pet refreshments, but you will want to include at least some of the following items:

Jars of Pickles	Jars of Cheese
Stuffed Olives	Pâté de Fois Gras
Ripe and Green Olives	Anchovy Paste
Pimentos	Sardines
Almonds	Shrimp
Celery	Chicken
Tiny Onions	Lobster
Mayonnaise	Crab
Chili Sauce	Clam Bouillon
Worcestershire Sauce	Tomato Juice
Mushroom Catsup	Jar Honey
East Indian Chutney	Maple Syrup
Preserved Ginger	Jams
Preserved Kumquats	Nuts
Tinned Cookies	Cluster Raisins
Fruit Cake	

Toasted sandwiches are sure to be liked by your guests. There are several delightful and extremely efficient electric stoves made especially for toasting sandwiches at the table. Whether you use one of these clever stoves or prepare the sandwiches in the kitchen here are some particularly interesting ones to try.

Southern Sandwich

Make these sandwiches in individual portions. Use 3 slices of bread for each sandwich. For the filling chop ¾ cup shrimps and ¾ cup lobster. Combine. Add 4 tablespoons mayonnaise. Put 4 tablespoons of this filling between 2 slices of bread. Spread the third slice with anchovy paste. Press the 3 slices firmly together. Remove the crusts with a sharp knife. After the necessary number of sandwiches are assembled toast first on one side and then the other. Cut diagonally across with a sharp knife. This amount of filling will make 6 sandwiches.

Snappy Sandwich

Mash 1 snappy cheese with 1 tablespoon of Worcestershire sauce and 1 tablespoon cream. Spread thin slices of bread with the mixture. Press together in pairs. Remove the crusts. Toast. This should make the filling creamy. Cut into thin strips with a sharp knife. Serves 6.

Rolled Salamagundi

Chop 1 tablespoon of parsley. Chop ½ cup chicken and ½ cup ham very fine. Combine and add 1 tablespoon of softened butter. Dust with pepper. Spread thin slices of bread with this mixture. Remove the crusts and roll. Toothpicks are useful to hold the roll together. Toast. Serve these with jelly, olives and pickles. Serves 8.

Biscuits

Tiny tea biscuits may be used to make delicious sandwiches. Sweet fillings are particularly good, such as honey and nuts, shaved maple sugar, guava jelly or marmalade. The biscuit dough should be made ahead of time, set in the refrigerator and baked when you need them.

Sandwich Biscuit

Sift 2 cups of flour with 4 teaspoons of baking powder and 1 teaspoon salt. Measure ½ cup cream. Beat it with 2 eggs. Combine the liquid with the flour. Roll thin and cut with a small cutter. Bake and fill with sandwich material while warm and serve warm. Makes 24 biscuits.

Holiday Cookies

The fancy cookie cutters sold wherever kitchenwares are

carried are used to shape these cookies. The shapes run all the way from stars, crescents, triangles and hearts to small amusing animals.

2 Cups Flour	Pinch Salt
½ Cup Sugar	2 Teaspoons Baking Powder
2 Egg Yolks	1 Teaspoon Vanilla
½ Cup Shortening	4 Tablespoons Milk

Cream the butter and sugar with the vanilla. Add the egg yolks. Beat. Add the sifted dry ingredients a little at a time alternately with the milk. Knead and place in the ice box to chill. Roll out ¼ inch thick. Cut with the different shaped cookie cutters. Use currants for the eyes of the animals or leave them plain. Decorate the others with bits of candied cherry, angelica or citron. Some may be decorated with chopped pistachio nuts. The colored sugar that is so attractive or tiny seed-like candies may be sprinkled over others. These decorations should be put on the cookies before baking. Some might be baked plain and iced with colored icing. The icing is made with 1 cup of sifted confectioners' sugar combined with 2 tablespoons cream and a few drops of flavoring. Divide it into several portions and tint with vegetable or fruit coloring. Frost the cookies while warm. Bake the cookies in a moderate oven (375° F.), for 10 minutes or until a pale golden color. Makes 3 dozen cookies.

Gingers

1 Cup Molasses	1 Teaspoon Cinnamon
¼ Cup Brown Sugar	¼ Teaspoon Cloves
½ Cup Shortening	3 Teaspoons Baking Powder
1 Egg	½ Teaspoon Salt
3 Cups Flour	¼ Teaspoon Soda
1 Teaspoon Ginger	

Melt the shortening. Mix with the molasses and sugar. Add the egg and beat. Add the dry ingredients which have been sifted together. Chill well. Roll out and cut. This is the dough that the gingerbread dolls of our childhood were made from. If you want to try your artistic ability, use a sharp knife to cut the figures and add currants for eyes and nose.

Holly Cakes

2 Tablespoons Water
3 Eggs
1 Cup Sugar
1 Cup Flour

1 Teaspoon Baking Powder
Vanilla
Lemon

Beat the egg whites well. Add the sifted sugar, a little at a time. Add beaten yolks. Beat. Add the baking powder and flour sifted together, alternately with water. Beat between each addition. Flavor with a few drops of lemon and vanilla extract. Bake in gem pans in a moderate oven (350° F.), for 15 minutes. Frost. Decorate before the icing has hardened with tiny red candies and angelica or citron cut thin with the scissors to simulate leaves. Makes 12 cakes.

Icing

1 Egg White
1 Tablespoon Water
1 Cup Confectioners' Sugar

Vanilla
Lemon Extract

Beat the egg white stiff. Add the sifted confectioners' sugar alternately with the water a little at a time. Flavor with a few drops of vanilla and lemon extract.

Mulled Loganberry Juice

4 Cups Loganberry Juice
2 Cups Grapefruit Juice
2 Cups Water

6 Whole Cloves
Small Piece Stick Cinnamon
Small Bit of Whole Mace

Combine ingredients. Simmer 5 minutes. Strain. Serve hot in tall glasses with a cherry and quarter of a slice of orange. Serves 8.

CHAPTER XXXII

HOLIDAY DINNERS

If there is one time of year more than another when we are intrigued by cooking it is at the approach of the Holidays. Everyone's mind, whether they cook or not, turns to feasting. I like that little undercurrent of pleasant anticipation that is in the air. Its glamour gives color to our lives and lifts them out of the prosaic. In books, pages of description have been devoted to these same holiday dinners and perhaps they have stimulated our imagination. Or perhaps it is some childish memory of the excitement and preparation that went forward at our house at the holiday season. The rich spiciness of the air days before the big day, and then, when the day finally arrived that unforgettable, delectable aroma that filled the house to its farthermost corner—the turkey roasting! Many were the trips to the kitchen to peep into the oven and view the rich brown beauty there sizzling deliciously.

Here are the dinners. One serves turkey, the other two are given in case you wish to have duck or chicken instead. Full directions for preparing these dishes will be found under the several classifications in the Recipe Section.

Turkey Dinner for Four

Mushroom Soup
Roast Turkey, Oyster Dressing
Mashed Potatoes   Giblet Gravy
                Peas
Olives   Hot Rolls   Cranberry Sauce
Jellied Tomato Salad   Stuffed Celery
Mince Pie   French Ice Cream
Assorted Fruit   Coffee   Nuts and Raisins

Duck Dinner for Four

Tomato Juice Cocktail
Roast Duck, Walnut Dressing
Tiny Lima Beans with Celery   Mashed Sweet Potatoes
Currant Jelly
Pickles   Olives   Radishes
Hot Rolls
Alligator Pear and Orange Salad
Fruit Cake   Ice Cream
Fruit
Assorted Mints   Coffee   Salted Nuts

Chicken Dinner for Four

Oysters on the Half Shell
Roast Chicken   Poultry Dressing
Mashed Potatoes
Giblet Gravy
Glazed Onions   Fringed Celery
Red Cinnamon Apples
Ripe Olives   Pickles
Hot Rolls
Asparagus Salad
Ice Cream or Hard Sauce   Plum Pudding
Cluster Raisins   Candy
Coffee

CHAPTER XXXIII

BUFFET SUPPERS

An Easy Way Out for the Large Party

The buffet supper is a delightful way to entertain, if the number of your guests exceeds the seating capacity of your dining table.

The buffet supper may either be served in place of the evening meal or as a late supper.

The dining table should be made as large as possible. The food to be served is set upon it together with plates, napkins and silver, and the guests allowed to help themselves. Unless, of course, there is a roast to be carved, when the host should carve and serve it.

Small tables set about the room so that the guests may have a place to set their plates are convenient.

When the supper is finished the food and dishes are removed and the dessert brought in together with the coffee.

Make the table attractive with flowers or fruit. If a salad is used arrange it on large platters and serve French dressing and mayonnaise in separate dishes.

Buffet Supper Menus

Broiled Lobster
Potato Chips   Hot Buttered Rolls
Mayonnaise   French Dressing
Vegetable Salad   Pickles
Frozen Pudding
Cake   Coffee

Vegetable Salad

For the salad use crisp, chilled lettuce, thinly sliced tomatoes, sliced cucumbers, cooked string beans, cooked asparagus and cooked beets. Arrange the lettuce so that it will cover the platters. Place the cooked vegetables in separate piles on the lettuce. Decorate the salad with the cucumbers and the tomatoes.

Decoration

Place 1 platter at each end of the table. The scarlet lobster should be heaped upon one central dish which occupies the center of the table. The other dishes grouped about so that they may be easily reached.

Apple green candles and a large bowl of flame colored zinnias would make an attractive table decoration to accompany this supper.

Another Buffet Supper

Fried Chicken
Creamed Potatoes   Hot Corn Bread
Raspberry Jelly
Asparagus Salad with Egg Slices
Mayonnaise   French Dressing
Mixed Pickles
Lemon Sherbet
Cake
Coffee

Fried Chicken

Purchase tender chickens cut for frying. Select a large pan. Put enough water into the pan so that it will be an inch in depth. Light the gas. When the water is boiling, lay the chicken in. Cover and cook for 20 minutes, turning occasionally. Remove the chicken and liquid from the pan. Heat 3 tablespoons butter in the pan. Flour the chicken, dust with salt and pepper. Brown well in the butter. Cook 30 minutes, keeping the gas flame low.

Asparagus Salad

Arrange crisp chilled lettuce so that it will cover a large round chop plate. Lay cooked asparagus stalks on the lettuce in circles so that the tips point toward the edge of the plate. Decorate the salad with slices of hard boiled eggs, strips of pimento and stuffed ripe olives.

Buffet Supper Menu

Chicken with Mushrooms and Sweetbreads
Stuffed Tomatoes   Deviled Eggs
Cranberry Jelly
Sweet Pickles   Celery   Ripe Olives
Hot Baking Powder Biscuits
Pineapple Ice
Cake
Coffee

Chicken with Mushrooms and Sweetbreads

Purchase two chickens weighing 3 lbs. each, cut for fricasseeing; 4 sweetbreads and 1 lb. of mushrooms. Cook the chicken and sweetbreads 1 hour. Cool and cut up the meat in small pieces. Into a saucepan put 4 cups of rich milk. Blend ½ cup flour with ½ cup butter. Add to the milk. Put over the flame and stir until thick. Wash and cut up the mushrooms for the sauce. Add the chicken, sweetbreads and mushrooms to the sauce. Season with salt and pepper. Heat a casserole in the oven. Put the creamed mixture into it and bake 25 minutes. Serves 12.

Serving

The tomatoes, scooped out and stuffed with chopped celery, cucumbers and tomatoes and mixed with salad dressing, are arranged in the center of 2 round chop plates which have been covered with water cress. The deviled eggs are placed around the edge. Place one of these dishes at each end of the table. In the center place the casserole dish. If it is not a decorative casserole, the chicken may be served on a large platter decorated with parsley.

Buffet Supper Menu

Roast Ham
Macaroni Salad   Hot Buttered Rolls
Currant Jelly
Olives   Pickles   Celery   Radishes
Ice Cream
Assorted Cakes
Coffee

Macaroni Salad

Boil 1 package of macaroni. Cool it. Mix the macaroni with 1 can of tuna fish, 1 cup of stuffed olives, sliced, 2 cups of diced celery, 2 cups of diced cucumbers, 6 tomatoes cut into small pieces, 1 cup of cheese cut into small cubes. Mix and moisten with French Dressing. Cover a large platter with crisp lettuce. Arrange the salad on it. Decorate it with sliced tomatoes and stuffed olives. Serves 12.

Serving

Put cracked ice in the center of a chop plate. Arrange the olives, pickles, celery and radishes upon it. Place it in the middle of the table. Put 4 candles about the chop plate, and a bowl of flowers at each end. Put the platter of ham at one end of the table and the macaroni salad at the other.

SECTION FIVE

RECIPES

CHAPTER XXXIV

SOUPS

Soup Stock

3 lbs. Beef from Shank
1 Sliced Onion
1 Teaspoon Sugar
2 qts. Cold Water
2 Stalks Celery
1 Carrot

3 Sprigs Parsley
1 Onion
2 Peppercorns
1 Teaspoon Salt
1/8 Teaspoon Pepper
2 Cloves

Have the butcher crack the bone and cut the meat into pieces. Sear the meat in a hot frying pan with onion and sugar. When very brown remove to soup kettle. Add bones and water. Bring slowly to the boiling point. Skim. Simmer gently for 3 hours. Add celery, carrot, parsley, onion, peppercorns, salt, pepper and cloves. Simmer for 1 hour. Strain through a sieve. Cool. Skim the fat from the top. Store in the refrigerator. Soup stock may also be made from the bones and meat left from roasts, chickens and leftover vegetables. This soup stock and the following one are the basis for all clear soups. Variety is achieved by the different ingredients added.

Quick Method Soup Stock

1 lb. Round Steak Ground
1 Slice Onion

1/4 Bay Leaf
4 Tablespoons Chopped Carrot

SOUPS

1 Teaspoon Sugar	4 Slices Onion
6 Cups Cold Water	2 Whole Cloves
4 Sprigs Celery Leaf	1 Teaspoon Salt

Brown 3 tablespoons of meat with onion and sugar. Remove to soup kettle. Add the rest of the meat and the cold water. Bring slowly to the boiling point. Add the seasoning listed above. Cook slowly for 15 minutes. Strain through a fine sieve. Cool and skim the fat from the top. This will keep several days in the refrigerator.

Mushroom Soup

Wash and slice 6 mushrooms into thin slices. Cook for 5 minutes in 1 cup of water. Add 3 cups of soup stock and heat together. Add salt and pepper. Serve with cheese crackers. Serves 4.

Alligator Pear Soup

Peel an alligator pear. Cut one quarter of it into thin crescents. Let the slices simmer in 4 cups of soup stock for 10 minutes. Add salt and pepper. Serve with saltines that have been buttered, sprinkled with paprika and heated in the oven. The remainder of the alligator pear may be served in salad at another meal. Serves 4.

Borsch (Russian Soup)

1 Cup Cabbage	¼ Teaspoon Salt
3 Cups Soup Stock	Pepper
2 Cooked Beets Chopped Fine	Juice of ½ Lemon
½ Cup Beet Juice	

Put the cabbage through the food chopper. Cook it for 10 minutes in 2 cups of water. Add the cooked cabbage and liquid to the soup stock. Add the chopped beets to the soup stock together with the beet juice and seasonings. Heat and serve with 2 tablespoons of whipped cream on top of each plateful. The Russians use a sour cream for this. Rye or Russian bread should accompany this soup. Serves 4.

Lobster Bisque

Heat 2 tablespoons of butter in a pan. Do not brown. Add the meat from a 1 pound lobster or 1 can of lobster. Cook 3 minutes. Stir into this 3 cups of thin cream or rich milk. Dust with salt and pepper. Serve very hot with finger rolls that have been split, buttered and toasted. Serves 4.

Oyster Soup

Into a saucepan put 1 cup of hot water. Add 2 dozen oysters. Heat thoroughly, but do not boil. Be sure they are hot. In another saucepan heat 3 cups of thin cream or rich milk. Combine with the oysters. Add 1 teaspoon of butter, salt and pepper. Serves 4.

Lima Bean Soup

Put 1 can of lima beans through a sieve. Add them to 3 cups of soup stock. Blend 1 tablespoon of butter with 1 tablespoon of flour. Add to the soup together with salt and pepper. Cook 5 minutes. Add croutons to each portion, sprinkle with minced parsley and serve with slices of lemon dusted with paprika. Serves 4.

Croutons

To make croutons to be served with this soup cut stale bread into cubes. Sauté these in melted butter and turn them frequently as they fry so that they will be browned on all sides equally.

Vegetable Soup

Shred ½ carrot, ½ onion, 2 pieces of celery. Boil rapidly 10 minutes in 2 cups of water. Add to 3 cups stock. Serve with saltines. Serves 4.

Onion Soup

Brown 2 large onions cut in thin slices in 2 tablespoons of butter. Cook 5 minutes or until tender. Add to 4 cups hot soup stock. To each portion add 1 slice of bread toasted and 1 tablespoon of orange juice or cooking sherry. This may be served in individual casseroles. Serve very hot. Pass grated parmesan cheese to be sprinkled on the soup at the table. Serves 4.

Cream of Mushroom Soup

Wash ½ pound mushrooms. Cut them fine. Cook them for 5 minutes in 4 tablespoons butter. Do not brown. Stir into this 4 teaspoons flour. Add 4 cups of thin cream or rich milk and ¼ teaspoon salt. Cook 5 minutes. Serves 4.

Tomato Soup

Strain the juice from 1 large can of tomatoes. Add 3 cups of stock to the juice. Heat thoroughly. Serve with a slice of lemon and croutons. The tomatoes remaining may be scalloped. Serves 4.

Cream of Tomato Soup

Heat 2 cups of tomato juice in a saucepan with ⅛ teaspoon soda, 1 slice of onion, 2 cloves, ¼ teaspoon salt and a small bit of bayleaf. When hot add 2 cups of thin cream or rich milk. Add 1 tablespoon butter. Strain and serve very hot. Serves 4.

Cream of Onion Soup

2 Onions Peeled and Minced Fine
3 Tablespoons Butter
1 Tablespoon Flour

4 Cups Thin Cream
¼ Teaspoon Salt
Pepper

Heat but do not brown the butter. Heat the minced onions in the butter. Cover and cook for 5 minutes so that it steams but does not brown. Stir in the flour. Add the cream, salt and pepper. Cook 10 minutes. Pass grated parmesan cheese when soup is served. Serves 4.

Potato Soup

Peel and slice 1 potato in very thin slices. Peel and slice a small onion in thin slices. Cook rapidly in 2 cups of boiling water for 15 minutes. Add 3 cups of thin cream or rich milk and ¼ teaspoon of salt. Heat. Add 2 tablespoons of butter. Dust with pepper. Sprinkle each portion with minced parsley. Fresh mint leaves, finely chopped, may be substituted for the parsley. Serves 4.

Cream of Celery Soup

Slice into very thin slices, enough celery to make 2 cups. Cook in 3 cups of boiling water for 15 minutes. Add 2 cups of thin cream and ¼ teaspoon salt. Dust with pepper. When hot add 2 tablespoons of butter. Dust each serving with paprika and add a sprig of parsley. Left over cooked celery may be utilized for this soup. Serves 4.

Cream of Spinach Soup

Heat 2 cups of water. When boiling add 1 cup of shredded spinach and 2 thin slices of onion. Boil 5 minutes. Add 2 cups of thin cream, ¼ teaspoon of salt. Dust with pepper.

Heat and serve. For variety this soup may be served in small casseroles. Lay a thin slice of cheese on the top of each portion. Melt the cheese slightly in the oven. Serves 4.

Cream of Asparagus Soup

Heat 2 cups of water. When boiling add ½ cup of shredded asparagus tips. Boil 10 minutes. Add 3 cups of thin cream of rich milk, 1 tablespoon of butter and ¼ teaspoon of salt. Heat and serve very hot. Serves 4.

Fish Chowder

Boil 4 cups of water. Add 2 cups of raw potatoes chopped. Cook 15 minutes. In another saucepan boil 1 cup water. Add 1 minced onion. When the potatoes are done, add the onion. Lay on top of this 1 pound of filet of sole or filet of haddock and on top of this 2 slices of salt pork. Simmer for 10 minutes. Add 2 cups of cream or milk. Heat. Remove the salt pork. Add salt and pepper. Serve the chowder very hot poured over pilot biscuit. Serves 4.

Bouillabaisse

1 lb. Filet of Sole cut in Pieces
4 Tablespoons Butter
Meat of 1 Small Lobster or
1 Can Lobster Meat
1 Cup Shrimps
1 Onion Sliced Thin
2 Tablespoons Minced Celery
Juice of 1 Lemon

2 Thin Slices Lemon Peel
2 Cups Boiling Water
2 Cups Soup Stock
4 Tablespoons Cooking Sherry
   or Orange Juice
¼ Teaspoon Salt
¼ Teaspoon Curry Powder

Heat the butter in a pan. When hot but not brown add the filet of sole, lobster, shrimps, onion, celery. Cook in the butter 5 minutes. Add the lemon juice, lemon peel, and boiling water. Cook covered for 10 minutes. Add the soup stock, sherry or orange juice, salt and curry powder. Heat. Pour over slices of toast into hot bowls. Serves 4.

Clam and Chicken Bouillon

Mix 2 cups of clam bouillon with 2 cups of chicken bouillon. Heat thoroughly. Serve hot with 1 tablespoon of whipped cream on each portion.

Luncheon Soup

2 Tablespoons Butter
1 Sliced Onion
2 Tablespoons Minced, unpeeled Apple
2 Tablespoons Minced Celery
1 Cup Minced Boiled Potato
½ Cup Minced Ham
½ Teaspoon Curry Powder
2 Cups Water
Juice of ½ Lemon
1 Teaspoon Grated Lemon Peel
½ Teaspoon Salt
2 Cups Rich Milk

Heat the butter in a saucepan at gentle heat. Add the onion, apple, celery. Cook covered for 5 minutes. Add the boiled potato, ham, curry powder and water. Simmer 5 minutes. Add the lemon juice, lemon peel, salt and milk. Simmer 5 minutes. Serve with squares of toast and grated cheese or crackers and cheese. Decorate with minced parsley and a slice of lemon that has been dusted with paprika. Serves 4.

Clam Bouillon

Wash the clams thoroughly before using. For ½ peck clams use 3 cups cold water in a kettle which can be tightly covered. Steam the clams until the shells are well opened. Strain the liquor through cheesecloth and cool. Season to taste.

Chicken Bouillon

4 lbs. Chicken
2 qts. Cold Water
1 Blade Mace
1 Teaspoon Salt
1 Slice Onion
1 Teaspoon Sugar
½ Teaspoon Celery Seed (Celery Tops may be substituted.)
¼ Teaspoon Pepper

Wash the chicken. Cut the meat into pieces, removing all flesh from the bones. Put through the meat chopper. Brown the sugar in your soup kettle. When it has burned add the chicken meat. Stir for a moment, then add the water and chicken bones. Bring to boiling point in covered kettle. Skim. Simmer gently for 2 hours. Add the celery tops or celery seed, mace, 1 bay leaf and the slice of onion. Simmer gently 30 minutes. Strain. Season with salt and pepper.

Beet Soup

Mince 1 medium sized can of beets fine. Add ½ cup of water to the juice. Simmer the beets and liquid 10 minutes. Strain. Add 1 cup chicken bouillon, 2 cups thin cream, ¼ teaspoon salt. Dust with celery salt. Add whipped cream to the top of each serving. Sprinkle with minced parsley. Serves 4.

CHAPTER XXXV

SEA FOOD AND FISH

Oyster Loaf

Cut the tops from 4 soft rolls. Scoop out the center. Butter them inside. Put into the oven to warm. Drain the liquor from 1 quart of oysters. Heat 1 tablespoon butter in a large pan. Put the oysters in, keeping them separated. When the edges curl dust with salt and pepper. Fill the rolls. Sprinkle with minced parsley. Put 1 teaspoon of butter on top. Replace the covers of the rolls. Heat in a quick oven (400° F.) for 10 minutes. Garnish with lemon cups. Pass mushroom sauce with them. The lemon cups are made by cutting the lemons in half. Remove the pulp with a grapefruit knife. Cut the edges with a fruit decorator or cut into points with a sharp knife. Fill with Chili sauce. The bottoms of the lemon cups should have a thin piece cut off so that they will stand erect. A small loaf of bread may be substituted for the rolls. Serves 4.

Mushroom Sauce

½ lb. Mushrooms
4 Tablespoons Butter
1½ Cups Milk
3 Tablespoons Flour
¾ Teaspoon Salt

Wash and slice the mushrooms. Cook them in 1 tablespoon of the butter in covered pan. Do not brown. Make a cream sauce in the double boiler using the milk, 3 tablespoons of butter, the flour and the salt. Blend the butter, salt and a seasoning of pepper. Add the milk next. Place over hot water, stirring well as it cooks. Cook 10 minutes. Beat vigorously. Add the hot mushrooms to the sauce. Dust with pepper.

To Open Oysters and Clams

Put a short, thin, flat knife back of the shell where it is hinged together. Push forward until the knife cuts the strong muscle. When this is cut the valves may be separated from each other. Wash in cold water to remove any bits of shell that may cling to the oysters or clams. Some of these may have to be loosened with the fingers. Look at each one carefully to be sure the shell has not clung to the meat.

Roasted Clams

Purchase clams in their shells. Wash and scrub them. Allow them to stand for several hours covered with water. Put ½ cup of cornmeal in the water. This will insure a freedom from sand. The clams open the shell slightly to feed upon the cornmeal and this releases the sand which often collects in the shell. Heat the oven very hot (450° F.). Place the clams in a dripping pan. When the shells open they are done. This takes about 15 minutes. Drain the liquor from the pan. Strain it and serve in cups along with melted butter. Mussels are treated in the same way, except that they have ½ cup of cooking wine, 1 tablespoon minced parsley and 1 tablespoon minced chives added to the pan they are cooked in.

Fried Scallops

Drain 1 quart of scallops. Let stand in a dressing made with 2 tablespoons olive oil, juice of 1 lemon, ½ teaspoon salt, ¼ teaspoon pepper, 1 teaspoon minced parsley. Let stand 1 hour. Beat 1 egg with 1 tablespoon of water. Dip the scallops in it. Dip in sifted dry bread crumbs. Fry in deep fat heated until it will brown a cube of bread in 1 minute (375° F.). Use a fat thermometer to test the fat. Fry a few at a time until they are golden brown. Keep hot in the oven. Drain on soft paper. Serve with strips of browned bacon, slices of lemon and parsley. A frying basket is a convenience in frying foods in deep fat. Serves 4.

Baked Shrimps

1 Pint Shrimps
2 Tablespoons Butter
2 Tablespoons Flour
½ Cup Cooking Wine
   or Orange Juice
1½ Cups Milk
Lemon Peel
½ Teaspoon Salt
2 Eggs Well Beaten
Cracker Crumbs

Wash and drain the shrimps. Heat the butter in a pan and heat the shrimps in this. Stir in the flour. Add the milk. Stir well and cook until bubbling. Add the wine or orange juice, a bit of lemon peel, salt, pepper and a sprinkling of mace. Stir in the eggs which must be well beaten. Place in an open casserole. Cover the top with buttered cracker crumbs. Bake 20 minutes in a moderate oven (375° F.).

Crab Croquettes

1 Cup Crab Meat
1 Cup Cooked Filet of Sole
⅓ Cup Butter
½ Cup Flour
1 Teaspoon Salt
2 Cups Cold Milk

Flake the meat and mix the crab with the filet of sole. Make a white sauce by blending the butter, flour and salt. Add to the milk. Stir over the fire with a wire whisk, stirring constantly. When the ingredients are blended and thickened slightly cook for 10 minutes in a double boiler. Dust with pepper. Add the crab and fish. Spread in a shallow dish. Cool and place in the refrigerator to get thoroughly cold.

Form into croquettes. Dip in dry sifted bread or cracker crumbs. Then in a beaten egg that has been diluted with 1 teaspoon of water. Dip again in the crumbs. Fry in a basket in deep, hot fat. The fat should be heated until it will brown a cube of bread in 1 minute (375° F.). Decorate with parsley and lemon. Fresh green peas should accompany the croquettes. Cream sauce with minced parsley may be served with them. Serves 4.

Lobster with Cauliflower

1 Head Cauliflower
Juice of 1 Lemon
1 Pint Water
3 Tablespoons Butter
1 Cup Lobster Meat
3 Tablespoons Flour
2 Cups Milk
1 Teaspoon Salt

Wash and trim the head of cauliflower. Leave it whole. Soak in cold water with the lemon juice. Put pint of water in a saucepan and add ½ teaspoon salt. Stand the cauliflower erect with the flower side up. Steam for 30 minutes. Remove to a chop plate. Surround with lobster sauce. For the lobster sauce heat the butter in a pan. Stir in lobster meat. When hot stir in the flour. When blended add the milk and ½ teaspoon salt. Dust with pepper. Serves 4.

Lobster in Butter

Heat 2 cups of fresh lobster meat in 4 tablespoons of melted butter. Serve with shell beans and boiled sweet potatoes. If you wish to economize on lobster, it may be mixed with an equal amount of meat from cooked filet of flounder.

Baked Mackerel

Have the mackerel split and the tail and head removed. Place in a buttered utility dish. Dot with bits of butter.

Sprinkle with salt and pepper. Add ¾ cup of milk. Bake in a hot oven 25 minutes (400° F.).

Baked Shad

1 Shad (about 4 pounds)
2 Tablespoons Shortening
1½ Cups Bread Crumbs
1 Teaspoon Chopped Onion
1 Teaspoon Chopped Parsley
½ Teaspoon Salt
⅛ Teaspoon Pepper

Have the shad cleaned and slit for stuffing. Season inside and out with salt and pepper. Melt the shortening. Add the bread crumbs, onion, parsley, salt and pepper. Stuff the shad with this dressing. Sew the fish together at the slit place. Grease a glass oven proof platter. Lay the fish in it. Brush with melted shortening. Place in a hot oven for 15 minutes (450° F.). Reduce the heat. Bake 45 minutes (400° F.). Serve on the platter on which it was baked.

Boiled Salmon

2½ Pounds Salmon Steak
1 Onion, Chopped
¼ Cup Celery, Chopped
1 Teaspoon Parsley, Chopped
¼ Cup Carrot, Chopped
½ Bay Leaf
1 Teaspoon Salt
⅛ Teaspoon Pepper
1 Tablespoon Vinegar
2 Quarts of Water

Heat the water to the boiling point. Add the vegetable, salt, pepper, bay leaf and vinegar. Wrap the fish in cheese-cloth. Tie securely. Drop into the boiling water. Reduce the heat. Simmer 30 minutes. Remove from the water. Remove cheese-cloth. Serve on a hot platter decorated with parsley and lemon.

Filet of Sole

1½ Pounds Filet of Sole
Salt
1 Egg
2 Tablespoons Water

Pepper   2 Tablespoons Cooking Fat
1 Cup Fine Bread Crumbs

Sprinkle the filet with salt and pepper. Dip in crumbs. Then in the egg beaten with the water. Dip again in crumbs. Heat the fat in the frying pan. When hot, cook the fish in this for 10 minutes or until brown on both sides. Garnish with parsley and lemon. Serve with Tartar Sauce.

Tartar Sauce

To 1 cup of mayonnaise add 2 tablespoons of chopped parsley, 2 tablespoons chopped sour pickle, 2 tablespoons chopped olives and 1 teaspoon capers.

For additional recipes for sea food cocktails, cooked seafood and fish, see index.

CHAPTER XXXVI

MEATS

Minute Steak

These steaks are cut from the tenderloin, about ½ inch thick. They should be broiled close to the gas flame for 3 minutes. Turn them often. Serve on a platter with bunches of water cress at each end. Slices of lemon dusted with paprika may accompany this. Sautéd sliced tomatoes take about 3 minutes and mashed potato cakes the same length of time. A dinner including these may be prepared very quickly.

Ham in Milk

Purchase a slice of boiled Virginia ham ½ inch thick. Spread it with prepared mustard. Heat ½ cup of milk. Lay the ham into this. When the milk cooks away add a little more. Cook 10 minutes. Serve surrounded with rings of red apple and pineapple.

Cut rings of red apple. Add rings of pineapple. Dust with cinnamon. Sprinkle with sugar and bits of butter. Bake in a pan or casserole which contains enough water to just cover the bottom of the dish. Bake 10 minutes.

Lamb Stew

Lamb Steak or Lamb Chops
2 Tablespoons Butter
1 Cup Minced Celery
1 Cup Minced Carrots
1 Onion Sliced
1 Tablespoon Flour
2 Cups Water

Heat the butter in a frying pan. In this cook the celery, carrots and onion. Cook 2 minutes. Stir in the flour and add the water. Salt and pepper. When thickened transfer to a saucepan. Cut the meat in small pieces. The bones may be used for soup stock. Dust the meat with flour. Sauté in butter and place on top of the vegetables. Cover and cook slowly for 25 minutes. Add more water if it cooks away. Pork, veal or beef may be used instead of lamb. Any meat left over from a roast will serve.

Thick Steak

Purchase a porterhouse steak 2½ inches thick. This may take the place of roast beef. Broil 25 minutes. Turn every 5 minutes. Serve surrounded by mounds of cooked vegetables and potatoes. Horseradish mixed with fresh cream and a very little French mustard should accompany this.

Swiss Steak

1½ Pounds Round Steak
2 Tablespoons Melted Fat
⅓ Cup of Flour
½ Teaspoon Salt
Pepper
1½ Cups Cooked Tomatoes
1 Cup Hot Water

Sift flour and salt together. Pound it into the steak. Dust with pepper. Melt the fat in a heavy pan. When hot, brown the steak thoroughly. Add the tomatoes and the hot water. Cover closely. Simmer on top of the stove for 3 hours. The steak may be cooked in a covered casserole in the oven, if you prefer, for 3 hours at a moderate temperature (325° F.).

Beef Stew with Vegetables

2 Pounds Top Round of Beef
2 Tablespoons Cooking Fat
1½ Teaspoons Salt
3 Cups Water
1 Cup Cooked Tomatoes
6 Small Onions

⅛ Teaspoon Pepper
6 Tablespoons Flour

1½ Cups Sliced Carrots
1 Tablespoon Chopped Parsley

Cut beef in even pieces. Sprinkle with 3 tablespoons of the flour and a small amount of the salt and pepper. Heat the fat in a heavy pan. Brown the meat in it, turning so it will brown evenly. Add the water, tomatoes and parsley. Simmer 1 hour. Add the rest of the vegetables, salt and pepper. Simmer for 1 hour after the vegetables are added. Mix 3 tablespoons of flour with ⅓ cup of water. Stir to a smooth paste. Thicken the gravy with this. Other vegetables may be added.

Pot Roast

4 Pounds Round of Beef
2 Tablespoons Flour
2 Tablespoons Cooking Fat
1 Teaspoon Salt
⅛ Teaspoon Pepper
2 Cups Hot Water

½ Bay Leaf
Sprig of Parsley
½ Cup Sliced Carrots
½ Cup Celery, Sliced
1 Onion, Minced

Sprinkle the meat with salt and pepper. Dust with the flour. Heat fat in a heavy frying pan. Thoroughly brown the meat, turning so that all will be evenly browned. Put meat in a saucepan. Add bay leaf, vegetables and hot water. Cover closely. Simmer 4 hours. Turn occasionally. Mix 2 tablespoons of flour with ⅓ cup of water. Make a gravy with the liquid in the pan. Add salt and pepper to taste.

Veal Cutlets

Purchase 1 pound of veal steak cut from the leg. Cut into pieces for serving. Flatten them slightly. Dust with salt, pepper and flour. Beat 1 egg with 1 tablespoon cold water. Dip the cutlets in the egg then in sifted dried bread or cracker crumbs. Put 4 tablespoons cooking fat or butter in a frying pan. Brown the cutlets well. Add ½ cup of hot water or stock. Cover closely. Cook gently for 30 minutes. Veal Cutlets may be breaded and baked in a utility dish in a hot oven (400° F.) for 30 minutes.

Fricassee of Veal

2 Pounds Veal Cut for Fricasseeing
1 Onion
¼ Cup Sliced Carrot
¼ Cup Sliced Celery

Salt and Pepper
4 Tablespoons Butter
5 Tablespoons Flour
¼ Bay Leaf

Cover the meat with boiling water. Add the bay leaf and vegetables. Simmer gently for about 1 hour or until the meat may be easily removed from the bone. Discard the bone. Salt and pepper the meat, sprinkle with flour. Brown delicately in 2 tablespoons of the butter. Add 2 tablespoons of butter to the frying pan in which the meat was browned after removing the meat. Stir into the butter 4 tablespoons of flour. Add 2 cups of the strained broth from the meat. Stir until thickened. Season with salt and pepper. Pour the sauce around the meat.

Roast Leg of Veal

Dust the meat with salt and pepper. Place in a roasting pan. Lay strips of salt pork over the top to supply the fat the meat lacks. Place the meat in a hot oven (525° F.) for 15 minutes. Reduce the heat to a moderate temperature (350° F.). Roast 30 minutes to the pound after the temperature has been reduced. Veal should be roasted in a covered, self-basting roaster. To make the gravy pour off all but 4 tablespoons of fat in the roasting pan. Stir in 4 tablespoons of flour. Add 2 cups of water. Stir until thickened. Season with salt and pepper.

Veal Steak

1 lb. Veal Steak
4 Thick Slices Wholewheat Bread
1 Cup Hot Water
1 Tablespoon Walnut Meats
1 Tablespoon Butter
¼ lb. Mushrooms
1 Egg
1 Cup Rich Milk

Dust the steak with flour, salt and pepper. Brown in butter. Moisten the bread with hot water. Add walnut meats, butter and mushrooms, salt and pepper. Combine with the egg. Stir together. Spread the steak with the dressing and lay in a hot casserole. Cover with the milk. As the milk cooks away add more hot milk if necessary. Dust flour over all. Bake covered for 25 minutes at 350° F. Serve surrounded by the pan gravy. For relishes use celery, radishes, sweet pickles and grape jelly. Serves 4.

English Mutton Chops

Have the chops cut 2 inches thick. Broil 20 minutes. Turn them often. Serve with large baked potatoes which have been split open and pieces of butter inserted. Dust the potatoes with paprika. Surround the chops with sliced tomatoes sprinkled with minced parsley and buttered cauliflower. English mustard pickle makes a good relish.

East Indian Curry

5 lbs. Fricasseeing Chicken
2 Apples
2 Onions
2 Tablespoons Butter
1 Tablespoon Curry Powder
2¼ Cups Chicken Stock

Peel and slice in thin slices the apples and onions. Brown them in a frying pan with the butter. Add curry powder which has been mixed with ¼ cup chicken stock. Stir and add the rest of the chicken stock. Add the meat of the chicken which must be cut in pieces. Cook in water 30 minutes. Cook slowly for 1 hour additional, adding more chicken stock if it cooks away. Remove the chicken. Thicken the liquid. Add salt. Serve on a large chop plate, surrounded by plain boiled rice and sautéd tomatoes. Pass East Indian chutney, crisp celery and radishes with the curry. Add a tablespoon of chutney syrup to the gravy when it is made.

Meat Loaf

1½ lbs. Ground Beef
1 Onion Chopped
1½ Tablespoons Minute Tapioca
2 Teaspoons Salt

1 Egg
¾ Cup Tomatoes
4 Tablespoons Chili Sauce
Pepper

Mix all ingredients, except Chili sauce, together thoroughly. Put into greased loaf pan. Spread Chili sauce on top. Bake 45 minutes in a moderate oven (375° F.).

Baked Steak

Tender Steak
2 Onions
2 Carrots
1 Cup of Celery

¼ lb. Mushrooms
2 Cooked Beets
½ Cup Radishes

Brown each vegetable separately in butter and place in a baking dish. Dust the steak with flour, salt and pepper. Brown in butter. Lay it on top of the vegetables. Pour a cup of water into the frying pan. When hot pour the liquid over the vegetables. Dust the steak with more flour. Cover and cook 20 minutes. More hot water should be added to the vegetables if it boils away. The water should be boiling when added.

Pork Tenderloin

The pork tenderloin should be cut into rounds. Dust with flour, salt and pepper. Brown in hot butter. Add the juice of

1 lemon, 1 cup of thin cream and 1 slice of onion. Cook covered, slowly for 20 minutes. Sprinkle with minced parsley when ready to serve. Mushrooms may be added. Accompany this with mounds of spinach, stuffed eggs, mashed potatoes, radishes and India relish.

Deviled Roast Beef

Use a slice of left over roast beef about 1½ inches thick. Spread with French mustard and Worcestershire sauce. Brown in butter, turning often for 10 minutes.

Roast Turkey with Oyster Dressing

Have the butcher prepare and dress the turkey for stuffing. Singe it over an open flame. To stuff an 8 pound turkey you will need 1 large loaf of bread. Cut the bread into slices. Butter it. Remove the crusts. Cut into cubes. Moisten the bread with 1 pint of oyster liquor. Add 2 teaspoons salt, ½ teaspoon pepper and 2 dozen oysters. Stuff the turkey at the crop and lower opening. Thread a trussing needle or large darning needle with heavy twine. Sew up the openings. Run 2 metal skewers through the wings and body on either side to hold them close to the body. Tie the legs together at the ends. Run the needle and twine through the tail and fasten it to the ends of the legs. Tie the loose skin at the end of the neck and pull the neck back and fasten in the back. Rub the turkey with softened butter. Dust with salt and pepper. Put into a very hot oven (450° F.) until it is well browned. Add 1 cup of water to the pan. Reduce the heat to 350° F. or a moderate oven. Roast for 3 hours after it has browned. Baste every 15 minutes with the liquid in the pan adding more if it cooks away. Remove the string and skewers before serving. Decorate the platter with bunches of parsley. You may use a covered roasting pan if you prefer it. The cooking time is the same.

Giblet Gravy

Cook the liver, heart and gizzard in 1½ cups of hot water for 30 minutes. Save the broth. Chop them fine. Pour the fat from the pan in which the turkey has been roasting, saving 6 tablespoons. Add 5 tablespoons flour. Stir until it browns. Add 3 cups of water and 1 cup of broth from the giblets. Stir until smooth and thickened. Cook 10 minutes. Add the giblets and 1½ teaspoons salt. Dust with pepper.

Veal Kidney

2 Veal Kidneys
Flour, Salt, Pepper
3 Tablespoons Butter
¼ lb. Sliced Mushrooms
1 Slice Onion
1 Tablespoon Minced Parsley
4 Tablespoons Cooking wine or juice of 1 Orange
1 Cup Soup Stock
Thick Slices Toasted Bread

Heat a casserole in the oven. Cut the kidneys into small pieces. Pour boiling water over them. Drain and dust with flour, salt and pepper. Cook 3 minutes in hot water. Remove to hot casserole. Put in frying pan the mushrooms, onion, minced parsley. Salt and pepper. When this has cooked a minute and is hot add the orange juice or cooking wine and the soup stock. When boiling, pour into the casserole. Bake covered for 20 minutes. Add the thick slices of toast to the casserole. Dust with grated cheese. Heat a moment and serve. Serves 4.

Shepherd's Pie

Put any kind of roast meat through the food chopper. Add gravy. Put into a casserole. Cover the top with mashed potatoes. Bake 20 minutes.

Broiled Duckling

Young duckling should be chosen. Have them split. Broil

25 minutes under a gas flame. Turn frequently. Serve with orange sauce. Serve ½ duck for each person.

Orange Sauce

1 Cup Orange Juice
1 Teaspoon Grated Orange Peel
¼ Cup Water
Juice of ½ Lemon

⅛ Teaspoon Paprika
¼ Teaspoon Salt
2 Tablespoons Butter
2 Tablespoons Flour

Blend the flour and butter. Stir into the combined liquid. Cook in a double boiler and stir until thickened. Chopped fresh mint may be added.

Fried Chicken

Have the butcher cut a chicken for frying. Dust with flour, salt and pepper. Brown in butter. Add 1 cup of milk. Cook covered 25 minutes. If the milk cooks away add more, a little at a time. Serve with celery, olives, currant jelly, tiny lima beans, avocado salad, mashed potatoes and hot rolls.

Roast Chicken, Poultry Dressing

To serve four people purchase two 3 pound roasting chickens prepared for stuffing. For the dressing melt 4 tablespoons butter in a skillet. Add 8 cups soft bread crumbs. Stir until hot. Add ¼ cup minced celery, 2 tablespoons minced onion and ½ cup of hot water. Add 2 teaspoons salt, 2 teaspoons poultry seasoning and ¼ teaspoon pepper. Remove from the fire. When the dressing has cooled slightly add 1 well-beaten egg. Singe the chickens. Stuff and truss them according to the directions for roast duck in the following recipe. Put the chickens in a pan in a hot oven at 450° F. When they are well browned add 1 cup of water. Reduce heat to 350° F. Roast at that temperature for 1 hour. Baste every 15 minutes. Follow the directions for giblet gravy in the Turkey recipe.

Roast Duck

For a dinner for four people you will need two 2½ pound ducks. Have the butcher dress the ducks and prepare them for stuffing.

Light the broiler flame so that the oven will be hot for the ducks. Singe them over a gas flame. Make the dressing as follows: Cut a loaf of bread into slices, discarding the crusts. Butter the bread and cut the slices into small cubes. Add 1 tablespoon of minced parsley, 1 teaspoon salt, 1 tablespoon minced celery, ⅛ teaspoon pepper and ¼ pound of broken walnut meats. Mix well and fill the ducks with the dressing. Thread a trussing needle with twine. Fasten the wings of the duck close to the body with needle and twine or metal skewers. Fasten the legs together at the ends. Run the needle through the tail and fasten the tail to the legs. Dust with salt and pepper. Broil under the gas flame until the ducks are well browned, turning often. Place the ducks in a pan in the oven. Add 1 cup of water to the pan. Roast 40 minutes in a hot oven at a temperature of 400° F. Baste with the liquid in the pan every 10 minutes. Add more water if it cooks away. Use a covered roasting pan if you prefer it.

Casserole of Chicken

2 Tender 3 lb. Chickens	4 Tablespoons Flour
2 Slices Onion	3 Cups Water
½ lb. Mushrooms	4 Tablespoons Cooking Wine or
1 Thin Slice Lemon Peel	Juice of 1 Orange
4 Tablespoons Butter	Salt and Pepper

Either a glass or earthenware casserole may be used. Heat the casserole. Cut chickens into pieces for serving. Dust with flour, salt and pepper. Brown the chicken in hot butter in a frying pan. Lay the meat in the hot casserole. Cook the onion, mushrooms and lemon peel in frying pan. Add butter and stir in the flour. Add water and wine or orange juice. Salt and pepper. When this has thickened pour it over the chicken in the casserole. When the liquid in the casserole is bubbling reduce heat to 300° F. and cook for 3 hours. Longer cooking will not harm this dish if it is cooked slowly. Serves 4.

Lamb Cutlets

Purchase loin lamb chops cut ½ inch thick. Remove the fat and bone leaving only a round of meat. Use the bones for soup stock. Dust the meat with salt and pepper and flour. Brown in butter with a slice of onion and 1 tablespoon of minced celery. Dust more flour over the meat and cook covered for 20 minutes. Serve on a platter surrounded by thin slices of orange with the peel left on and cooked halves of pears. Dust chopped mint over the fruit and decorate the platter with sprigs of fresh mint. Creamed carrots and endive salad should accompany the lamb.

Baked Ham Casserole

Cover the bottom of a casserole with slices of pineapple. Peel and cut into lengthwise slices 3 large sweet potatoes. Core and cut crosswise 3 red apples. Lay over the sweet potatoes. Put a thick slice of ham over all. Add 1 cup of pineapple juice and cook covered for 2 hours in a slow oven, (300° F.). Uncover and add bits of brown sugar and butter. Brown under the broiler flame. Marshmallows may be added to the top and toasted. Serves 4.

Steak with Onions

Broil a steak 1 inch thick for 10 minutes, close to the flame, turning every 3 minutes. Slice and sauté 6 large onions in a skillet in 4 tablespoons of butter. Stir them often until they are tender and beginning to brown. Add 1 cup of soup stock. Add pepper, salt, 1 teaspoon Worcestershire sauce and 1 tablespoon of chutney. Serve the steak on a bed of water cress with radish roses about it and the onion sauce covering the steak. Serves 4.

Baked Ham

Put a large kettle of water to boil. Scrub the ham with a stiff brush. Reduce the heat of the water until it is simmering. Place the ham in the water; it should just cover it. Simmer 30 minutes to the pound. Let the ham stand in the water after it has finished cooking until it is partially cool. Remove from the water. Cut away the outside skin. Sprinkle with 1 cup of brown sugar. Stick cloves into the ham 1 inch apart. Place 1 cup of cider in an oven pan. Bake the ham 1 hour in a slow oven (300° F.). This may be served either hot or cold.

Tamale Pie

2 Cups Cooked Chicken or Beef
1 Tablespoon Minced Bacon
1 Onion Sliced
1 Ground Green Pepper
1 Cup Ground Celery
2 Tablespoons Butter
2 Tablespoons Flour

4 Cups Water
1 Bouillon Cube
½ Teaspoon Salt
1 Teaspoon Chili Powder
1 Cup Tomatoes
1 Cup Cornmeal

Brown the minced bacon in a casserole. Add the onion, green pepper and ground celery. Cook in the oven while you are preparing the other ingredients. Heat the cooked chicken or beef in a skillet with the butter. Stir the flour into this and add 2 cups of water, the bouillon cube, salt and the Chili powder. When it has thickened add the tomatoes. When hot add this to the casserole. Stir well. For the cornmeal mixture place 2 cups of water in a saucepan and add salt. When it boils sift into this, stirring constantly, the cornmeal. Cook until it is thick. Spread over the meat in the casserole. Cook in a slow oven (300° F.) for 40 minutes. Serves 6.

Stuffed Pork Chops

4 Thick Pork Chops (cut for stuffing)
1½ Cups Cooked Rice
2 Chopped Pimentos
Pepper and Salt

Wipe chops, stuff with chopped pimento and rice. Place in hot skillet and brown on both sides. Cover and reduce heat. Cook 1 hour.

Stuffed Cabbage

Mix 1 pound of ground round steak with 1 roll soaked in milk. Add 1 teaspoon of salt, 1 egg and 1 teaspoon minced parsley. Stuff the outer leaves of cabbage. Roll up and tie with thread. Cook in a casserole in the oven with slices of onion, ½ pint of thin cream and 1 cup of stock. Cook about 1 hour in a slow oven (300° F.). This may be cooked in a double boiler. Serves 4.

Chili Con Carni

1 lb. Ground Round Steak
1 Can Kidney Beans
1 Can Tomatoes
2 Onions Chopped
1 Green Pepper Chopped
1 Cup Celery Chopped
4 Teaspoons Chili Powder
2 Teaspoons Salt
2 Cups Cooked Rice
4 Cups Water

Combine the ingredients listed above. The water should be boiling when added. Cook over hot water in a cooker for 2 hours. This Chili may also be cooked in a fireless electric cooker. It is an excellent dish to serve as a supper for 10 people for the hostess without a maid. With a salad, jelly, radishes, dessert and coffee it is a complete meal with a minimum of last minute rush. If the electric cooker is used the Chili might be carried in the car for a picnic supper.

Veal and Olives

Flour 1 lb. of veal steak. Dust with salt and pepper and sauté in a frying pan in 2 tablespoons of butter. When it is brown add 1 bottle of stuffed olives sliced thin. Place the steak and olives in a casserole. Add 2 cups of water to the pan. Add to casserole. Bake for 1 hour. The water may cook away and the veal brown when more hot water should be added and the process repeated. Make a gravy from the contents of the casserole. Serves 4.

Casserole of Pork Chops

Use a large flat covered casserole. Heat in the oven. Brown the pork chops in butter in a frying pan. Lay in the hot casserole. Put whole sliced pineapple around them together with large cooked prunes stuffed with stuffed olives. Core small red apples. Remove a part of the center and chop. Add 1 cup of bread crumbs and a few currants. Just moisten with pineapple juice. Stuff the apples. Place in the casserole. Add 1 cup of hot cider. Cook covered in a slow oven (300° F.) for 40 minutes. Serve in the casserole.

Chicken Pie

2 Tender 3 lb. Chickens	1 Egg Yolk
1 Cup Carrot Balls	⅛ Teaspoon Salt
1 Cup Small White Onions Peeled	⅛ Teaspoon Thyme
	1 Cup Soft Bread Crumbs
1 Tablespoon Cream	1 Tablespoon Cream

The chickens should be cut for fricasseeing. Cook them 30 minutes in 6 cups of water. Save the water they were cooked in. Remove skin from chickens. Boil the carrot balls, which can be prepared with a vegetable cutter, for 5 minutes. Boil the onions for 5 minutes. Make forcemeat balls with the bread crumbs which have been moistened with the cream and egg yolk. Add salt and thyme. Form into balls the size of marbles. Arrange the carrots, onions and forcemeat balls in the bottom of an open casserole. Lay the chicken over it. Truffles may be added if you like. Make a gravy from the broth: Mix a little broth with 4 tablespoons flour and ½ teaspoon salt. Stir until smooth. Add to the broth. Cook 5 minutes, stirring continuously. Pour over the chicken. Make puff paste. (See recipe under Pastry.) Roll ¼ inch thick. Cover the top of the casserole. Make slits in the top. Add a roll of puff paste around the edge. When the pie is put in the oven temperature should be hot (450° F.). After 15 minutes reduce the heat to 350° F. Bake 1 hour longer. Serves 6.

Hamburger Brochette

Put ¼ lb. bacon through a food chopper. Add 1 lb. ground round steak. Wash 12 large mushrooms. Chop stems and add to meat. Make the meat into cakes. Place 1 mushroom on a metal skewer. Add a meat cake. Then another mushroom cap and another meat cake, etc. Finish with mushrooms. Broil 15 minutes. Turning occasionally. Serves 4.

Lamb Pot Roast

4 lbs. Shoulder of Lamb
1 Cup Celery
2 Onions Sliced
2 Tomatoes Sliced
4 Minced Carrots
1 Thin Slice Garlic

Have the butcher bone the lamb and remove every trace of fat. Have the meat rolled and bound in a compact mass. Brown it in butter until a rich, deep brown. Place in a kettle. Surround this with the vegetables. Add 2 cups of water to the pan the meat was browned in. Pour over the vegetables.

Add more hot water if necessary. The water should half cover the pot roast. Cook slowly for 2 hours. Remove the meat. Make a sauce of the vegetables and liquid in the pan by adding 2 tablespoons of flour mixed with 4 tablespoons of water. Serve with broiled eggplant. The recipe for this is given under Vegetables.

CHAPTER XXXVII

VEGETABLES

Cauliflower au Gratin

1 Cauliflower
1 Tablespoon Lemon Juice
2 Tablespoons Butter
4 Tablespoons Flour
2 Cups Cold Milk
½ Cup Grated Cheese

Wash the cauliflower. Remove the green leaves. Cut into flowerets. Soak in cold water with the lemon juice. Boil 20 minutes. While the cauliflower is boiling make the sauce: Blend the butter with the flour. Add the cold milk. Cook in a double boiler. Stir until blended and then stir occasionally. Add the grated cheese. Remove cauliflower to utility dish. Dress with the cream sauce. Sprinkle top with buttered cornflakes. Bake in a moderate oven (350° F.) about 10 minutes until the flakes are brown. Serves 4.

Leeks

Wash 2 bunches of leeks. Remove the outer leaves. Cut off green stalks. Cook in boiling water until they are tender, about 25 minutes. Lightly toast bread with the crusts removed. Drain the leeks. Arrange on toast. Pour melted butter over them. Dust with salt and pepper.

Casserole of Summer Squash

Peel 2 summer squashes. Cut in small pieces and cook 20 minutes in boiling salted water. Drain, mash, add 1 tablespoon butter, 4 tablespoons cream and 2 tablespoons minced ham. Remove to utility dish. Cover top with buttered cornflakes. Bake in a moderate oven until the cornflakes are brown. Serves 4.

Carrot Cups with Peas

Scrape large carrots. Cut in 1 inch slices crosswise. Scoop out the center. Steam 20 minutes or until they are tender. Fill with tiny green peas, heated. Decorate with a sprig of parsley. Serve on the meat platter surrounding broiled steak, chops or a roast.

Glazed Onions

Peel 1 quart of small white onions. Cook 20 minutes in boiling water. Drain. Place 2 tablespoons butter in a saucepan. Melt. Add the onions with 2 teaspoons powdered sugar. Shake occasionally until the butter has been absorbed and the onions are golden brown. Add 1/4 cup water. Cook until the water is absorbed.

Lima Beans and Tomatoes

1 Can Green Lima Beans	1 Teaspoon Chopped Green Pepper
1/2 Can Tomatoes	

1 Small Onion Chopped or Lemon Rind from ¼ Lemon
    Sliced Salt and Pepper
1 Tablespoon Butter

Sauté onion and green pepper in butter, add lima beans, tomatoes, lemon rind, salt and pepper. Cover and cook 30 minutes over a low flame.

Broccoli

Remove leaves and hard stock from broccoli. Separate the flowerets or cut into sections with a knife. Cook 20 minutes in boiling water. When it is partly cooked add 1 teaspoon salt for every quart of water. Drain and serve with melted butter or Hollandaise sauce.

Hollandaise Sauce

2 Egg Yolks 8 Tablespoons Butter
1 Tablespoon Lemon Juice ½ Cup Boiling Water
¼ Teaspoon Salt

Beat the egg yolks with the lemon juice and add salt. Add 2 tablespoons of butter. Stir constantly over hot water. When blended add 2 tablespoons of butter and repeat, then add 4 tablespoons of butter. When well blended add the half cup boiling water a little at a time, stirring constantly. Dust with white pepper or a few grains of cayenne.

Baked Tomatoes

Mix 1 can of tomatoes with 1 cup corn. Add 1 tablespoon minced onion, 1 teaspoon grated lemon peel, 1 teaspoon salt, 12 stuffed olives sliced, 1 tablespoon butter and pepper. Bake in a buttered casserole 30 minutes at 375° F. Serves 6.

Tiny Lima Beans with Celery

Wash and slice in thin slices 1 bunch of celery. Cook in boiling water for 15 minutes. Drain. Add 1 can of tiny lima beans. Place in a double boiler and heat thoroughly. Dust with salt and pepper. Add ½ cup of cream and butter.

Stuffed Onions

6 Large Onions
2 Tablespoons Minced Bacon
1 Apple Chopped
2 Cups Soft Bread Crumbs
½ Teaspoon Salt
1 Teaspoon Grated Lemon Peel
⅛ Teaspoon Ginger

Peel the onions. Boil 10 minutes. Drain. Scoop out the centers and save the onion removed. Fill the onions with the following dressing: Brown the bacon until a delicate brown. Add the chopped apple, bread crumbs, 4 tablespoons of minced onion centers. Season with salt, lemon peel, ginger and a little pepper. Pile this in the onion cups. Bake in buttered utility dish in a moderate oven (375° F.) for 40 minutes. Put 1 teaspoon of catsup in the center of each onion. Serve around a roast of pork. Serves 6.

Artichokes

Wash and trim the hard ends from artichokes. Boil in a large quantity of salted water to which has been added the juice of 1 lemon. Cook 1 hour. Serve either hot or cold, one to a person with a side dish of Hollandaise sauce in which to dip the tender lower portion of the leaves and the bottom. The recipe for Hollandaise sauce is given in the recipe for broccoli. Mayonnaise or a boiled dressing may be served instead of the Hollandaise sauce.

Green String Beans

Buy young stringless green beans. Cut the beans across slantwise into very sliverlike pieces. Soak at least 1 hour in ice water. Plunge into violently boiling water to which has been added 1 teaspoon of salt. Cook the beans until tender. About 20 minutes. They may be served plain or decorated with one tablespoon of minced sweet red pepper. Chopped mint is a variation, or melted sweet butter.

Lemon Butter Potatoes

Peel potatoes. Cut them into balls with a vegetable cutter. Boil 20 minutes in salted water. Cream 4 tablespoons of butter. Add ½ tablespoon of lemon juice a little at a time. Add 1 teaspoon finely minced sweet red pepper and 2 teaspoons of minced parsley. Chives may be substituted for the parsley.

Spaghetti With Meat Sauce

1 Small Package Spaghetti
¼ Clove of Garlic
2 Tablespoons Butter
1 lb. Chopped Beef
½ Cup Cooking Wine or Orange Juice
1 Cup Soup Stock
½ Cup Chopped Carrot
½ Cup Chopped Celery
½ Bay Leaf
1 Onion

Boil the spaghetti in boiling salted water for 20 minutes. Serve with the following sauce: Chop the onion and the garlic. Brown in butter. Add the chopped beef. Brown and add the wine or orange juice, soup stock, carrot, celery, bay leaf, salt and pepper. Cook 1 hour over very slow flame. Add more soup stock if the liquid cooks away. Press through a sieve. Pour over the hot spaghetti. Pass grated Parmesan cheese with this at the table. Serves 4.

Macaroni with Caper Sauce

1 Package Macaroni
3 Eggs
2 Tablespoons Flour
1 Tablespoon Minced Parsley
1 Pint Milk
½ Teaspoon Salt
1 Can Tomato Soup
1 Cup Water
1 Bottle Capers
1 Cup Cheese

Cook the macaroni in boiling salted water. Drain it. Beat the eggs. Add the flour and beat together. Add the parsley, milk, salt and pepper. Pour into a casserole and bake 40 minutes. Make the sauce with the tomato soup, 1 cup water, bottle of capers and 1 cup cheese. Heat in a double boiler, stirring occasionally. Serves 6.

Potatoes in Butter

Light the gas oven. Heat a casserole. Slice peeled potatoes into very thin slices. Put a layer of potatoes in the casserole, dot with bits of butter. Salt and pepper. Repeat until the dish is full. Cover closely. Bake 20 minutes in the oven.

Mashed Potatoes

Heat a saucepan of water. Peel and slice 6 potatoes. Boil 20 minutes. Heat ½ cup cream in a pan. Put the hot potatoes through a ricer into the cream. Add salt and pepper. Beat until light and creamy. Heap in a mound. Serve with bits of butter melted on the top. Sprinkle with parsley. Serves 2. The same amount of milk with 1 tablespoon butter can be substituted for the cream.

Potato Cakes

For 1 pint mashed potatoes use 1 egg and 1 tablespoon flour. Beat all together and form into cakes. Dip into flour and brown in butter. This mixture may be cooked in an omelet pan, browned on both sides and served in one big cake. This needs 8 minutes to brown. Serves 2.

Potato Soufflé

Beat the yolks of 3 eggs into 1 pint mashed potatoes in a buttered baking dish. Add salt and pepper, 1 tablespoon minced parsley, 1 tablespoon minced ham. Beat the whites of 3 eggs stiff. Fold into the potato mixture. Bake 25 minutes in a moderate oven (375° F.). Serve immediately. Serves 4. Another method is to place the dish in a pan of hot water in oven. Bake at 325° F. for 60 minutes.

Sauté Mashed Potatoes

Sauté left-over mashed potatoes in butter. Stir and brown 5 minutes.

Minced Potatoes

Peel and chop 6 raw potatoes. Heat 1 large tablespoon butter in a frying pan. Brown the potatoes. Keep them covered. Stir occasionally. Cook 20 minutes. Minced onion may be added.

Potatoes O'Brien

Chop 6 boiled potatoes. Put into a casserole 1 layer

potatoes, sprinkle with 1 tablespoon chopped onion, 1 tablespoon chopped green peppers, 2 tablespoons grated cheese. Salt and pepper. Dot with cubes of butter. Repeat until all the potatoes are used. Bake 20 minutes at 375° F. Brown top. Serves 4.

Casserole Potatoes

Cut peeled raw potatoes into thin slices. Boil 10 minutes. Drain the potatoes. Put them into a warm casserole. Sprinkle with cheese and bits of ham. Bake in an oven 20 minutes.

Creamed Potatoes

6 Potatoes
4 Tablespoons Flour
4 Tablespoons Butter
1 Pint Milk
½ Teaspoon Salt
Parsley

Peel the potatoes. Cut into dice. Drop into boiling water and cook 15 minutes. While they are cooking prepare the following sauce: Blend the flour and the butter. Put the milk in the top of a double boiler. Add the flour and butter and salt. Stir constantly, as this is easily burned. Join the parts of the double boiler and finish cooking over hot water until the potatoes are ready. Drain potatoes and add to the cream sauce. Sprinkle with minced parsley. Serves 4.

Browned Potatoes

Peel 4 potatoes and cut lengthwise into ¼ inch slices. Put these into a saucepan of boiling, salted water. When the potatoes have cooked 10 minutes, fry 2 slices of bacon in a frying pan. Add a little butter and brown the potatoes in the frying pan, keeping each slice separate. Turn the slices until browned on both sides. Serves 2.

Scalloped Potatoes

Heat 2 tablespoons butter in a frying pan. Peel 6 potatoes and cut into small pieces. Heat them in the pan. Add 1 pint milk. Cover the pan and cook. The milk will cook into the potatoes. Watch carefully and add more milk in small amounts from time to time. Turn occasionally. Mince the potatoes with a knife as they cook. When done they will be covered with a light brown, creamy sauce. This will take about 20 minutes. Serves 4.

Parsley Potatoes

Heat water in a saucepan. Scrub 4 potatoes, but do not peel. Cut lengthwise into ¼ inch slices. Put the slices into a colander over the boiling water and cover closely. Steam 15 minutes. Serve with bits of butter, salt and pepper. Minced parsley or chives may be sprinkled over. Serves 2.

Sweet Potatoes with Apples

3 Sweet Potatoes	½ Teaspoon Salt
1 Cup Water	¼ Teaspoon Nutmeg
1 Cup Sugar	3 Tablespoons Butter
3 Sliced Apples	Marshmallows optional

Peel and cut the potatoes into slices. Boil 10 minutes. Boil 1 cup water with cup sugar. Add the apples, salt and nutmeg. Cook 8 minutes. Stir into this the butter. Drain the potatoes. Arrange them in a baking dish. Begin with a layer of potatoes, then a layer of apples and continue until dish is filled. Pour the liquid over them. Bake 10 minutes in the oven. Marshmallows may be laid over the top at the last and cooked until they are puffed. Serves 4.

Candied Sweet Potatoes

6 Sweet Potatoes
½ Cup Brown Sugar
Butter, Salt and Pepper
1 Cup Water

2 Teaspoons Lemon Juice
Bit of Lemon Rind
Mace to Season

Peel the potatoes. Cut into cubes and parboil in boiling water 10 minutes. Drain and remove to a shallow dish. Add the brown sugar, bits of butter, salt and pepper and cup of water. Add lemon juice, a little lemon rind and sprinkling of mace. Cook 10 minutes in the oven. Serves 4.

Baked Stuffed Potatoes

Scrub large potatoes. Bake 45 minutes. Remove from the oven. Butter the skins. Cut across the top of each potato. Scoop out centers. Mash the potato with butter, salt and paprika. Return to the skins. Place half of a small sausage in the center. Bake for 20 minutes or until the sausage is cooked. Decorate with sprigs of parsley.

Cauliflower

Cut 1 head of cauliflower into small pieces. Drop into boiling salted water. Cook 15 minutes. Serve with the following sauce:

Lemon Sauce

Beat 2 eggs with salt and pepper and the juice of 1 lemon. Add 1 cup hot milk. Cook in a double boiler until it thickens. Add 1 tablespoon minced parsley. The same amount of chives or capers may be used, if you like. Serves 4.

Cabbage with Apple

Heat 4 cups water. Chop enough cabbage to fill 4 cups. Chop fine 1 unpeeled apple. Add the apple and cabbage to the boiling water. Boil rapidly 5 minutes. Add 1 tablespoon butter, salt and 1 teaspoon paprika. Add 1 cup thin cream and 1 tablespoon lemon juice. Cook 5 minutes longer and serve. Serves 4.

Scalloped Cabbage

Heat 2 tablespoons butter in a frying pan. Cut 1 quart cabbage into small bits. Cook in the butter and add 1 cup milk. Stir occasionally. As the milk cooks away add more, a little at a time. Salt and pepper. Cook 20 minutes. When it is finished the cabbage is a brown, creamy mass with very little liquid.

Chopped Eggplant

Chop 1 eggplant, 1 tomato, 1 slice onion, 1 piece celery. Heat 3 tablespoons butter in a frying pan. Put the vegetables in this. Add 1 cup water or stock. Cook 10 minutes. Serves 4.

Asparagus

Wash and remove the hard ends from a bunch of asparagus. Cook the tips in boiling water 20 minutes. Serve on triangles of toast and pass melted butter. Asparagus tips may be cut into ½ inch slices, which reduces the time of cooking. Drain and serve dressed with hot cream. Serves 4.

Sliced Tomatoes

Slice 6 tomatoes and dip into flour, salt and pepper. Brown 8 minutes in a pan in butter. Make a sauce for them as follows:

VEGETABLES

Stir 1 tablespoon flour and 1 tablespoon butter together in the pan in which the tomatoes were cooked. Add 1 cup water and cook until thickened. Serve the tomatoes on a dish, and pour the sauce over them. Serves 4.

Mushrooms

Heat 2 tablespoons butter in a frying pan. Wash and cut into pieces 1 pound of mushrooms. Cook in the butter 3 minutes. Add 2 cups chicken broth and cook 2 minutes longer. These are very good served on slices of toast. Serves 4.

Spinach with Mushroom Sauce

Wash 1 pound spinach. If washed in warm water the sand will loosen much quicker. Remove the roots. Be sure to free each leaf of sand. Drop into 1 cup boiling water which has been salted. Cook 10 minutes. Lift from the water. Drain and chop. Serve with mushroom sauce, made as follows:

Mushroom Sauce

½ lb. Mushrooms	1 Pint Rich Milk
3 Tablespoons Butter	2 Tablespoons Flour

Cook, but do not brown, the mushrooms in 2 tablespoons butter. Add the milk. Blend 1 tablespoon butter with the flour. Add to the milk and cook 8 minutes. This should be prepared while the spinach is cooking so that the whole dish is finished within 10 minutes. Serves 4.

Endive on Toast

Heat 1 pint water in a saucepan. Add 1 pound endive, cut lengthwise. Boil 15 minutes. Dress with cream and butter. This may be served on slices of buttered toast or on thin slices of bread spread with anchovy butter. Pour some of the hot cream over the bread. Serves 4.

Broiled Eggplant

Heat a large kettle of boiling salted water. Boil an unpeeled eggplant in this for 15 minutes. Remove from the water. Slice in ½ inch slices. Place in a pan. Dot with butter, dust with salt and pepper. Broil under a flame until a rich brown. Turn and dot with butter and brown. The broiling takes 10 minutes.

CHAPTER XXXVIII

LUNCHEON DISHES

Omelet Soufflé

1 Cup Milk
1 Tablespoon Butter
1 Tablespoon Flour
¼ Teaspoon Salt
4 Eggs

2 Sliced Tomatoes
2 Stalks Celery
¼ Cup Sliced Stuffed Ripe Olives
Roquefort Cheese

Make a white sauce of the milk and the butter rubbed with the flour. Add salt. Cook in a double boiler until thick. Beat the egg whites stiff. Add the egg yolks and ¼ cup of the white sauce. Bake in a casserole 10 minutes in moderate oven (375° F.).

In another casserole place the sliced tomatoes, celery cut fine and the sliced stuffed olives. Cover with ¾ cup of the white sauce. Add slices of roquefort cheese to the top. Cook in oven. When the cheese is melted pour over the omelet. Serves 2. Hearts of lettuce salad may be served with this. Have brown sugar cookies for dessert.

Bacon and Vegetables

Mince 2 slices bacon. Brown in a pan. Add 1 pint cooked green beans, 1 large tomato cut into pieces, 1 package snappy cheese. Add 1 cup water. Cook 10 minutes. Serve on triangles of whole wheat bread sautéd. Decorate the platter with pickled beets. Serves 4.

Pineapple salad and apricot jam with cream finish this luncheon.

Eggs a là King

1 Green Pepper Cut in Narrow Strips, 1 inch long
½ Cup Mushrooms—Sliced
½ Cup Pimentos—Cut in Narrow Strips, 1 inch long
3 Tablespoons Butter
2 Tablespoons Flour
¼ Teaspoon Salt and Pepper
1 Cup Warm Milk
6 Eggs Hard Cooked

Sauté vegetables in butter. When done add flour and stir till smooth. Add the warm milk gradually. Cook over a low heat stirring constantly until thick. Cut cooked eggs in quarters and add to sauce.

Hot Turkey Sandwiches

Heat 1 tablespoon butter in a frying pan. Cook 2 tablespoons celery and 2 slices onion 2 minutes. Add 2 cups turkey meat cut fine, 2 cups gravy. Heat well. Serve on individual plates, spread on thin triangles of fresh, white bread. Beside this sandwich serve a spoonful of cranberry sauce, curls of celery, olives and turkey dressing. Serves 4.

Tomato and Bacon

Toast rounds of bread lightly on 1 side. On the untoasted side place 1 slice tomato, 1 slice bacon, 1 slice cheese. Broil under the gas flame 5 minutes.

Corn Beef and Potato Cakes

Mix 1 cup mashed potatoes with 4 slices corned beef which has been cut into shreds. Add 1 tablespoon minced parsley. Heat 1 tablespoon butter in a pan and warm the mixture in this. When hot, stir in 1 egg. Brown and serve surrounded by parsley and stuffed olives. Serves 2.

Serve cabbage-and-apple salad. For dessert, sliced peaches and cream.

Eggplant with Lamb

Chop 1 small eggplant. Heat in 1 tablespoon butter. Add 2 tomatoes cut fine, a slice of onion and 2 cups chopped, cooked lamb. Cook 10 minutes longer in the oven. Serve on a bed of dressed water cress with sliced hard-boiled eggs and slices of lemon. Serves 4.

Sliced oranges with cocoanut and honey make a good dessert with this luncheon.

Oyster Sandwich

Heat 1 tablespoon butter in a frying pan. Sauté rounds of bread in this. Keep the bread warm in the oven. Dip each oyster into cream and then into bread crumbs. Sauté them in butter. Add a little cream to them. Let it cook away and brown slightly. Add ½ cup cream, so that there may be a little brown liquor.

Put a round of bread on each plate. Lay the oysters on the bread and pour a little of the gravy over each. Serve hot with jelly, celery and sweet pickles.

Sweetbreads en Brochette

Wash 2 sweetbreads. Plunge into boiling, salted water. Add the juice of ½ lemon. Boil gently 20 minutes. Drain. Cover with cold water. Remove the membrane and separate the sweetbreads into small pieces. String on metal skewers, alternating sweetbreads with 1 inch slices of bacon. Brush with melted butter. Place in a frying pan and dust with sifted bread crumbs. Broil 10 minutes, turning them occasionally. Serve on the skewers. Chicken livers are prepared in the same way except that they are boiled for 5 minutes. Serves 4.

For a first course with the sweetbread luncheon serve avocado cubes in cocktail glasses. Cover with fresh grapefruit juice and decorate with preserved cherries.

Stuffed Eggplant

1 Eggplant
¼ Cup Chopped Onion
1 Cup Leftover Cooked Meat, Chopped
½ Cup Minced Ham
1 Cup Mushrooms
¼ Teaspoon Salt
⅛ Teaspoon Pepper
4 Tablespoons Butter
Buttered Bread Crumbs

Cut the top from the eggplant. Scoop out the pulp leaving a shell ½ inch thick. Wash the mushrooms. Chop them with the eggplant. Add the onions. Sauté the vegetables in the butter for 10 minutes. Add the chopped meat, ham and seasoning. Fill the eggplant. Cover the top with buttered crumbs. Bake in a buttered dish, uncovered. The temperature should be hot for the first 10 minutes (400° F.). Reduce the heat to a moderate temperature (375° F.). Bake for 25 minutes at that temperature.

Kale

Remove the root and the heavy part of the leaf. Wash and soak in warm water. Lift carefully from the water. Cook, closely covered, in 2 cups of boiling water which has had 1 teaspoon salt added to it. Cook 35 to 40 minutes. Drain. Chop. Season with salt, pepper and butter. Decorate with sliced hard-boiled eggs.

Stuffed Peppers

4 Green Peppers
1½ Cups Chopped Cooked Meat (Any Variety left over meat)
½ Cup Cooked Rice
¼ Teaspoon Salt
⅓ Cup Stock
1 Small Onion, Chopped
⅛ Teaspoon Pepper
Buttered Cracker Crumbs

Wash the peppers. Cut the tops from them. Remove the seeds. Stuff with the meat, rice, salt, pepper, onion and stock combined. Cover with buttered cracker crumbs. Place in an uncovered casserole. Add ½ cup of water. Bake in a moderate oven for 40 minutes (350° F.).

Stuffed Tomatoes

Cut a thin slice from the tops of 6 large tomatoes. Scoop out the pulp with a teaspoon. Chop and add ½ cup of bread crumbs, ½ teaspoon of salt and pepper and 2 tablespoons melted butter. Fill the tomato shells. Bake in a buttered, uncovered casserole for 20 minutes in a hot oven (400° F.).

Scalloped Tomatoes

3 Cups Cooked Tomatoes
⅛ Teaspoon Pepper
½ Teaspoon Salt
2 Teaspoons Grated Onion

2 Cups Bread Crumbs
4 Tablespoons Butter
½ Chopped Green Pepper

Add the green pepper, salt, pepper and onion to the tomatoes. Cover the bottom of a greased baking dish with bread crumbs. Add one half of the tomatoes and bits of butter. Cover with crumbs. Add the rest of the tomatoes, bits of butter and cover with crumbs. Dot with butter. Bake uncovered for 25 minutes in a moderate oven (375° F.).

CHAPTER XXXIX

SALADS

Mayonnaise

2 Egg Yolks
½ Teaspoon Salt
¼ Teaspoon Mustard
½ Teaspoon Sugar

1 Tablespoon Lemon Juice
1 Tablespoon Vinegar
2 Cups Olive Oil
1 Teaspoon Hot Water

Have all ingredients cold. Mayonnaise mixers which add the oil drop by drop and electric beaters are a convenience in mixing mayonnaise. Lacking these, use a cold bowl and a rotary beater. Beat the egg yolks until lemon colored. Add sugar, mustard and salt sifted together. Beat. Add the lemon juice and vinegar. Beat. Add the olive oil, 1 teaspoon at a time, beating between each addition. When the mayonnaise begins to thicken add the olive oil ¼ cup at a time. When it is thick add the hot water to bind it. When serving, lemon juice may be added. For cream mayonnaise add lemon juice and whipped cream.

Boiled Dressing

4 Egg Yolks
2 Tablespoons Salt
6 Tablespoons Sugar
2 Tablespoons Flour

1½ Cups Thin Cream, or rich milk
3 Tablespoons Butter
½ Cup Vinegar

Beat the egg yolks in the top of the double boiler. Mix salt, sugar and flour together. Stir into the egg yolks. Add the thin cream and butter. Put over hot water in the double boiler.

SALADS

Cook until the butter is melted, stirring constantly. Add the vinegar. Cook, stirring often until thick. When you wish to use the sauce thin with cream.

Fruit Salad Dressing

Beat the yolks of 4 eggs. Add the juice of 2 lemons. Beat. Add 1 cup of sugar and beat well. Add the whites of 4 eggs, beaten stiff. Cook in a double boiler over hot water, until thick. Cool. When serving combine with whipped cream.

Lemon Mayonnaise

1 Egg
1 Teaspoon Salt
4 Teaspoons Sugar
Juice of 1 Lemon
2 Cups Olive Oil

Beat the egg for 2 minutes. Add salt, sugar and lemon juice. Beat this together. Add olive oil, 1 teaspoon at a time, beating between each addition. Beat until thick. You may color the dressing pale green or rose by the addition of a tiny bit of vegetable coloring. Whipped cream may be added when using. This is particularly good for fruit salad.

Jellied Mayonnaise

To each cup of mayonnaise add 2 teaspoons of gelatine, softened in 1 tablespoon of cold water and dissolved in 3 tablespoons of boiling water. This may be hardened in a flat sheet. Cut into squares or diamond shaped pieces with a sharp knife. Or use a fancy cutter. The mayonnaise may be chilled in fancy moulds if you like.

Russian Dressing

For Russian dressing add 2 tablespoons of Chili sauce to 1 cup of mayonnaise.

French Dressing

1 Onion	2 Teaspoons Salt
1 Cup Olive Oil	2 Teaspoons Sugar
⅓ Cup Vinegar	1 Teaspoon Paprika

Peel the onion and cut into quarters. Put this in a glass jar and add ingredients listed above. In place of the sugar 1 tablespoon pineapple juice may be substituted. Cover the jar and keep it in the refrigerator. When you wish to use the dressing add a small piece of ice to the jar, screw on the top and shake until it is creamy.

Vegetables for Salads

Lettuce or any raw vegetables used in the making of salads should be washed, cut into pieces for serving and kept wrapped in a piece of cheese cloth against the ice. If you have an iceless refrigerator, leave it whole and put in a covered container kept for that purpose. Cook vegetables for salads in boiling salted water. Keep in the refrigerator in bowls ready for use.

Jellied Tomato Salad

Boil together 1 large can of tomatoes, 1 cup of water, 1 tablespoon grated onion, 1 teaspoon salt, ¼ teaspoon paprika, 4 whole cloves, a small piece of bay leaf. Soften 3 tablespoons of gelatine in ½ cup of water. Add to the boiling tomatoes and stir until the gelatine dissolves. Strain and pour into wet individual moulds. This should harden on ice for several hours. Serve on lettuce with mayonnaise.

Alligator Pear with Orange Salad

Peel and slice 4 oranges in thin circles. Arrange the slices on salad plates in a circle, with overlapping edges. Peel alligator pear. Cut into balls with vegetable cutter. Place in the center of the salad. Decorate the top with a maraschino cherry. Pass the dressing at the table. For the dressing mash the bits of alligator pear left from the balls. Add it to 1 cup of mayonnaise dressing together with ½ cup whipped cream, 1 tablespoon lemon juice and 2 tablespoons maraschino syrup from the cherries. Blend. Add 1 maraschino cherry cut into bits.

Chicken Salad

3 Cups Diced Chicken
1 Cup Celery Finely Cut
½ Cup Pineapple in Thin Slices
½ Cup Sliced Ripe Stuffed Olives
½ Cup Salted Almonds

Mix the chicken meat with the celery. Add the pineapple which has been cut into thin, finger-like slices. Add the almonds, and olives. Let this marinate in French dressing in the ice box for 1 hour. Drain. Arrange in salad bowl. Mask with mayonnaise. Decorate with capers, sliced ripe olives and salted almonds.

Avocado and Crab Salad

1 Cup Crab Meat
½ Cup Celery
½ Cup Orange Cubes
¼ Cup French Dressing
1 Tablespoon Catsup
3 Ripe Avocados
Large Green Olives
Shrimps

Mix the crab meat, celery and orange cubes. Marinate in the French dressing with the catsup added. Cut the pears in half, remove the seeds and peel them. Fill the halves with crab meat. Mask the meat with mayonnaise. Serve on crisp lettuce. Make a slit and remove seeds from large green olives. Insert a half shrimp in the slit. Use these to decorate the salad. Serves 6.

Endive Salad

½ lb. Endive
5 Tablespoons Olive Oil
3 Tablespoons Vinegar
½ Teaspoon Salt
1 Tablespoon East Indian Chutney

Wash the endive. Cut it into strips and chill. Dress with French dressing made with the olive oil, vinegar, salt and chutney. Arrange endive on salad plates. Beat the dressing well. Dress the endive with it. Serve with saltines spread with cream cheese and 1 teaspoon currant jelly in the center of each.

Ambrosia Salad

1 Can Seedless Grapes
3 Oranges
1 Grapefruit
6 Slices Pineapple
1 Bottle Maraschino Cherries
1 Cream Cheese
1 Cup Lemon Mayonnaise
½ Cup Whipped Cream
Lettuce

Drain the seedless grapes. Peel the oranges and grapefruit. Cut the fruit into squares, discarding the white, pithy portions. Cut the pineapple into dice. Slice the maraschino cherries. Drain all the fruit well. For the dressing blend the cheese with lemon mayonnaise and add whipped cream. Put together just before serving. Serve in nests of chilled lettuce. Serves 6.

Anchovy Salad

2 Cooked Beets
1 Cup Tiny Lima Beans
½ Minced Cucumber
1 Cup Cooked Cauliflower
5 Tablespoons Olive Oil
2 Tablespoons Tarragon Vinegar
1 Teaspoon Anchovy Paste
½ Teaspoon Salt
1 Hard Boiled Egg Chopped
Bit of Garlic
Rolled Anchovies
Stuffed Olives

Mince the beets and add the beans, cucumber, and the cooked cauliflower which is cut into pieces. Arrange the vegetables on lettuce and dress with the following dressing: Olive oil, vinegar, anchovy paste, salt, chopped hard-boiled egg. Rub a bowl with bit of garlic and put a piece of ice in it when you beat up the dressing. When creamy pour over the vegetables. Decorate with rolled anchovies and stuffed olives. Serves 6.

Stuffed Red Peppers

7 Sweet Red Peppers
1 Pint Water
1 Cup Vinegar
½ Cup Sugar
4 Whole Cloves
2 Unpeeled Apples Chopped Fine

2 Cups Cabbage Chopped Fine
1 Cup Cream
½ Teaspoon Salt
4 Teaspoons Sugar
2 Tablespoons Orange Juice
4 Tablespoons Lemon Juice

Remove the seeds from peppers, leaving them whole. Boil 5 minutes in water, vinegar, ½ cup sugar and 4 cloves. Drain and chill. Stuff 6 peppers with the following mixture:

Chopped apples, cabbage and one pepper chopped fine. Dress this with the following:

Cup cream, salt, 4 teaspoons sugar, orange juice, lemon juice. Beat thoroughly until stiff. Mix with the chopped ingredients. Stuff the peppers. Serve with toasted cheese crackers. Serves 6.

Pineapple and Honeydew Salad

4 Cups Honeydew Melon Balls
Pimento Cheese
8 Slices Pineapple
Rings of Green Pepper
Stuffed Ripe Olives Sliced

1 Cup Mayonnaise
¼ Cup Pineapple Juice
2 Tablespoons Lemon Juice
½ Cup Whipped Cream

Arrange a bed of lettuce on a chop plate. In the center place a mound of melon balls which can be cut with a vegetable cutter. Place 1 teaspoon pimento cheese in each center of the slices of pineapple. Arrange the slices around the melon mound. Decorate with the green pepper rings, which should be chilled, and slices of stuffed olives. Serve with dressing of mayonnaise, pineapple juice, lemon juice and whipped cream combined. Serves 4.

Frozen Tomato Salad

2 Teaspoons Gelatine
2 Cans Tomato Soup
1 Cup Whipped Cream
Lettuce

1 Cup Cottage cheese
1 Tablespoon Chopped Pistachio Nuts

Dissolve the gelatine in 2 tablespoons water. Dissolve this over hot water. Add the tomato soup. Chill. Add the whipped cream and place in trays of the automatic refrigerator for 3 hours. If you do not use an automatic, place in covered moulds and pack the moulds with equal parts of cracked ice and salt and keep covered 3 hours. Cut into cubes. Serve on lettuce with cheese balls which have been combined with the chopped pistachio nuts. Serve with mayonnaise.

Waldorf Salad

Chop 2 red apples. Add 1 cup chopped celery and 2 tablespoons nut meats. Moisten with mayonnaise. Serves 4.

The Waldorf salad may be enhanced by serving surrounded by tomato cubes as described in the recipe preceding.

Frozen Fruit Salad

2 Teaspoons Gelatine
½ Cup Mayonnaise
1¼ Cups Fruit Finely Cut

1 Cup Whipped Cream
Maraschino Cherries

Dissolve the gelatine in 3 tablespoons of cold water. Melt over boiling water. Add the dissolved gelatine to the mayonnaise. Add the fruit. Oranges, pineapple, green grapes and maraschino cherries are suitable fruits. The fruit should be chilled and drained before using. Add the whipped cream which must be stiff. Pour into refrigerator trays. Decorate the top with halves of maraschino cherries. Chill 2 hours. Cut into portions and serve on crisp lettuce. Serves 4.

Frozen Cheese with Fruit

Salad	Dressing
2 Packages Cream Cheese	½ Cup Olive Oil
1 Cup Grapefruit Juice	¼ Cup Grapefruit Juice
¼ Cup Powdered Sugar	1 Teaspoon Lemon Juice
½ Teaspoon Paprika	½ Teaspoon Salt
1 Tablespoon Gelatine	½ Teaspoon Paprika
1 Cup Whipped Cream	
Fresh Fruit	

Mash the cream cheese and blend with the grapefruit juice and sugar. Add this to the cheese gradually and add the paprika. Dissolve the gelatine in 3 tablespoons cold water. Melt over hot water. Add the whipped cream and the melted gelatine to cheese. Place in a tray of the automatic refrigerator and let stand 2 hours. If you do not use an automatic this may be packed in a covered mould and buried in equal parts of crushed ice and salt and let stand 2 hours. Turn out on a decorative chop plate. Surround with fresh fruit such as seeded cherries, sliced peaches, pineapple and oranges. Serve with French dressing made of the olive oil, grapefruit juice, lemon juice, salt and paprika. Beat this until creamy. Serves 6.

Tomato and Mushroom Salad

Peel and chill 6 large tomatoes. Scoop out the centers, mix with an equal quantity of canned button mushrooms chopped. Add 2 tablespoons of chopped olives. Mix with French dressing. Serve on water cress or lettuce. Serves 6.

CHAPTER XL

DISHES FOR THE ELECTRIC WAFFLE IRON

Care of the Electric Waffle Baker

Before heating a new waffle baker, oil the grids thoroughly, using a pastry brush and olive oil. Close and heat. The first waffle cleans the grid and should be discarded. It may be necessary to oil the grids the second time the appliance is used. If it overheats, oil it again as if it were a new waffle baker. Use a wire brush for cleaning the waffle grids.

Waffles

2 Cups flour
4 Teaspoons Baking Powder
2 Eggs

1 2/3 Cups Milk
4 Tablespoons Butter

Heat the waffle iron for about 10 minutes. If it is a modern electric iron the indicator will show when it is ready to use. It should be hot enough so that the batter will sizzle the instant it hits the iron.

Sift the flour with baking powder. Beat the eggs well. Add the beaten eggs and milk to dry ingredients. Beat well. Add the butter which has been melted and mix. Pour or ladle the batter over the iron evenly. It should just cover it. Bake 3 minutes or until brown. Serves 4.

A paper-thin slice of bacon may be laid across the waffle and baked with it. Another variation is the cinnamon waffle made with this recipe by adding 1 teaspoon cinnamon with the flour.

Cornmeal Waffles

1½ Cups Water
½ Cup White Cornmeal
1½ Cups Milk
3 Cups Flour
4 Teaspoons Baking Powder

1 Teaspoon Salt
3 Tablespoons Sugar
3 Egg Yolks
⅓ Cup Butter Melted
3 Egg Whites Beaten Stiff

Boil the water. Stir into this the white cornmeal. Cook 10 minutes. Remove from fire. Add the milk and beat well. Sift the flour with the baking powder, salt and sugar. Add to the cooked mixture. Beat well. Add the egg yolks. Beat. Add the melted butter. Beat. Add the egg whites which should be beaten stiff. Bake on a hot waffle iron. Serve with butter and maple syrup or honey. Serves 4.

Note: If you use honey it should be warmed over hot water. When it is warm add 2 tablespoons orange juice and 1 teaspoon cocoanut to each cup honey. Use while warm.

Raised Waffles

1 Yeast Cake
1 Cup Milk
1 Teaspoon Salt
1 Tablespoon Sugar

2 Tablespoons Butter
2 Cups Sifted Flour
2 Egg Yolks Beaten
2 Egg Whites Beaten Stiff

Dissolve the yeast cake in ¼ cup lukewarm water. Heat but do not boil the milk with salt and butter. Add ¾ cup cold water to make the mixture lukewarm. Beat in sifted flour. Add the egg yolks. Beat. Add the egg whites beaten stiff. Cover and place in a warm spot to raise for 1½ hours. Bake on a hot waffle iron. After the batter has risen it may be kept in a refrigerator if covered. This recipe serves 4.

Short Cake

2 Cups Flour
4 Teaspoons Baking Powder
½ Teaspoon Salt

2 Tablespoons Sugar
6 Tablespoons Butter
¾ Cup Milk

Sift the flour, baking powder, salt and sugar together. Blend the butter with this. Add the milk. Bake on a hot waffle iron. For serving use two sections of a waffle with a filling of crushed, sweetened strawberries between. Add more strawberries on top. Serve cream with this at table. Serves 4.

Sweetened sliced peaches or sweetened sliced oranges may be substituted for the berries. Serve with whipped cream.

Chocolate Waffle Cake

¾ Cup Butter
1 Cup Sugar
4 Egg Yolks
1 Cup Flour
½ Cup Cocoa
2 Teaspoons Baking Powder
⅓ Cup Milk
¼ Cup Chopped Nut Meats
1 Teaspoon Vanilla
4 Egg Whites

Cream the butter with the sugar. Beat the egg yolks and add to the creamed mixture. Sift together the flour, cocoa and baking powder. Add alternately with the milk. Beat between each addition. Add the chopped nut meats. Flavor with vanilla. Beat the egg whites stiff. Fold into the batter. Bake on a hot waffle iron. In serving use a waffle for top and bottom and put ice cream between for filling. Put whipped cream on top.

Maryland Cream Waffles

2 Cups Flour
4 Teaspoons Baking Powder
½ Teaspoon Salt
2 Teaspoons Sugar
2 Eggs
⅓ Cup Melted Butter
1¾ Cups Milk

Mix and sift dry ingredients together; add milk which has been mixed with beaten egg yolks. Add melted butter. Beat until all lumps have disappeared, and you have a smooth creamy mixture. Cut and fold in beaten egg whites.

When heat indicator of the electric waffle baker shows

that iron has been sufficiently preheated, pour the batter into center of iron from a pitcher or ladle, allowing the batter to come to the edge of the iron. Bake 3 to 6 minutes until the iron has ceased to steam. In case you have an automatic electric waffle baker, until the automatic control shows that waffle is finished. Serve piping hot. Restrain your curiosity and don't lift the cover during the cooking.

Gingerbread Waffles

2 Cups Flour
½ Teaspoon Ginger
1 Teaspoon Soda
1 Egg
1 Teaspoon Baking Powder
¾ Cup Molasses
¾ Cup Milk
4 Tablespoons Melted Butter

Mix all the dry ingredients except the soda together. Dissolve the soda in milk, add molasses and egg, melted butter. Fold into dry ingredients. Bake in waffle iron. Serve with whipped cream or cream cheese.

Waffle Cake

¼ Cup Butter
½ Cup Powdered Sugar
1 Egg
⅓ Cup Milk
1 Cup Flour
1 Teaspoon Baking Powder
½ Teaspoon Vanilla

Cream the butter and sugar. Beat the egg. Add milk to the egg. Beat. Sift the flour and baking powder together. Add the liquid ingredients alternately with the dry ingredients to the creamed mixture. Beat between each addition. Flavor with vanilla. Drop by spoonfuls on each section of the waffle iron. When this is served spread with a mixture of butter creamed with confectioners' sugar. Use 1 cup sugar with ½ cup butter. Dust with cinnamon. Whipped cream which has been sweetened and flavored may be served with the waffles. Crushed fruit with whipped cream is good.

CHAPTER XLI

HOT BREADS

Muffins

2 Egg Whites
2 Egg Yolks
4 Tablespoons Sugar
⅔ Cup Milk

2 Cups Flour
4 Teaspoons Baking Powder
3 Tablespoons Butter

Light the gas oven. Put the buttered muffin pans to heat in it. Beat the egg whites in mixing bowl until stiff, but not dry. Add the egg yolks. Beat. Add the sugar. Stir into this mixture alternately with the milk, the flour which has been sifted with the baking powder. Beat between each addition. Melt the butter and add it. Bake 15 minutes in hot oven (450° F.). When baked in a shallow pan or an earthen or glass casserole this becomes Breakfast Bread.

If you wish variety add ½ teaspoon powdered ginger or ½ teaspoon cinnamon to the recipe. Interesting fruits to add are 1 teaspoon chopped preserved ginger or 1 teaspoon orange marmalade.

For cheese muffins, add ½ cup of grated cheese.

Pineapple muffins, add ½ cup well drained and crushed pineapple.

Makes 8 muffins.

Muffins

2 Cups Flour
4 Teaspoons Baking Powder
½ Teaspoon Salt
2-4 Tablespoons Sugar

1 Cup Milk
1 Egg Slightly Beaten
3 Tablespoons Shortening

Mix dry ingredients, add gradually, milk, egg well beaten, and melted butter. Bake in buttered gem pans—20-25 minutes at 400° F.

For Whole Wheat: Substitute ¾ cup whole wheat flour for 1 of wheat.

For Fruit Muffins: Add small amount of the flour to ½ cup fruit and add last.

Graham Muffins With Dates

4 Tablespoons Sugar	4 Teaspoons Baking Powder
4 Tablespoons Butter	⅔ Cup Milk
1 Cup White Flour	2 Eggs
1 Cup Graham Flour	½ Cup Stoned Dates Cut Up

Light the gas oven. Heat buttered muffin pans. Cream the sugar and butter. Sift together the white flour, graham flour and baking powder. Add dry ingredients alternately with the milk, beating between each addition. Beat the eggs. Add them to the mixture. Beat. Add the dates which should be in small pieces. Bake 15 minutes at 450° F. For variety add 1 teaspoon vanilla and a sprinkling of mace. This recipe may be used for plain graham muffins by omitting the dates. Makes 8 muffins.

Corn Bread

4 Tablespoons Butter	1 Cup Flour
2 Egg Whites	1 Cup Cornmeal
2 Egg Yolks	4 Teaspoons Baking Powder
4 Tablespoons Sugar	⅔ Cup Milk

Light the gas oven. Put the butter into a pan, glass baking dish or casserole. Melt it in the oven. Beat the egg whites stiff. Add the yolks. Beat. Add the sugar. Sift together the flour and cornmeal and the baking powder. Add the dry ingredients and the milk alternately to the egg mixture. Beat well between each addition. Add the melted butter. Turn into the pan. Bake 25 minutes at 400° F. This may be baked in muffin pans. Serves 4.

Bran Muffins

1 Cup Flour
1 Cup Bran
4 Teaspoons Baking Powder
4 Tablespoons Brown Sugar
2 Eggs

4 Tablespoons Molasses
1 Cup Milk
4 Tablespoons Butter
Vanilla

Light the oven. Sift the flour and baking powder together. Add the brown sugar and bran. Beat the eggs. Add the molasses and milk. Beat the liquid ingredients into the dry mixture. Add the butter which has been melted. Flavor with vanilla. Bake in hot, well-buttered muffin pans for 10 minutes at 400° F. Then reduce the heat to 350° F. for 15 minutes longer. Makes 8 large muffins or 12 small ones.

Spoon Bread

Heat 1½ cups of milk. Stir ¾ cup of cornmeal into this. Cook until thick, stirring constantly. Add the yolks of 3 eggs that have been beaten until light. Remove from the fire. Fold in the stiffly beaten whites of 3 eggs. Bake in an earthen or glass baking dish at 375° F. for 35 minutes. Serve in the dish in which it is baked. Break with a fork and lift out with a spoon. The Spoon Bread may be baked in small casseroles which should have a teaspoon of butter or other cooking fat added to each dish. Serves 6.

Pancakes

2 Cups Flour
6 Teaspoons Baking Powder
2 Eggs

1 Cup Milk
4 Tablespoons Butter

Sift the flour and baking powder together. Beat the eggs. Add milk to them and beat again. Beat this into the flour mixture until light and smooth. Add the butter melted. Brown in butter in a pan or on a well greased griddle.

For fruit pancakes add ½ cup of any fruit such as blackberries, blueberries or raspberries. Serves 2.

Cornmeal Pancakes

2 Cups Milk
4 Tablespoons Butter
1 Cup Cornmeal
2 Tablespoons Flour
2 Eggs

Heat the milk and the butter together. After you have removed this from fire stir in cornmeal and flour. Beat the eggs into this mixture. Heat butter in a frying pan. Brown the cakes in it. Serve with honey or maple syrup and with sausages. Serves 2.

French Pancakes

Mix together 1 cup of milk, 1 egg and 1 cup of sifted flour. Beat with a rotary beater for 2 minutes. Heat 1 tablespoon of butter in a frying pan. When hot pour in enough batter to just cover the bottom of the pan. When delicately brown on the bottom dust the top with powdered sugar and cinnamon. Roll up, keeping the filling in the center. Jelly or jam may be used instead of the spice and sugar. The pancakes may be baked, rolled, kept hot and reheated in orange sauce. The heating should be done at the table on an electric stove with a pan. Serves 2.

Orange Sauce

Cream 6 tablespoons butter with ¾ cup of sugar. Beat 1 egg with ¼ cup cream, juice of 1 orange and juice of ½ lemon. Beat all together in a double boiler. Add the grated rind of 1 orange. Cook until thick and transparent. Stir often.

Scones

2 Cups Flour	2 Eggs
4 Teaspoons Baking Powder	2 Tablespoons Sugar
⅔ Cup Milk	2 Tablespoons Butter

Sift the flour and the baking powder. Add the milk. Beat the eggs well and add together with sugar and the butter melted. Drop on a hot griddle in oblong shape. Turn often. Bake about 5 minutes. This amount makes 12 scones.

A little powdered mace added to the batter is good.

Serve the scones with honey or jam. They are delicious when split and toasted for tea.

Baking Powder Biscuit

2 Cups Flour	2 Tablespoons Shortening
4 Teaspoons Baking Powder	¾ Cup Milk
½ Teaspoon Salt	

Sift the flour, baking powder, and salt together. Add the shortening. Blend this with the flour, using the tips of the fingers or a pastry blender until it is the consistency of cornmeal. Add the milk, a little at a time. Knead lightly together for 10 seconds. Pat into shape and roll on a floured board to the thickness of 1 inch. Cut into rounds. Bake 15 to 20 minutes in a hot oven (450° F.). Makes 12 biscuits.

Baking Powder Biscuit

2 Cups Flour	4 Tablespoons Shortening
4 Teaspoons Baking Powder	½ to ¾ Cup Milk
½ Teaspoon Salt	

Mix dry ingredients together. Cut shortening into dry

ingredients. Add enough milk to make a soft dough. Roll or pat out. Cut with floured biscuit cutter. Bake 15 to 20 minutes in oven (425° F.).

Envelope Biscuit

1 Egg
¾ Cup Milk (About)
2 Cups Flour
4 Teaspoons Baking Powder

½ Teaspoon Salt
1 Teaspoon Sugar
2 Tablespoons Butter

Break the egg into a measuring cup. Beat with small egg beater. Pour in enough milk to make cup ¾ full. Sift the flour and baking powder, salt and sugar together. Blend the butter with the dry mixture. Add the liquid gradually. Knead until well blended, about 20 seconds. Roll out ½ inch thick on a pastry board. Cut into rounds, spread with melted butter and fold over, envelope fashion. Place in a pan. Spread on top with melted butter and prick with a fork. Bake in a quick oven (450° F.) for 15 minutes.

For variety sprinkle the inside of the rolls with grated cheese. Grated pineapple that has been thoroughly drained of juice may be used also. Spread a small teaspoonful in center of the round and fold over. Makes 12 biscuits.

Popovers

1 Cup Flour
½ Teaspoon Salt
1-2 Eggs

1 Teaspoon Melted Butter
1 Cup Milk

Mix flour and salt, add eggs and milk and beat all for two to three minutes. Add melted butter. Have popover pans very hot and greased. Half fill with batter. Bake in a very hot oven (475° F.) for 25 minutes, reduce heat to 350° F. and leave for 20 minutes. Serve immediately.

Maple Sugar Bread

2 Eggs
1 Cup Milk
2 Cups Flour
4 Teaspoons Baking Powder
½ Teaspoon Salt
1 Cup Maple Sugar
2 Tablespoons Butter

Light the gas oven. Heat 2 buttered shallow pans. Glass, earthenware or metal may be used. Beat the whites of the eggs stiff. Add the yolks. Beat. Sift the flour, baking powder and salt together. Add the milk alternately with the flour to the eggs, beating hard between each addition. Crush the maple sugar and stir into the batter. Add the butter melted. Bake 20 minutes in a moderate oven (350° F.). Serves 4.

Raisin and Nut Bread

3 Cups Bread Flour
¾ Cup Sugar
5 Teaspoons Baking Powder
1 Teaspoon Salt
6 Tablespoons Butter Melted
2 Eggs
1 Cup Milk
¾ Cup Nuts
1 Cup Raisins

Mix the dry ingredients together and add raisins and nuts. Beat eggs slightly and add milk. Mix liquid with the dry ingredients. Add melted butter. Beat all together. Put in greased loaf pan and allow to stand 20 minutes before baking. Bake 45 minutes to 1 hour in oven at 350° F.

Fritter Batter

1 Cup Flour
¼ Teaspoon Salt
⅔ Cup Milk
2 Eggs
1 Tablespoon Butter
Pineapple or Apple Slices

Sift the flour and salt together. Add the milk gradually. Beat in the egg yolks. Add the butter melted. Add the egg whites beaten stiff. Dip slices of pineapple or cored apple in this and fry in deep fat. The fat should be heated until it will brown a cube of bread in 1 minute, or 375° F. on your fat thermometer. Cook until a delicate brown. Serve with broiled ham or sausage.

This fritter batter may be kept in a mechanical refrigerator. The ingredients to make different types of fritters may be added as wanted. Beside the pineapple and apple fritters, there are corn, rice, cheese or banana fritters. For the corn add 1 cup of drained corn to the fritter batter and fry at 375° F. The rice fritters have 1 cup of cooked rice added to the batter and are fried at the same temperature. The cheese fritters are made with ½ cup of grated cheese added. Banana fritters have 1 cup of finely cut bananas added.

CHAPTER XLII

YEAST BREADS

White Bread

6 Cups Sifted Flour
2 Compressed Yeast Cakes
1 Cup Milk
2 Tablespoons Shortening
1 Tablespoon Salt
2 Tablespoons Sugar

Dissolve the yeast cakes in ½ cup of lukewarm water. Heat but do not boil the milk with shortening, salt and sugar. Add 1 cup of cold water. This cools the milk to lukewarm. Add the yeast. Stir the flour into the liquid. Stir until smooth and elastic. Half fill a buttered bread pan with the dough. Butter the top and cover it. Set in a warm place. When the dough has doubled in bulk bake in a hot oven (400° F.) for 10 minutes. Reduce the heat to 375° F. and bake for 30 minutes longer. When the bread has finished baking remove it from pan onto a wire rack. Butter the top of the loaf while warm. Let it stand uncovered until cool.

Cinnamon Bread

Roll a piece of white bread dough (made as in the recipe preceding) about 1 inch thick. Cream 1 cup of brown sugar with ⅓ cup butter and ½ teaspoon cinnamon. Spread on the dough. Fold up the dough like a jelly roll, the cinnamon sugar and butter inside. Cut 1-inch slices crosswise. Place these in a buttered pan and set to rise in a warm place. When double in bulk, bake 20 minutes in an oven at a temperature of 350° F.

Date Bread

For this, use the same dough as in the recipe for white bread. Add to the dough 1 cup stoned dates. This is enough for 1 loaf. Bake as in the recipe for white bread.

Cinnamon Cake

½ Cup Milk
2 Tablespoons Butter
½ Cup Sugar
½ Teaspoon Salt
1 Yeast Cake

2 Cups Sifted Flour
2 Eggs
Cinnamon
Currants
Candied Orange and Citron

Heat the milk with the butter. Stir into this the sugar and salt. Add ½ cup cold water. Dissolve the yeast in this lukewarm liquid. Stir in the flour. Add the eggs well beaten. Beat the mixture thoroughly. Butter a round tube pan. Put into it a layer of the batter. Sprinkle with cinnamon, a few currants, slices of orange and citron. Cover with batter. Repeat this until the dish is filled. Keep enough plain batter for the top. Sprinkle the top layer with sugar and cinnamon. Let rise until double in bulk. Bake in a hot oven (400° F.). After 10 minutes reduce the heat and bake at 325° F. for 35 minutes. Serve warm, cut in slices with lots of butter.

Sally Lunn

2 Eggs
2 Tablespoons Melted Butter
½ Teaspoon Salt

½ Cup Milk
1 Yeast Cake
2 Cups Sifted Flour

Beat the egg whites stiff. Add the yolks and beat. Add to this the butter melted and salt. Make the milk lukewarm and combine with ½ cup lukewarm water in which the yeast has been dissolved. Add to the egg mixture. Stir in the flour and beat thoroughly. Half fill a buttered bread pan with dough.

Let it rise in a warm place until doubled in bulk. Put in a hot oven (400° F.). After 10 minutes reduce the heat to 325° F. and bake 30 minutes longer. Serve warm, cut in slices with plenty of butter.

Graham Bread

1 Cup Milk	3 Cups White Flour
2 Tablespoons Butter	3 Cups Graham Flour
4 Tablespoons Sugar	(All Graham Flour May be
1 Tablespoon Salt	Used if Desired.)
Yeast Cake	

Heat the milk with the butter, sugar and salt. Add 1 cup of cold water. Dissolve the yeast cake in this lukewarm liquid. Combine and stir into this the flour. Beat well. Half fill a buttered bread pan. Put to rise in a warm place. When double in bulk place in a hot oven (400° F.) for 10 minutes. Reduce the heat to 325° F. and bake 30 minutes longer.

Gluten or rye bread may be made in the same way by substituting either flour for the graham in the above.

Ice Box Rolls

1 Cup Milk	1 Cake Compressed Yeast
½ Cup Sugar	8 Cups Sifted Flour
½ Tablespoon Salt	2 Eggs
3 Tablespoons Shortening	

Heat but do not boil the milk with the sugar, salt and shortening. Soak the yeast cake in ¼ cup of lukewarm water. Add 1 cup of cold water to the hot milk, which should cool it to lukewarm. Add the dissolved yeast cake to it. Stir in 4 cups of well sifted flour. Beat well. Add the eggs and beat well. Let rise until double in bulk. Then add gradually 4 cups sifted flour, mixing between each addition. Knead well until smooth and elastic. Butter the top of the dough with softened butter and set in a warm place well covered until the dough has doubled in bulk. Knead down for a moment in the bowl. Cover well and place in the refrigerator. The action of the yeast is particularly effective when it has been well chilled. The beauty of these ice box rolls is that just the right amount of dough may be pinched off for a current meal and the rest covered, left in the bowl and used when it is desired. This is particularly true of an iceless refrigerator where the cold is more intense than in other types.

When baking the dough, pinch off the desired amount, shape into small round rolls. Place in a buttered pan. Cover and set in a warm place until they have tripled in bulk.

Bake in a hot oven (400° F.) for 20 minutes.

Some of the other varieties of rolls that may be made from this dough are: Clover leaf rolls, Parker House rolls, and braided rolls. Your ingenuity will suggest others.

For clover leaf rolls shape the dough into small marbles with softened butter. Place in buttered muffin pans 3 in each section. Set in a warm place and let triple in bulk. Bake in a hot oven 20 minutes at 400° F.

For Parker House rolls, roll the dough ¼ of an inch thick. Cut with a round, floured cutter. Spread with softened butter, crease down the center with a knife. Fold over envelope fashion. Place in a buttered pan. Cover. Set in a warm place. Let triple in bulk. Bake for 20 minutes at 400° F.

For braided rolls. Roll dough. Cut into strips of uniform length. Shape between the palms and braid. Place on a buttered pan about 1 inch apart. Set in a warm place. When tripled in bulk bake in a hot oven at 400° F. for 20 minutes.

CHAPTER XLIII

PIES

Puff Paste

Puff paste is seldom used for pie crust, but it has many other uses such as patty cakes, tarts, French pastry or as a crust for meat pies. Several recipes given in other parts of this book call for puff paste.

Recipe: Wash ½ pound of butter. Cut it into 4 portions. Measure 2 cups of flour. Blend ¼ of the butter with the flour. Add just enough ice water to hold it together. Knead it about 1 minute. Chill for 30 minutes in the ice box. Roll out ½ inch thick. Flatten out one of the pieces of butter. Place it in the center of the dough. Fold the edges of the paste over the butter. Roll out. Sprinkle with flour. Fold again and roll. Chill in the ice box for 30 minutes. Dust with flour. Roll again, ½ inch thick. Add another quarter of the butter. Fold the edges over. Roll out. Chill. Repeat until all the butter is used. Chill thoroughly in the ice box before baking. Bake puff paste for 10 minutes in a hot oven (450° F.). Reduce the heat to a moderate oven (325° F.). Bake until the paste is dry and flaky.

Pie Crust

The pastry for all pies is made exactly the same. Sift 1½ cups of flour with ½ teaspoon salt. Blend ½ cup of lard with this, using a fork or pastry blender. When it is like cornmeal, add 4 tablespoons cold water. Do not use more water. Make this amount do. Too much water makes a tough crust. Work lightly together into a ball. Turn onto a floured pastry board. Divide into 2 portions. Roll the pastry ⅛ inch thick. Fit the pastry neatly over the pie plate, leaving about 1 inch projecting over the rim of the pan. Use any desired filling. Moisten the edges of the pastry with cold water. Fit the top crust over the pie. Press the edges together firmly. Trim the overhanging pastry even with the edge of the pan. Mark the rim with a fork or a pastry marker. Put the pie in a hot oven (450° F.) for 10 minutes. Bake in a moderate oven (325° F.) for the rest of the time the recipe needs. Before putting the pie into the oven cut slits in the top crust to allow the steam to escape. A larger amount of dough may be made by increasing the ingredients, keeping their proper proportions. The pastry dough may be kept in an iceless refrigerator indefinitely. Wrap in a towel or heavy waxed paper and use as wanted. If the pastry dough is chilled before using, the heat is more effective and makes a lighter crust.

Apple Pie

Peel, core and chop 5 large apples. Add 1 cup of sugar and 1 tablespoon flour. Mix well. Fill a pastry lined pie plate and cover with pastry. Place in a hot oven (450° F.) for 10 minutes. Bake 20 to 30 minutes in a moderate oven (325° F.). There is a difference in the cooking time of apples. Test the apples with a fork. If they are tender and transparent, they are done. Cinnamon and bits of butter may be sprinkled over the apples before the top crust is added. Serves 4.

Cherry Pie

Mix 3 cups of stoned pie cherries with 1 cup sugar and 1 tablespoon of flour. Fill a pastry lined pan. Dot with 2 tablespoons butter. Add top crust. Bake 10 minutes in a hot oven (450° F.). Reduce heat and finish baking 25 minutes in a moderate oven (325° F.).

Cranberry Pie

Chop 2 cups cranberries. Add 1 cup of sugar and 1 tablespoon flour. Mix well. Turn into a pie plate lined with uncooked pastry. Over the top cross strips of pastry so that squares of the cranberries show through. Bake for 10 minutes in a hot oven (450° F.). Reduce heat to moderate oven (325° F.) for 20 minutes longer.

Rhubarb pie is made in the same way with chopped rhubarb substituted for the cranberries.

Berry Pies

This recipe will do for any berry pie such as blueberry, raspberry, loganberry or blackberry. For 4 cups of berries use 1 cup of sugar and 1 tablespoon flour. Stir together and bake between 2 crusts; or strips of pastry may be laid over the top to form an open design. Bake in a hot oven (450° F.) for 10 minutes. Reduce heat to 325° F. and bake for 20 minutes longer.

Cranberry and Pineapple Pie

Put 2 cups of cranberries through the food chopper. Add 1 cup of drained, crushed pineapple and 1 cup of sugar. Line a pie tin with pastry. Add the filling. Cover the top with strips of pastry. Bake 10 minutes in a hot oven (400° F.). Finish baking in moderate oven (350° F.) for 20 minutes.

Orange Pie

FILLING
1 Cup Orange Juice
3 Tablespoons Lemon Juice
1 Cup Sugar
⅓ Cup Flour
½ Teaspoon Salt
1 Orange Rind
3 Egg Yolks
3 Tablespoons Butter

MERINGUE
3 Egg Whites
6 Tablespoons Sugar
1 Teaspoon Vanilla

Add the lemon juice to the orange juice. Mix ½ cup sugar with the flour and salt. Grate in the rind of 1 orange. Add the liquid to the dry ingredients. Cook over hot water for 10 minutes, stirring occasionally. Beat the egg yolks. Beat in ½ cup sugar. Remove the orange mixture from the fire. Beat in the eggs. Add butter. Cook for 3 minutes, beating constantly. Cool.

At serving time place the orange filling in a pie shell that has already been baked. Whip the egg whites stiff. Add 6 tablespoons sugar and vanilla. Pile this on the pie. Set in a very hot oven (500° F.). Brown the top delicately. This should take 3 minutes or less. Watch it carefully.

Lemon Pie

1 Cup Sugar
¼ Teaspoon Salt
6 Tablespoons Flour
1½ Cups Boiling Water
6 Tablespoons Lemon Juice
Grated Rind of 1 Lemon
1 Tablespoon Butter
2 Eggs

Mix sugar, salt and flour together. Add water and cook in double boiler until clear. Add lemon juice, grated rind, and butter. Add egg yolks and cook 2 minutes. Pour in baked pie shell. Cover with meringue. Bake 25 minutes in oven (325° F.).

Meringue

2 Egg Whites   4 Tablespoons Sugar

Beat egg whites stiff. Add sugar and beat again. Spread on top of pie.

Rhubarb Pie

FILLING
3 Heaping Cups Cut Rhubarb
1¼ Cups Sugar
3 Tablespoons Flour
2 Tablespoons Butter

PASTRY
1½ Cups Flour
½ Cup Shortening
¼ Teaspoon Salt
Cold Water

Mix flour, salt and shortening together with dough blender until mealy. Add cold water slowly, enough to hold dough together. Place in refrigerator in covered pan and chill. Roll out three fourths of pastry, place on pie pan for bottom crust.

Mix rhubarb, sugar and flour together and put in pan. Dot with butter. Roll out remaining dough and cut in strips. Place strips lattice fashion over top of filling. Press edges together and trim. Bake in oven (400° F.) for 10 minutes. Reduce the heat to 375° F. for 20 minutes.

Lemon Meringue Pie

Put 1 cup sugar into the top of a double boiler. Add 1 cup boiling water and the juice of 2 lemons. Blend 3 tablespoons butter with 3 tablespoons flour. Combine with the liquid and cook in the double boiler until slightly thickened. Stir constantly. Add the well-beaten yolks of 3 eggs. Cook 10 minutes. Stir occasionally. This is allowed to stand until very cold. The pie should not be put together until a few minutes before it is eaten. A shell of pastry which has been previously baked is the crust. (Bake the crust at 450° F. for 10 minutes. Reduce the heat to 325° F. for 10 minutes.) The filling is put into this. Beat the whites of 3 eggs until stiff. Add 6 tablespoons sugar. Pile this meringue on the pie. It should be placed in a hot oven (500° F.) for 3 minutes or less. Watch it. Remove when a delicate brown on top.

Custard Pie

Beat the yolks of 3 eggs. Add 6 tablespoons sugar. Beat well. Combine with 1 pint milk. Beat the whites until stiff. Add to the liquid. Pour this into a pie pan lined with uncooked pastry. Sprinkle the top with nutmeg. This pie may be turned into cocoanut custard by omitting the nutmeg and sprinkling the top with cocoanut. Bake 10 minutes, at 450° F., reducing the heat, after the first 10 minutes to

325° F. Bake 20 minutes at this heat. Test with a silver knife inserted in the center. When it comes out clean the custard is done.

Rich Pumpkin Pie

Mix 4 tablespoons flour, 2 tablespoons cinnamon, 1 tablespoon mace and 1 level teaspoon cloves with 2 cups brown sugar. Add to 1 quart steamed mashed pumpkin. Beat in the yolks of 4 eggs. Add ½ cup cream, ½ cup melted butter and ½ cup molasses. Fold in the beaten whites of 4 eggs. This recipe will make 2 small pies or 1 very large pie. Pour the mixture into tins lined with uncooked pastry. Put into an oven at 450° F., and at the end of 10 minutes reduce the heat to 325° F. for 20 minutes. Bake until the custard is set. Whipped cream may be served on top of this.

Pumpkin Pie

Pastry	Filling
1½ Cups Flour	2 Cups Cooked Pumpkin
½ Teaspoon Salt	1 Cup Brown Sugar
½ Cup Shortening	¾ Teaspoon Ginger
Cold Water	¾ Teaspoon Cinnamon
	1 Teaspoon Salt
	2 Eggs
	1½ Cups Milk

Mix sifted flour and salt together. Cut in shortening by means of a dough blender. Add cold water gradually, until enough has been added to make a stiff dough. Flour rolling pin and pastry board and roll the pastry out lightly. Line pie plate.

Mix pumpkin, brown sugar, ginger, cinnamon and salt together. Beat eggs slightly and add milk to them. Add to pumpkin mixture and stir well. Pour into pastry lined pie pan. Bake in oven (450° F.) for 15 minutes and at 350° F. for 1 hour or until custard is set.

Date Pie

Line a pie plate with pastry. For the filling beat the yolks of 2 eggs. Add ¾ cup sugar and beat. Add 2 tablespoons flour mixed with ¼ teaspoon cloves, ¼ teaspoon nutmeg and 1 teaspoon cinnamon. Add to the egg and sugar. Blend. Add 1 cup of cream and 1 cup of stoned dates cut fine. Beat the whites of 2 eggs stiff. Add to the mixture. Put the filling in the pastry. Sprinkle the top with cocoanut. Bake for 10 minutes in a hot oven (450° F.). Reduce heat and bake 30 minutes longer in a moderate oven (325° F.).

Lemon Chiffon Pie

Mix 2 tablespoons of butter with 1 cup of sugar. Stir into this the yolks of 2 eggs, well beaten. Add 3 tablespoons flour. Beat. Add 1 cup of milk. Beat. Add the juice and grated rind of 1 lemon. Fold in 2 stiffly beaten egg whites. Pour into a pie plate lined with uncooked pastry. Bake 10 minutes in a hot oven (450° F.). Finish baking for 20 minutes in a moderate oven (325° F.).

Cream Pie

Blend 3 tablespoons of butter with 6 tablespoons of flour. Heat 2 cups of milk in a double boiler. Add the butter and flour. Beat until it thickens. Continue cooking, beating occasionally. Beat the yolks of two eggs well. Beat into them ½ cup of sugar. Dip some of the hot mixture over them. Add to the mixture in the double boiler. Beat as it cooks. When thick and transparent remove from the fire and cool. Chill in the refrigerator. When wanted put the filling into a previously baked crust. Bake the crust in a quick oven for 10 minutes (450° F.). Reduce heat to moderate and bake 10 minutes (325° F.). Beat the whites of 2 eggs stiff. Add 4 tablespoons sugar. Flavor with 1 teaspoon vanilla. Pile the meringue on top of the filling. Brown quickly in a hot oven (500° F.). This takes but a few moments. Watch carefully. This operation should be done quickly because long cooking melts the filling. Chocolate cream pie is made by adding 1 square of bitter chocolate to the cream while cooking it.

CHAPTER XLIV

CAKES

Angel Food

8 Whites of Eggs
1 Teaspoon Cream of Tartar
1 Cup Sifted Flour
1 Cup Sifted Sugar
1 Teaspoon Vanilla
¼ Teaspoon Salt

Beat the whites of 8 eggs slightly. Add the salt and cream of tartar. Beat until stiff. Add the sifted sugar gradually, beating between each addition. Sift the flour 3 times. Fold lightly into the mixture. Add the vanilla. Turn the batter into an ungreased tube pan. Bake 60 minutes in a moderate oven at 325° F. Turn the pan upside down on a wire rack. Let the cake cool in the pan.

Icing

1½ Cups Sugar
⅛ Teaspoon Cream of Tartar
½ Cup Hot Water
1 Teaspoon Vanilla
1 Slice Candied Pineapple
1 Slice Candied Orange
Angelica
Candied Cherries
2 Egg Whites

Put the sugar in a saucepan. Add the cream of tartar and the hot water. Stir over a low flame until dissolved. Boil the syrup without stirring until it will spin a thread when dropped from a spoon or until the thermometer registers 238° F. Beat the whites of the eggs until they are stiff and dry. Pour the syrup onto the egg white in a thin steady stream, beating constantly as you pour. Beat until the frosting is thick enough to spread. Add the pineapple and orange cut into bits. Stir into the frosting. Spread on the cake with a spatula. Decorate with candied cherries and angelica cut into thin slices.

Chocolate Cake

2 Eggs
1 Cup Sugar
½ Cup Milk
1 Cup Flour

½ Cup Cocoa
4 Tablespoons Butter
1 Teaspoon Vanilla
2 Teaspoons Baking Powder

Break the eggs into a mixing bowl. Beat well. Add the sugar gradually, beating well after each addition. Sift the flour, baking powder and cocoa together. Add alternately with the milk. Beat between each addition. Melt the butter. Add to the batter. Beat. Flavor with vanilla. Bake in a loaf pan for 40 minutes at 350° F.

Icing

1 Egg White
1 Tablespoon Water
2 Cups Confectioners' Sugar

1 Teaspoon Vanilla
1 Cake Bitter Chocolate

Put the egg white into a bowl. Add the water. Beat slightly. Add the sifted sugar gradually. Beat between each addition. Continue beating after the sugar is all used until thick enough to spread. Flavor. Spread on the top and sides of the cake with a spatula. Melt the chocolate in the double boiler. Cover the icing with a thin layer of hot chocolate. For variety the chocolate may be flavored with a few drops of essence of peppermint. Orange flavoring may also be used to flavor the chocolate.

Cocoanut Cake

4 Tablespoons Butter
1 Cup Sugar
2 Eggs
½ Cup Milk

1½ Cups Flour
2 Teaspoons Baking Powder
1 Teaspoon Vanilla

Soften the butter. Stir the sugar into it gradually. Add the yolks of the eggs. Beat vigorously. Sift the flour and baking powder together. Add alternately with the milk. Beat between each addition. Add the vanilla. Beat the whites of the eggs stiff. Fold into the batter. Bake in 2 layers in a moderate oven (375° F.) for 20 minutes.

Cocoanut Icing

2 Egg Whites
1 Cup Granulated Sugar
1 Teaspoon Vanilla

Beat the whites of the eggs till white and foamy. Add the sugar gradually. Flavor with vanilla. Beat until thick. Ice the layers. Sprinkle cocoanut over them.

Walnut Spice Cake

1 Cup Brown Sugar
¼ Cup Softened Butter
½ Cup Sour Milk
3 Egg Yolks
½ Teaspoon Soda
1¼ Cups Flour
½ Teaspoon Allspice
½ Teaspoon Nutmeg
½ Teaspoon Cinnamon
1 Cup Seeded Raisins
1 Cup Broken Walnut Meats

Cream the sugar with the softened butter. Add the egg yolks. Beat. Add the milk with the soda dissolved in it. Beat well. Sift the spices with the flour. Add the dry ingredients to the liquid. Beat for 1 minute. Add the nuts and raisins. Bake in a loaf in a moderate oven for 40 minutes at a temperature of 375° F.

Walnut Icing

1½ Cups Granulated Sugar
½ Cup Hot Water
⅛ Teaspoon Cream of Tartar
3 Egg Whites
1 Teaspoon Vanilla
12 Walnut Halves

Place the sugar and cream of tartar in the saucepan. Add the boiling water. Stir over a low flame until dissolved. Boil without stirring until the liquid will spin a long thread when dropped from the side of a spoon. Or boil until a thermometer registers 238° F. Pour the syrup in a thin stream over the stiffly beaten egg whites stirring constantly while pouring. Flavor. Beat until thick enough to spread. Cover the top and sides of the cake. Decorate the frosting with the walnut halves.

Caramel Cake

½ Cup Butter
1 Cup Sugar
2 Cups Flour
3 Teaspoons Baking Powder

⅔ Cup Milk
1 Teaspoon Vanilla
3 Egg Whites

Cream the butter. Add the sugar. Cream until light and fluffy. Sift the baking powder with the flour. Add alternately with the milk, a little at a time, beating vigorously between each addition. Flavor with vanilla. Beat the egg whites stiff. Fold into the batter. Bake in layers in buttered pans in a moderate oven (375° F.) for 20 minutes.

Caramel Frosting

1½ Cups Brown Sugar
½ Cup Cream
3 Tablespoons Butter

1 Teaspoon Vanilla
½ Cup Chopped Pecans

Place the sugar, cream and butter in a saucepan. Boil until a little of the syrup forms a soft ball when dropped into cold water or to 238° F. Remove from the fire. Add the vanilla. Cool slightly. Beat until creamy and thick enough to spread. Add the chopped nuts. Put the frosting between and on top of the cake. Frost the sides. Chopped figs may be substituted for the nuts.

Lady Baltimore Cake

½ Cup Butter
1 Cup Sugar
2 Cups Flour
3 Teaspoons Baking Powder

⅔ Cup Milk
2 Eggs
½ Teaspoon Almond Extract

Cream the butter. Add the sugar gradually and cream until light and fluffy. Add egg yolks. Beat vigorously. Sift the baking powder with the flour. Add to the creamed mixture alternately with the milk. Beat well between each addition. Flavor with almond. Beat the egg whites stiff. Fold into the batter. Bake in layers for 20 minutes in a moderate oven (375° F.).

Lady Baltimore Frosting

1 Pound Sifted Confectioners' Sugar
3 Egg Whites
¼ Teaspoon Cream Tartar
½ Teaspoon Almond Extract

1 Cup Chopped Raisins
¼ Cup Chopped Pecans
2 Tablespoons Chopped Citron
2 Tablespoons Chopped Candied Cherries

Beat the egg whites with the cream of tartar until white and foamy. Add the sugar gradually. Beat well between each addition. Flavor. When nearly thick enough to spread, add the chopped ingredients. Put between the layers and on the top and sides of the cake. Boiled frosting may be used for this icing and the fruit and nuts added to it.

Butterfly Cakes

3 Eggs
1 Cup Sugar
1½ Cups Flour
2 Teaspoons Baking Powder

1 Teaspoon Vanilla
3 Tablespoons Water
½ Pint Whipped Cream
3 Tablespoons Powdered Sugar

Beat the yolks of the eggs until lemon colored. Add the sugar gradually. Beat well between each addition. Sift the baking powder with the flour. Add alternately with the water. Beat the egg whites stiff. Fold into the batter. Flavor. Bake in buttered shallow pans about 4 inches in diameter in a moderate oven (350° F.) for 15 minutes. These cakes should be served individually. Split each cake in two, crosswise. Divide the top portion in two. Sweeten the whipped cream with the powdered sugar. Flavor with vanilla. Place the whipped cream on opposite edges of the lower cake. The cream should be an inch high. Rest the 2 top pieces on the whipped cream so that the edges will be elevated. The center dips down to resemble a butterfly. Decorate the center of the cake with whipped cream to represent the body of the butterfly. Dust the top of the cake with powdered sugar.

Ice Cream Cake

½ Cup Butter
1 Cup Sugar
3 Eggs
½ Cup Milk
½ Teaspoon Salt

2 Cups Flour
3 Teaspoons Baking Powder
1 Teaspoon Vanilla
Salted Almonds
Candied Cherries

Cream butter and sugar until light and fluffy. Add the well beaten egg yolks. Beat. Sift flour, baking powder and salt together. Add alternately to creamed mixture with the milk. Beat between each addition. Beat in the vanilla. Fold in the stiffly beaten egg whites. Turn into well buttered individual Mary Ann cake pans. Bake 20 minutes in a moderate oven (375° F.). Let cool inverted on a wire cake rack. Loosen edges and remove from pans. At serving time fill the center with ice cream. Decorate with salted almonds and cherries. Hot butterscotch sauce may be served with it.

Devil's Food

½ Cup Butter
2 Cups Brown Sugar

1 Cup Sour Milk
3 Squares Bitter Chocolate

2 Eggs
2 Cups Flour
1 Level Teaspoon Soda
1 Teaspoon Vanilla
½ Teaspoon Salt

Cream the butter and sugar until light and fluffy. Beat into this the eggs, one at a time. Beat well. Melt the chocolate. Beat into the egg mixture. Sift the soda with the flour. Add alternately with the sour milk. Beat well between each addition. Flavor with vanilla. Bake in layers for 30 minutes in a moderate oven (350° F.). Put the layers together with white icing.

Devil's Food Icing

2 Cups Confectioners' Sugar
3 Egg Whites
½ Teaspoon Cream of Tartar
1 Teaspon Vanilla

Sift the sugar. Add the cream of tartar to the egg whites. Blend. Stir the sugar into the unbeaten whites a little at a time. Beat between each addition. Add vanilla. Beat until smooth and creamy and of a consistency to spread.

Cocoanut Cake

½ Cup Butter
1 Cup Sugar
3 Eggs
2½ Cups Flour
3 Teaspoons Baking Powder
¾ Cup Milk
2 Cups Grated Cocoanut
1 Teaspoon Vanilla
½ Teaspoon Salt

Cream the butter and sugar until light and fluffy. Beat the egg yolks until lemon colored. Beat into the creamed mixture. Sift the flour and baking powder together twice. Add alternately to batter with the milk. Beat well between each addition. Add vanilla. Beat. Add grated cocoanut. Fold in the stiffly beaten egg whites. Bake in a moderate oven for 40 minutes (350° F.).

Cocoanut Icing

3 Egg Whites
2 Tablespoons Orange Juice
2 Cups Sifted Confectioners' Sugar
1 Tablespoon Grated Orange Peel

1 Cup Cocoanut
¼ Cup Orange Juice
Candied Orange Peel cut in quarters

Beat the eggs slightly with 2 tablespoons of orange juice. Add the sugar gradually. Beat well between each addition. Beat until thick enough to spread. Add the grated orange peel. Frost the top and sides of the cake. Soak the cocoanut in ¼ cup orange juice. Cover the top of the cake. Decorate with quarters of candied orange peel.

Sponge Cake

1 Cup Sugar
½ Cup Water
3 Eggs

1½ Cups Flour
1 Teaspoon Baking Powder
1 Teaspoon Vanilla

Sift the sugar. Add ¼ cup water. Stir. Add the well beaten yolks of the eggs. Beat. Sift the flour and baking powder together twice. Add to the mixture alternately with ¼ cup of water. Beat well between each addition. Beat in the vanilla. Fold in the stiffly beaten whites of the eggs. Bake 40 minutes in a moderate oven (350° F.). This cake may be served unfrosted and dusted with powdered sugar, or the top may be coated with a thin layer of melted bitter chocolate.

White Almond Cake

½ Cup Butter
1 Cup Sugar
⅔ Cup Milk
½ Teaspoon Almond Extract

2 Cups Flour
2 Teaspoons Baking Powder
4 Egg Whites

Sift the flour and baking powder together. Cream the butter and sugar until light and fluffy. Add the flour alternately with the milk. Beat well between each addition. Beat in the almond extract. Fold in the stiffly beaten whites of the eggs. Bake in a narrow oblong loaf pan 40 minutes in a moderate oven (350° F.).

White Almond Icing

¼ Cup Butter
1 Tablespoon Hot Coffee
1 Cup Confectioners' Sugar

¼ Teaspoon Almond Extract
1 Cup Almonds

Cream the butter. Add the hot coffee. Add the sugar a little at a time. Beat until thick enough to spread. Flavor. Blanch the shelled almonds by pouring boiling water over them. Allow to stand a few minutes. Drain. Pour cold water over them. Let stand. Remove the skins. Cut in half. Dry in the oven until crisp but not brown. Place the almonds in close even rows along the top of the cake.

Ginger Bread

1 Cup Brown Sugar
1 Cup Molasses
1 Cup Butter
1 Cup Sour Milk
2 Eggs
3 Cups Flour

1 Level Teaspoon Soda
1 Teaspoon Ginger
½ Teaspoon Mace
½ Teaspoon Cloves
½ Teaspoon Cinnamon

Melt slowly in a saucepan the sugar, butter and molasses. Allow to cool slightly. Stir in the sour milk. Beat into this the eggs. Beat vigorously. Sift the flour, spices and soda together. Beat into the liquid a little at a time. Beat well between each addition. Bake in a moderate oven for 45 minutes at a temperature of 350° F. This may be served warm, plain, or with whipped cream. A tablespoon of orange marmalade beaten into the cream adds variety.

Butter Cake (Layer or Cup Cake)

½ Cup Shortening
1 Cup Sugar
2 Eggs
2 Cups Flour
3 Teaspoons Baking Powder
½ Teaspoon Salt
½ Cup Milk
1 Teaspoon Vanilla

Cream the shortening. Add sugar gradually and cream until light and fluffy. Add eggs, one at a time and beat thoroughly. Add ⅓ of the flour which has been sifted with the baking powder and salt. Add ½ of milk, then ½ of remaining flour and rest of milk. Mix in remaining flour. Beat all together well. Pour into 2 greased layer cake pans and bake 25 minutes at 375° F.

Boiled Icing

1½ Cups Sugar
⅛ Teaspoon Cream of Tartar
½ Cup Water
½ Teaspoon Vanilla
2 Egg Whites

Stir sugar and water together until sugar is dissolved. Bring to boil and stir in cream of tartar. Allow to boil until candy thermometer registers 238° F. Do not stir after adding cream of tartar. When the thermometer registers 238° F. take saucepan from range and allow to cool while beating egg whites stiff. Then add syrup to egg whites in a thin stream, beating constantly. After syrup is added continue beating until stiff enough to spread.

Boston Cream Pie Filling

½ Cup Sugar
2 Tablespoons Cornstarch
⅛ Teaspoon Salt
1 Cup Scalded Milk
2 Beaten Egg Yolks
1 Tablespoon Butter
1 Teaspoon Vanilla

Heat milk in top of double boiler. Mix together sugar,

cornstarch and salt. Add to hot milk and cook until thick. Stir frequently. Add beaten yolks and butter and cook 2 minutes. Add vanilla. Cool mixture before spreading on the cake.

Chocolate Cake

BOILED MIXTURE:
½ Cup Milk
½ Cup Sugar
3 Squares Chocolate—Cook till chocolate is melted—bring to a boil—cool.

½ Cup Butter
1 Cup Sugar
3 Eggs
½ Cup Milk
2 Cups Flour
¾ Teaspoon Soda
1 Teaspoon Cream of Tartar

Cream shortening and add sugar gradually. Cream together until light and fluffy. Add eggs, 1 at a time. Beat well. Sift flour, baking soda and cream of tartar together. Add alternately with milk to mixture. Add boiled mixture. Beat all together. Bake in greased layer or loaf pans.

Chocolate Icing

3 Tablespoons Melted Butter
3 Cups Confectioners' Sugar
2 Tablespoons Orange Juice
Grated rind of ½ Orange

Pulp of 1 orange
1 Beaten Egg White
2½ Squares Melted Unsweetened Chocolate

Beat butter, sugar and orange juice together. Add egg white. Add chocolate last. Chocolate may be omitted for an orange icing. This amount will spread between 3 layers or will be enough for filling and sides of a 2 layer cake.

Cocoa Cake

1 Cup Confectioners' Sugar
2 Eggs
1 Cup Cream
1 Cup Flour

1 Cup Cocoa
6 Teaspoons Baking Powder
1 Teaspoon Vanilla

Sift the flour, baking powder, cocoa and sugar together. Beat the eggs. Add the cream and beat together. Add to the dry ingredients. Beat well. Add the flavoring. Bake in thin layers in well buttered pans in a quick oven (400° F.) for 10 minutes. Serve warm. Sift powdered sugar and cinnamon between the layers and on top. Sweetened, flavored whipped cream may be served with this, or hard sauce. Make the hard sauce with ½ cup of powdered sugar and ½ cup of brown sugar creamed with ½ cup of butter. Flavor with ½ teaspoon vanilla. Dust the top of the hard sauce with powdered mace.

Gommy's Cake

2½ Cups Flour
2½ Teaspoons Baking Powder
1½ Cups Sugar
2 Eggs
1 Cup Milk
1 Teaspoon Vanilla
½ Cup Butter
½ Teaspoon Cinnamon
½ Teaspoon Allspice
½ Teaspoon Mace

Sift the flour with the baking powder. Add the sugar. Sift together. Mix the softened butter with the eggs, milk and vanilla. Beat the liquid ingredients into the dry ingredients. Beat for 1 minute. If you have an electric beater use that. Remove ⅓ of the batter. Add the spices to it. Bake 2 white layers and 1 spiced layer in a moderate oven for 25 minutes (350° F.) Put the layers together with jelly. Ice the top and sides with white frosting.

Golden Cake

¾ Cup Butter
1 Tablespoon Hot Water
1¼ Cups Sugar
2½ Cups Pastry Flour
3 Teaspoons Baking Powder
8 Egg Yolks
¾ Cup Milk
1 Teaspoon Vanilla

This cake may be made when baking Angel Food to utilize the yolks left from the white cake. Cream the butter with the hot water. Add the sugar gradually. Cream until light and fluffy. Sift the flour and baking powder together 3 times. Beat the egg yolks until lemon colored. Add to the creamed butter and sugar. Beat. Add the flour alternately with the milk. Beat well between each addition. Flavor. Bake in a loaf pan for 45 minutes in a moderate oven (350° F.). This cake may be baked in layers for 25 minutes (375° F.).

Golden Cake Icing

2½ Cups Sugar
⅓ Cup Light Corn Syrup
½ Cup Water

1 Teaspoon Vanilla
2 Egg Whites

Place the sugar in a saucepan. Add the corn syrup and water. Stir over a low flame until the sugar is dissolved. Then boil without stirring until a little of the syrup will form a soft ball when dropped into cold water. Or boil to 238° F. Remove from fire. Pour in a thin steady stream onto the stiffly beaten egg whites, beating constantly. Flavor with vanilla. Beat until thick enough to spread.

Fruit Cake

1 Cup Butter
1 Cup Sugar
6 Eggs
2 Cups Flour
¼ Cup Orange Juice
½ Tablespoon Mace

½ Tablespoon Cinnamon
1 Tablespoon Nutmeg
2 Cups Seeded Raisins
2 Cups Currants
1 Cup Citron Cut into Thin Strips

Cream the butter and sugar until light and fluffy. Add the yolks of 6 well beaten eggs. Beat well. Sift the flour and spices. Add the orange juice to mixture. One fourth cup of cooking wine may be substituted for the orange juice. Stir in ½ of the flour and spices. Add the fruit. Mix well. Stir in the remainder of dry ingredients. Fold in the stiffly beaten whites of the eggs. Steam over boiling water for 3 hours in well buttered pans. Dry for 30 minutes in a slow oven (300° F.).

Frosted Raisin Spice Cake

2 Cups Flour
2 Teaspoons Baking Powder
½ Teaspoon Cinnamon
½ Teaspoon Ginger
¼ Teaspoon Cloves
½ Cup Sugar

½ Cup Milk
⅔ Cup Molasses
½ Cup Softened Butter
2 Eggs
½ Cup Chopped Seeded Raisins

Sift together the flour, baking powder, sugar and spices. Mix together in another bowl the beaten eggs, milk, molasses and softened butter. Beat. Stir the liquid ingredients into the dry ones. Beat for 1 minute. Add the chopped raisins. Bake in 2 layers for 35 minutes in a moderate oven (350° F.).

Frosting

2 Egg Whites
1 Cup Confectioners' Sugar
1 Cup Brown Sugar
1 Tablespoon Hot Coffee
1 Teaspoon Vanilla

1 Tablespoon Cocoa
¼ Cup Chopped Raisins
2 Tablespoons Chopped Candied Orange Peel

Beat the whites of the eggs slightly. Add a little at a time, the confectioners' sugar and the brown sugar sifted. Beat between each addition. Add vanilla, the hot coffee and the cocoa. Beat until of the consistency to spread. Add the raisins and orange peel. Nuts may be substituted for the orange peel. Spread between and on top of the layers.

Black Fruit Cake

½ Cup Butter
2 Cups Brown Sugar
1 Square Melted Bitter Chocolate
½ Cup Black Coffee
2 Tablespoons Molasses
2 Eggs
2 Cups Flour
3 Teaspoons Baking Powder
½ Teaspoon Cinnamon
¼ Teaspoon Mace
¼ Teaspoon Cloves
½ Cup Seeded Raisins
½ Cup Currants
2 Tablespoons Shredded Citron
2 Tablespoons Chopped Candied Orange Peel

Cream the butter and sugar together. Add the chocolate, melted. Beat. Add the coffee, molasses, and the well beaten eggs. Sift the flour, baking powder and spices together. Add the dry ingredients alternately with the fruit. Bake in a loaf pan for 1 hour. Put the cake in a cold oven. Raise the temperature to 350° F. Finish baking at that heat.

Birthday Cake

1 Cup Butter
2 Cups Sugar
¾ Cup Milk
3½ Cups Pastry Flour
3 Teaspoons Baking Powder
6 Egg Whites
1 Teaspoon Vanilla

Cream butter and sugar until light and fluffy. Add alternately, a little at a time, the milk and the flour which has been sifted 3 times with the baking powder. Beat hard after each addition. Beat the whites of the eggs stiff. Fold lightly into the batter. Add flavoring. Bake in a round cake pan. Put the cake in the oven at 300° F. and raise the temperature to 350° F. Bake at that heat. Bake 45 minutes.

Birthday Cake Icing

2 Cups Confectioners' Sugar
8 Tablespoons Cream
1 Teaspoon Vanilla

Sift the sugar. Stir it into the cream a little at a time. Add vanilla. Beat until thick. If it is not thick enough add more sugar. If too thick, a few drops of water. Spread on the cake, top and sides. Smooth with a knife dipped in hot water. Decorate both top and sides of cake with small candy gum drops cut in thin slices to simulate flowers and leaves. Just before carrying to the table add rosebud candle holders and tiny birthday candles lighted. Serves 16.

CHAPTER XLV

COOKIES

Chocolate Nut Kisses

1 Cup Chopped Walnut Meats
1¼ Cups Powdered Sugar
1½ Cups Grated Chocolate
5 Egg Whites

Mix the sugar and egg whites together for about 10 minutes until pure white and stiff. An electric beater simplifies this process. Mix in nuts and a trace of vanilla. Add the grated chocolate. Mix well. Drop in teaspoonfuls on a buttered paper placed on a pan or cookie sheet. Bake in a slow oven (300° F.) for about 15 minutes. Remove the paper to a moist towel. The kisses may be easily removed. Makes 6 dozen kisses.

Cream Cookies

1 Cup Rich Sour Cream
1 Cup Sugar
1 Egg
½ Teaspoon Soda
½ Teaspoon Vanilla
2 Cups Flour

Dissolve the soda in the cream. Add the sugar. Beat. Add the egg and beat. Flavor with vanilla. Add the sifted flour gradually. Place in the refrigerator to chill. Form into small balls with floured hands. Place in a pan. Sprinkle with sugar. Bake for 10 minutes in a quick oven (400° F.). A variety of cookies may be achieved at the same time by pressing candied fruits or nuts into the center of the cookies. Colored sugar or seedlike candies may also be sprinkled over them. Makes 3 dozen cookies.

Brownies

2 Eggs
1¼ Cups Brown Sugar
½ Teaspoon Vanilla
½ Cup Flour

2 Squares Unsweetened Chocolate, Melted
⅓ Cup Walnut meats, Cut in Pieces

Beat eggs well, add sugar. Add remaining ingredients. Spread evenly in a buttered shallow pan and bake in a moderate oven 20 minutes.

Hermits

1½ Cups Brown Sugar
1 Cup Butter
2½ Cups Flour
1 Teaspoon Soda
2 Teaspoons Cinnamon

3 Well Beaten Eggs
½ Teaspoon Salt
1 Cup Chopped Raisins
1 Cup Currants
1 Cup Chopped Walnuts

Cream the butter and sugar. Sift the flour with the soda, cinnamon and salt. Add the beaten eggs to the butter and sugar. Add part of the sifted dry ingredients. Mix well. Add the raisins, currants and nuts gradually. Mix well. Add the rest of the flour a little at a time. Drop in teaspoonfuls on a buttered, floured cookie sheet or pan. Bake in a slow oven (300° F.) for 15 minutes. Hermits will keep in a cookie jar for a long time, improving with age. Makes 6 dozen hermits.

Doughnuts

½ Teaspoon Shortening
1 Cup Sugar
1 Egg
3 Cups Bread Flour
4 Teaspoons Baking Powder

1 Teaspoon Nutmeg
¼ Teaspoon Cinnamon
1 Teaspoon Salt
1 Cup Milk
Extra Bread Flour

Cream shortening and sugar until blended then add beaten

egg. Measure and sift together 3 cups of flour and other dry ingredients. Add alternately with milk to sugar mixture. Beat well and add enough more flour to make a soft dough. Toss on floured board. Roll to ¼ inch thickness and cut. Fry in deep fat at 360° F. until brown. Drain on brown paper. When cool roll in sugar.

Grandmother's Cookies

1 Cup of Brown Sugar
⅔ Cup of Butter
¼ Cup Sour Milk
½ Level Teaspoon Soda
1 Teaspoon Cinnamon
½ Teaspoon Cloves
½ Cup Chopped Raisins
2¼ Cups of Flour
1 Egg Beaten

Cream the butter and sugar. Add the beaten egg. Blend. Add the sour milk with the soda dissolved in it. Add half of the flour sifted with the spices. Mix. Add the remainder of the flour. Chill in the refrigerator. This dough may be formed into a roll, wrapped in waxed paper and sliced into cookies or it may be rolled and cut with a cookie cutter. Bake in a hot oven on a cookie sheet for 10 minutes. Temperature 400° F. Makes eighteen cookies.

Chocolate Pecan Squares

1 Cup Sugar
2 Eggs
½ Cup Cream
½ Cup Cocoa
½ Cup Flour
½ Cup Broken Pecan Meats
3 Teaspoons Baking Powder

Beat the eggs light. Add ½ cup of cream. Sift flour, cocoa, sugar and baking powder together. Add gradually to the liquid. Beat well between each addition. Add nut meats. Bake in a square shallow pan for 10 minutes in a moderate oven (350° F.). Dust with powdered sugar and cinnamon. Cut into squares. Makes twelve cookies.

COOKIES

Drop Spice Cookies

½ Cup Softened Butter
1¼ Cups Flour
½ Cup Brown Sugar
2 Egg Yolks
2 Teaspoons Baking Powder

½ Teaspoon Cinnamon
½ Teaspoon Cloves
½ Cup Stoned Dates Cut in Pieces
Nut Meats

Mix the softened butter with the brown sugar. Beat in the egg yolks. Add the dry ingredients sifted together. Beat them in, a little at a time. Add the dates and a few nut meats. Drop in tablespoonfuls on a buttered cookie sheet. Bake in a moderate oven for 10 minutes (375° F.). Makes eighteen cookies.

Pecan Macaroons

3 Egg Whites
1 Cup Powdered Sugar
3 Tablespoons Flour

1½ Cups Chopped Pecans
3 Drops Vanilla

Beat the egg whites stiff. Add the sifted powdered sugar gradually. Fold in the flour. Add the vanilla and chopped nuts. Drop in spoonfuls on a buttered cookie sheet or pans. Bake 15 minutes in a moderate oven (350° F.) until a delicate brown. Makes 3 dozen macaroons.

Cry Babies

½ Cup Strong Hot Coffee
½ Cup Molasses
½ Cup Sugar
½ Cup Butter
2 Eggs

1 Teaspoon Baking Powder
1 Teaspoon Ginger
1 Teaspoon Nutmeg
4 Cups Flour
½ Teaspoon Soda

Melt the butter with the coffee. Add sugar, molasses and the well beaten eggs. Sift the spices, flour, baking powder and soda. Add to the liquid ingredients. Beat well. Chill.

Drop in tablespoonfuls on a well buttered baking sheet or pan. Bake 10 minutes in a moderate oven (350° F.). Frost while hot. Makes 4 dozen cry babies.

Frosting

2 Cups Sifted Confectioners' Sugar
8 Tablespoons Thick Cream
½ Teaspoon Vanilla

Stir the cream into the sifted sugar. Beat well. Add vanilla. Beat until thick enough to spread.

Ice Box Cookies

1½ Cups Butter
1⅓ Cups Sugar
3 Eggs
½ Teaspoon Salt
1 Teaspoon Soda
4 Cups Flour
1 Teaspoon Vanilla

Cream the butter and sugar until light and fluffy. Beat the eggs into the creamed mixture. Sift the dry ingredients. Add a little at a time beating well. Make into long rolls. Wrap in waxed paper. Chill thoroughly in the refrigerator. Slice across the roll with a sharp knife in thin slices. Bake the cookies on a buttered cookie sheet or in pans. The dough may be divided when it is made and fruit added to some of it. Chocolate, melted, changes another portion to chocolate cookies. Spices, nuts or cocoanut are other variations. Roll each in its own waxed paper. Bake as wanted. Pinwheel cookies are achieved by rolling two different varieties of dough separately. Lay one on top of the other. Roll jelly roll fashion. Wrap in waxed paper. When chilled slice across the loaf in thin slices with a sharp knife. Bake 10 minutes in a hot oven (400° F.).

CHAPTER XLVI

DESSERTS

Plum Pudding

1 Qt. Soft Bread Crumbs
2 Cups Chopped Suet
2 Cups Sugar
3 Teaspoons Baking Powder
¼ Teaspoon Soda
4 Eggs
½ Glass Non Alcoholic Cooking Sherry (Orange juice may be substituted.)
1 Lb. Currants
1 Lb. Raisins
1 Cup Citron Sliced Thinly
1 Teaspoon Cinnamon
1 Teaspoon Mace
½ Teaspoon Cloves

Mix the bread crumbs, suet and sugar. Add sifted baking powder and soda. Add the sherry or orange juice together with the yolks of the eggs well beaten. Blend well. Add spices and fruit and mix. Fold in the stiffly beaten egg whites. Put in a buttered mold. Steam over boiling water 3 hours. The water should boil under the steamer very hard. Add more water if it boils away. This pudding will keep indefinitely. When you wish to use it steam for 30 minutes over boiling water.

Hard Sauce

Beat ½ cup of butter until creamy. Add gradually, beating constantly, 1 cup of sifted powdered sugar. Flavor with 1 teaspoon of vanilla. Set on ice for several hours and when ready to serve sprinkle lightly with powdered mace.

Velvet Sponge Pudding

¼ Cup Flour
1 Cup Milk
¼ Cup Sugar

¼ Cup Butter
3 Eggs
1 Teaspoon Vanilla

Sift the flour. Add a little at a time the milk and blend well. Cook for 10 minutes in a double boiler. Stir occasionally. Add the sugar and butter while the mixture is hot. Cool slightly and add the yolks of the eggs well beaten. Beat the egg whites stiff. Fold into the mixture. Flavor with vanilla. Bake in a 1 quart pudding dish set in a pan of boiling water. Bake 35 to 40 minutes in a moderate oven (350° F.). Serve with velvet sauce. This recipe may be doubled if a larger pudding is wanted. Amounts given serve 4.

Velvet Sauce

Cream ½ cup of butter. Add gradually 1 cup of sifted powdered sugar. Add the yolks of 2 eggs beaten until lemon colored. Flavor with 1 teaspoon vanilla or ½ teaspoon vanilla and ½ teaspoon lemon extract. Beat into this ½ cup of thick cream.

Apple Dumplings

2 Cups Sliced Apple
2 Cups Water
1 Cup Sugar
1 Tablespoon Butter

2 Cups Flour
3 Teaspoons Baking Powder
½ Teaspoon Salt
¾ Cup Cream

Peel, core and slice the apples in thin slices. Place them in a saucepan with water, sugar and butter. When this boils drop in dumplings made as follows:

Sift the flour and baking powder together with the salt. Stir the cream into this. Drop the dumplings into the boiling liquid and cover closely. Cook for 20 minutes. Keep the liquid just boiling, but not violently lest the syrup burn. The apple dumplings may be cooked in the oven in a covered dish. A glass baking dish is convenient so that you may see through it. The oven should be moderate (350° F.). Remember that in cooking dumplings over liquid it is the steam that cooks them and the liquid should boil gently. Peaches, pears or apricots may be used instead of apples. Serves 6.

Pineapple Ice Box Cake

2 Level Tablespoons Granulated Gelatine
½ Cup Cold Water
1 Can Crushed Pineapple
¼ Teaspoon Salt

½ Cup Sugar
1 Tablespoon Lemon Juice
1½ Cups Cream
Lady Fingers

Soak gelatine in cold water about 5 minutes, dissolve over hot water and add pineapple, sugar, salt and lemon juice. Stir until all gelatine and sugar have dissolved. When it begins to thicken, beat and fold in whipped cream. Line sides and bottom of a round spring form mould with lady fingers. Cover with pineapple cream mixture, then alternate cakes and cream until mould is full. Place in ice box and let stand 3 or 4 hours. Unmould on a large cake plate and garnish with whipped cream and fruit in season. Serves 12.

Peach and Cherry Compote

Peel 2 peaches and cut into dice. Stone enough cherries to fill a cup. Combine the fruit. Cover with ¾ cup of powdered sugar. Add 4 marshmallows cut into pieces. Put into glasses and chill. Cover with whipped cream sweetened and flavored with some of the fruit juice. Serves 4.

Floating Island

Heat 2 cups of milk in a double boiler. Beat the yolks of 4 eggs. Add ¼ cup of sugar. Beat. Dip ⅓ cup of milk from the double boiler. Pour onto the eggs and sugar, slowly stirring until well blended. Add this mixture to the rest of the milk. Cook in double boiler 5 minutes, or until slightly thickened. Beat the whites of four eggs stiff. Add 6 tablespoons of sugar and 1 teaspoon vanilla. Flavor the yellow custard with 1 teaspoon vanilla. Remove to a serving dish. Drop the whites of eggs in tablespoons onto the hot custard. Serve cold. The top of the dessert may be decorated with bits of candied cherries and angelica. Serves 4.

Pineapple Upside Down Cake

2½ Cups Flour
½ Teaspoon Salt
4 Teaspoons Baking Powder
½ Cup Butter or Shortening
1 Cup Sugar
2 Eggs Well Beaten
1 Cup Milk
2 Teaspoons Vanilla
2 Tablespoons Butter
2 Cups Brown Sugar
8 Slices Pineapple Cut Fine
2 Cups Pecan Meats Slightly Broken

Sift flour once, measure, add salt and baking powder, and sift together 3 times. Cream butter thoroughly, add sugar gradually, and cream together until light and fluffy. Add egg, then flour alternately with milk, a small amount at a time. Beat after each addition until smooth. Add vanilla. Melt 2 tablespoons butter in a utility pan 14 x 9 inch. Add brown sugar. Stir until melted. On this, place pineapple and sprinkle nuts over top. Pour batter over contents of pan. Bake in a moderate oven (350° F.) 40 minutes. Loosen cake from sides and bottom of pan with spatula. Serve upside down on dish, with pineapple on top. Garnish with whipped cream, if desired.

Rice Pudding

1 Cup Washed Rice
1 Cup Milk
¼ Cup Sugar
½ Cup Raisins

1 Tablespoon Butter
2 Eggs
Vanilla
Nutmeg

In a large saucepan boil 2 quarts of water. Add the washed rice. Cook 20 minutes, drain and pour hot water over it. Drain again and return to the saucepan with the milk. Cook 10 minutes. Remove from the fire. Stir in while hot the sugar, raisins, butter and egg yolks. Flavor with vanilla and a sprinkling of nutmeg. Put into glasses.

Beat the egg whites stiff. Add 2 tablespoons of sugar. Flavor with 1 teaspoon vanilla and pile on top of pudding. Serves 6.

Baked Rice Pudding

½ Cup Rice
1 Pint Milk
¼ Cup Butter
4 Eggs

¼ Cup Sugar
¼ Teaspoon Cinnamon
¼ Cup Bread Crumbs
½ Cup Seeded Raisins

Boil the rice in salted water for 5 minutes. Strain through a sieve. Add rice slowly to boiling milk. Cook over a low flame until soft, without stirring. Stir the butter to a cream. Add the yolks of the eggs, sugar, cinnamon, bread crumbs and seeded raisins which have been well washed. Add to the rice which should be cooled. Then add to the whole the beaten whites of the eggs. Bake 1 hour in slow oven (300° F.). Serves 4.

Pears in Grenadine with Ice Cream

Heat 1 pint of grenadine in a saucepan. Drain 1 can of pears. Cook the fruit in the grenadine until it is a rich red.

Place the pears on a decorative dish, preferably of a contrasting color. A rich green or dull blue is effective. Serve the pears hot, placing one each on portion of ice cream.

Loganberry Pudding

Put into a saucepan 1 can loganberries. Stir into this ½ cup sugar mixed with 2 tablespoons cornstarch. Cook over hot water until the juice is thick and transparent. Pour into individual glasses. Serve cold with cream. Serves 6.

Strawberry Short Cake

1 Box Strawberries
1 Cup Powdered Sugar
1 Cup Flour
½ Teaspoon Salt
2 Tablespoons Butter
3 Teaspoons Baking Powder
¼ Cup Milk

Pick over the strawberries. Mash with a wire potato masher. Add powdered sugar. Make the short cake as follows:

Into a mixing bowl sift the flour and salt. Blend in the butter thoroughly. Add the baking powder. Stir the milk into this. Form into 4 biscuits. Bake 10 minutes in a hot oven (400° F.). Split the biscuits and put the halves together with crushed berries between and on top.

Sponge Cake Shortcake

Those who prefer a sweeter strawberry shortcake will find the sponge cake recipe given in the cake section. Whipped cream is usually added to the berries that top a cake of this kind.

Pineapple Cream

¾ Cup Preserved Pineapple
4 Marshmallows cut in bits
½ Cup Cream
1 Egg White
Juice of ½ Lemon

Cut the marshmallows into bits and mix with the pineapple. Combine the cream, the egg white and the lemon juice. Beat this stiff and mix with the pineapple. Pile into sherbet glasses. Serve cold. Decorate the top with bits of candied cherries. Serves 4.

Charlotte Russe

Into the bottom of each serving glass place a tablespoon of loganberry jam. Put 4 small lady fingers, standing upright into each glass. Fill the glasses with whipped cream, sweetened and flavored with vanilla. Top with a teaspoon of the jam or a candied cherry.

Orange and Banana Compote

Peel and slice 1 banana. Peel 1 orange, cut it into dice. Cut 1 piece of candied ginger into bits. Mix with the orange and banana and add 2 tablespoons honey. Arrange in glasses. Sprinkle the top with cocoanut. Serves 2.

Bavarian Cream

Heat 1 cup of milk in the double boiler. Add the yolks of 2 eggs beaten with 4 tablespoons of sugar. Add ½ tablespoon gelatine that has been softened in ¼ cup of cold water. Cook over hot water for 5 minutes. Beat the whites of 2 eggs stiff. Add to the custard. When cold, stir in ½ cup of whipped cream, measured before whipping. Place in refrigerator until jellied. Serve with crushed strawberries sweetened with powdered sugar. Any fruit, either cooked or fresh, may be used. Serves 4.

Grapefruit with Strawberries

Cut a grapefruit in half. Remove the fruit with a sharp

knife. Cut the pulp into small pieces. Mix with an equal quantity of strawberries and ½ cup of powdered sugar. Chill and at serving time pile into the grapefruit shell. Decorate with sprigs of mint. Serves 2.

Raspberry Compote

Press the juice from 1 pint of currants. Sweeten with 4 tablespoons of powdered sugar. Pile raspberries into sherbet glasses and chill. At serving time pour the juice over the raspberries. Serves 4.

Apricot Skillet Cake

Heat 1 tablespoon butter and ½ cup sugar in a heavy skillet. Add 1 can of apricots (any cooked fruit may be substituted). When hot pour a cake batter over it, and bake for 20 minutes in a moderate oven (350° F.).

Cake batter: Break 1 egg into a bowl and beat well. Add ½ cup sugar, 1 tablespoon melted butter, ⅓ cup of milk, and 1 cup of flour sifted with 1 teaspoon baking powder. Beat well, flavor with vanilla. Pour over the hot apricots. When the cake is done, turn it onto a serving dish with the fruit side up. Cover with whipped cream and decorate with cherries. Serves 6.

Cream Sponge Pudding

Whip ½ pint of cream, add 2 tablespoons sugar and 1 tablespoon lemon juice. Cut into bits 4 marshmallows, 1 tablespoon candied cherries, 1 tablespoon candied pineapple, 1 tablespoon candied ginger. Add to the cream. Flavor with vanilla. Chill in sherbet glasses and decorate the top with whole cherries. Serves 4.

Baked Pears

Put 1 can of pears in a baking dish. Pour over it 1 cup of loganberry juice. Add the juice of 1 orange and the grated orange peel and 1 tablespoon raisins. Bake for 20 minutes. Serve hot with cream. Serves 6.

Baked Custard

3 Eggs
¼ Cup Sugar

2 Cups Milk

Beat the whites of the eggs stiff. Add the sugar. Beat and add the egg yolks. When well mixed add the milk which has been made hot. Beat again and put into custard cups. Sprinkle the tops with powdered nutmeg. Place the cups in a pan of hot water and bake in a moderate oven (325° F.). When done a silver knife inserted in the center of the custard should come out clean. Serves 4.

Honeydew Melon with Ice Cream

For each portion cut a ring of honeydew melon crosswise. Remove the seeds and place a portion of ice cream in the center. Decorate the ice cream with bits of candied fruits or 2 tablespoons pineapple mint preserves.

Date Pudding

1 Cup Seeded Dates
1 Cup Walnut Meats
1 Cup Powdered Sugar
2 Eggs

5 Tablespoons Flour
1 Teaspoon Baking Powder
Vanilla

Put the dates and the walnut meats through a food chopper. Add the sugar and the eggs well beaten. Mix and add the flour and baking powder. Flavor with vanilla. Spread evenly in a large shallow pan, ¼ inch thick. Bake in a moderate oven (325° F.). While hot cut into narrow strips. Roll in powdered sugar. These may be eaten plain or if desired for pudding they may be broken into pieces and mixed with whipped cream. Serve piled in sherbet glasses. Serves 6.

Peach Fluff

Peel 4 peaches. Put them through a fruit ricer. Whip ½ pint cream. Sweeten it with 2 rounding tablespoons powdered sugar. Stir in the riced peaches. Pile in sherbet glasses. Decorate the top of each with a cherry and chill. Serves 6.

Cranberry Tart

Measure and sift 1 cup of flour with ½ teaspoon salt. Blend the flour with ⅓ cup lard. Add 3 tablespoons cold water. Roll the crust thin. Line muffin pans or a small pie plate with the pastry. Fill with cranberry sauce and decorate the tops with crossed strips of pastry. Bake in a hot oven (450° F.) until the crust is brown. Serves 4.

Jelly Roll

3 Eggs	1 Teaspoon Baking Powder
1 Cup Sugar	1 Teaspoon Vanilla
1 Cup Flour	

Beat the egg whites until stiff. Add the sugar gradually beating well between each addition. Beat into this mixture the egg yolks. Sift the flour with the baking powder and fold it into the eggs and sugar. Add 2 tablespoons water and the vanilla. Cover the bottom of a dripping pan with the batter. It should be about ½ inch thick. Bake in a slow oven (300° F.). Dip a tea towel in cold water and wring as dry as possible. Spread it on the table and turn the cake onto the towel. Spread with jelly and roll while hot.

Blueberry Pudding

1 Egg	1 Cup Flour
½ Cup Sugar	1 Teaspoon Baking Powder
4 Tablespoons Butter	½ Cup Blueberries
½ Cup Milk	

Cream the butter and sugar, add the beaten egg, flour and milk alternately, then the baking powder. Stir in the blueberries. Steam in small cups ½ hour. Serve with hard sauce. Raisins may be substituted for the blue berries. Serves 4.

Hard Sauce

See recipe under Plum Pudding.

Caramel Tapioca

Cook 4 tablespoons minute tapioca in 1 pint of milk. Use a double boiler. Cook 15 minutes. Add 1 cup of brown sugar, 1 teaspoon vanilla. Serve with cream. Serves 4.

Apple Compote

Place 1 cupful of sugar and 1 cupful of water in a saucepan to heat. When bubbling hot add 2 red apples that have been cored and cut into circles, about ¼ inch thick. Cook until transparent, about 15 minutes. Serve hot or cold with cream. Serves 2.

Baked Red Bananas

Use 1 red banana for every portion. Do not peel. Make a slit in the side the length of the banana. Break the pulp with a fork. Add 1 tablespoon of preserved ginger, cut into bits, to each banana. Bake in a pan in a moderate oven (375° F.) for 30 minutes. Serve hot.

Maple Custard

Beat the whites of 2 eggs. Add the yolks and 3 tablespoons of soft maple sugar. Dust with nutmeg and add 1½ cups of milk. Bake in custard cups in a pan of hot water in a moderate oven (325° F.).

Coffee Jelly

Cover 2 tablespoons of gelatine with ½ cup cold water and let it soften. Add ½ cup of sugar to 3 cups of strong, hot coffee. Add the gelatine to the coffee, strain and put in sherbet glasses. Set in the ice box to harden. Serve with brown sugar and cream. Serves 4.

Peaches in Honey

Peel 4 peaches. Slice thin. Mix them with 4 tablespoons honey. Serve in stemmed glasses. Serves 4.

Crushed Strawberries

Wash and stem 1 quart of strawberries. Add 1 cup of powdered sugar. Mash with a wire potato masher. Serve ice cold in sherbet glasses. Add a tablespoon of whipped cream to each glass just before serving. Serves 6.

Pears and Raspberries

Core 2 pears. Slice in circles and arrange on dessert plates. In the center of the pears place a mound of raspberries. Serve ice cold with sweetened whipped cream flavored with vanilla. Serves 2.

CHAPTER XLVII

QUICK DESSERTS

There are so many desserts that take but a few minutes to prepare that we should never omit a sweet from dinner or luncheon. Dessert is a food which gives us instant strength. Sweets should not be eaten in place of other foods, but they are a very necessary as well as a pleasant part of a meal. A simple dessert is preserved ginger, crackers, cheese, lemon wafers, vanilla wafers, nuts and raisins. Preserved kumquats might be substituted for the ginger.

Serve the preserves in their own ornamental jars. Arrange cookies, crackers and cheese on an attractive plate.

Apples and Cheese

Mix 2 ounces of Roquefort cheese, 1 tablespoon butter. Mash together. Add 4 tablespoons orange juice or 4 tablespoons cooking wine. Beat. Core, but do not peel red apples. Slice them crosswise. Spread with the cheese mixture. Cored sliced pears or rounds of pineapple may be substituted for apple. Nuts, raisins and black coffee should be served with this. Camembert cheese might be passed, instead of Roquefort, with the plain sliced apple and let each person spread their own.

Angel Food Whip

Break 6 pieces of Angel Food into very small pieces with a fork. Whip ½ pint of cream with 1 tablespoon grapefruit marmalade. Mix with the Angel Food. Pile into sherbet glasses. Decorate the top with a spoonful of quince preserves. Place in refrigerator while dinner is being eaten. Lady fingers or macaroons may be substituted for the cake. Serves 6.

Apple Butter and Pound Cake

Spread slices of pound cake generously with apple butter. Cover with sweetened whipped cream. Sprinkle with chopped pecan meats. Another method to use for this dessert is to cover the apple butter with a thick meringue and sprinkle with the pecans. Slip in the oven under the gas flame, watching it constantly until a delicate brown. This takes only a moment. Don't leave it, or it may burn. The proportion for the meringue is: For every white of egg beaten stiff add 2 tablespoons of sugar. Flavor with ¼ teaspoon vanilla.

Prune Whip

Put cooked sweetened prunes through a fruit press or grind them in a food grinder. Add 2 egg whites, a pinch of salt, 2 teaspoons lemon juice and a little of the grated rind. Beat with a rotary beater or in an electric beater until stiff. Pile in sherbet glasses and place in the refrigerator while the dinner is eaten, if this dessert is made at the last minute. It may be prepared ahead of time. Serve with cream sweetened and flavored with vanilla. Cooked figs, apricots or peaches may be used instead of the prunes.

Last Minute Dessert

This dessert is assembled in the kitchen just before it is served. It may be made in individual portions or in 1 large dessert and sliced at the table. For the individual portions use slices of any kind of unfrosted cake. For the larger dessert use a slice cut lengthwise of the cake or if the cake is round, cut across it. Pile the cake with ice cream. Cover with meringue at least 1½ inches thick. Completely cover the top and sides with meringue. Slip under the gas flame for a moment until a delicate brown. Serve immediately. For the meringue: For every egg white beaten until stiff, use 2 tablespoons of sugar and ¼ teaspoon vanilla.

Hot Chocolate Sauce

A quick and unusual hot chocolate sauce for ice cream is made by melting chocolate peppermints in a double boiler over hot water. Melt while preparing the meal, stirring to blend as it melts and leave in the double boiler to keep hot until you wish to serve it.

Honeydew Melon with Green Grapes

Cut honeydew melon into balls with a vegetable cutter. Add small seedless green grapes of the canned variety together with their juice. Chill thoroughly. Cantaloupe or watermelon may be used instead of the honeydew melon.

Cantaloupe with Raspberry Sherbet

Cut cantaloupe across the melon in 1 inch thick circles. Remove the skin. Pile the center with raspberry sherbet. Lemon sherbet may be substituted for the raspberry. Sprinkle the top of the lemon sherbet with crushed peppermint candy of the light brittle variety.

Figs and Apple Sauce

Slice skinless preserved figs in thin strips. There should be enough to fill 1 cup. Add ½ cup of fig syrup, 1 tablespoon lemon juice and 2 cups of cooked apple sauce. Heat together. Serve with cream sweetened with fig syrup. Serves 4.

Marmalade Rounds

Cut slices of bread with a large round cutter into rounds. Heat butter in a frying pan. Sauté the bread. Spread with ginger marmalade. Place a slice of rich American cheese on top. Soften under a broiler flame. Another variation of this dessert is to use mince meat instead of the marmalade. Spread the mince meat ¼ inch thick. Use either the melted cheese for the top or whipped cream.

CHAPTER XLVIII

CANDIES

Pralines

Place 2 cups of powdered sugar into a saucepan with 1 cup of maple syrup and ½ cup of cream. Stir until blended. Boil until a small amount of the mixture dropped into cold water will form a soft ball. If you use a thermometer it should reach 238° F. Remove from the fire. Let it cool until lukewarm. Beat until thick enough to drop onto oiled paper or a buttered dish. Just before it is finished stir in 2 cups of broken pecan meats. Drop from the spoon in cakes.

Cream Taffy

Place 2 cups of sugar with ½ cup of hot water and 1 tablespoon of vinegar into a saucepan. Stir over a low flame until dissolved. Boil without stirring until a small amount dropped into a glass of cold water will harden. Flavor with ½ teaspoon vanilla. Pour onto buttered plates. Let cool until it can be handled. Pull until the taffy is white and creamy. A square of bitter chocolate may be placed in the center of each piece of candy for chocolate taffy. The warmth melts the chocolate and it may be pulled into the taffy. Cut into 1 inch squares.

Fudge

Heat ⅔ cup of milk with 2 squares of bitter chocolate. Heat slowly and when the chocolate is melted beat for a moment with a Dover egg beater until the mixture is smooth and well blended. Add 2 cups of sugar and stir until it boils. Continue cooking without stirring until a little of the liquid will form a soft ball when dropped into a glass of cold water, or boil to 238° F. Flavor with vanilla, cool slightly and beat until thick and creamy. Pour onto a buttered plate and when cool mark into squares. Nuts may be added for nut fudge just before candy is poured out. For marshmallow fudge arrange marshmallows about 1 inch apart on a plate. Pour the fudge over them and when cool cut so that a marshmallow will be in the center of each piece.

Brown Sugar Fudge

Place 2 cups of brown sugar and 1 cup of granulated sugar in a saucepan. Add 1 cup of milk and 2 squares of bitter chocolate cut into small pieces. Cook until a little dropped into cold water will form a soft ball (238° F.). Add 1 tablespoon of butter and 1 teaspoon of vanilla. Cool slightly and beat until thick. Broken nut meats may be added just before the fudge is finished. Turn onto buttered plate and mark into squares when cool. Marshmallow fudge is made by stirring in cut marshmallow just as the beating is finished. One half pint of stiffly beaten whipped cream may be added just before finishing. Omit the marshmallows if cream is added.

Panocha

Put 3 cups of brown sugar into a saucepan. Add ¾ cup of milk and 2 large tablespoons of butter. Cook until a little dropped into cold water will form a soft ball (238° F.). Flavor with vanilla. Remove from the fire, cool slightly and beat until thick and creamy. Pour onto a buttered plate. Mark in squares when cool. Nuts or marshmallows may be added just before the candy is poured out to cool.

Divinity Candy

Combine 2½ cups of sugar with ½ cup of corn syrup and ½ cup of water. Cook until a little of the syrup will form a soft ball when dropped into cold water (238° F.). Pour the syrup in a thin stream on the stiffly beaten whites of 2 eggs, beating constantly as you pour. Flavor with ½ teaspoon of vanilla. Stir until thick. Add ½ cup of chopped walnut meats, 1 tablespoon of chopped candied orange peel, 1 tablespoon of chopped candied cherries and 1 tablespoon of chopped candied pineapple. Drop in spoonfuls onto a buttered plate. The fruit may be omitted and only the nuts used.

Walnut Creams

Beat the white of 1 egg slightly with 1 tablespoon of water. Add sifted confectioners' sugar, a little at a time, stirring between each addition. When the mixture is thick enough to knead put on a board and knead it. Flavor with a few drops of vanilla. Mould into individual candies. Press a half walnut into the center of each candy. A variation of this is made by using bits of candied fruit instead of the nuts.

Butterscotch

Put ½ cup of molasses into a saucepan. Add ½ cup of sugar and 6 tablespoons of water and ¼ pound of butter. Stir until the ingredients are thoroughly dissolved. Boil until brittle when dropped into water. Pour into shallow buttered plates and break when brittle.

Candied Grapefruit or Orange Peel

The grapefruit and the orange peel are made exactly the same. Peel the fruit. For this amount use 4 thin skinned grapefruits. Cover with water and cook until tender. Drain and remove the white portion with a teaspoon. Cut the skin into long thin strips. Boil 1½ cups of sugar with ⅔ cup of water until it will spin a thread. Cook the fruit in it 5 minutes. Drain and spread on waxed paper. Sprinkle with granulated sugar.

Sugared Pecans

Heat halved pecans very slowly in a pan. Dust with brown sugar and cinnamon and set in a warm oven for a few moments.

Pineapple Creams

Put 3 cups of sugar into a saucepan. Add 1 cup of milk, 2 teaspoons vanilla and 1 tablespoon of butter. Boil until a little dropped into a glass of cold water will form a soft ball (238° F.). Remove from the fire and beat until creamy. Add 1 cup of chopped candied pineapple. Pour into buttered pans, cool and mark into squares.

Maplelines

Measure 2 cups of powdered sugar, add 1 cup of shaved maple sugar and ¾ cup of cream. Cook until it will form a soft ball when a little is dropped into cold water, or boil to 238° F. Cool slightly and beat until thick and creamy. Drop from a spoon onto oiled paper.

CHAPTER XLIX

JAMS, JELLIES AND PICKLES

Cucumber Pickles

Wash cucumber pickles. Put them into an earthen jar with a cover. Mix together: 4 cups of cider vinegar, ¼ cup of salt, ¼ cup of dry mustard and ¼ cup of sugar. Pour over the pickles. Keep covered with the earthen lid in a cool place.

Cranberry Relish

Chop 1 cup of raw cranberries fine. Add ½ cup of sifted powdered sugar, ½ cup of orange juice and ⅛ teaspoon grated orange peel. Let get very cold in the refrigerator. Drain just before serving.

Cantaloupe Pickles

Slice the cantaloupe. Remove the seeds and peel. Cut into dice. Just bring the fruit to the boiling point in salted water. Use 1 teaspoon of salt for every quart of water. Drain the fruit. Measure the fruit. To every cup of fruit use ¼ cup of brown sugar, ¼ cup of vinegar, 1 teaspoon whole mace, 1 teaspoon whole cloves, 1 teaspoon whole cinnamon. Boil this sauce together for 5 minutes. Pour the hot sauce over the fruit. Keep in an earthenware crock with a cover, or seal in sterilized glass jars.

Currant and Mint Sauce

Cover 1 cup of stemmed washed currants with ⅔ cup of powdered sugar. Stir until well coated. [...] ice box for several hours. At serving time [...] ed mint.

Strawberry [...]

Remove the stems from stra[...] them. Mash them and boil 5 [...] measure of sugar. Boil 5 minu[...] glasses. Seal with melted paraffi[...] for raspberries, blackberries or l[...]

Gooseberry

Remove the stems from 1 pound [...] water. When the water is boiling hard, [...] Cook covered 5 minutes. Add 1 pint suga[...] utes longer. Put up in glasses as in preceding [...]

Apricots

Boil 1 pint water in a saucepan. Remove the stones fr[...] 24 apricots. Add them to the boiling water. Cover and cook 5 minutes. Add 2 measuring cups sugar and cook 3 minutes longer.

Cranberries

Heat 1 pint water in a saucepan. Add 1 pound cranberries to the water when it boils. Cook rapidly 5 minutes. Cover the pan while it cooks. Stir in 1 pint sugar and cook 3 minutes longer.

Peaches

Boil 4 cups water. Peel and slice enough peaches to make

4 cups. Add them to the rapidly boiling water. Cover and cook hard 5 minutes. Add 4 cups sugar. Cook 3 minutes longer.

Grape Jelly

Wash Concord grapes. Mash them and cook 10 minutes in a kettle. Strain the juice through a sieve. Measure the juice. For every measure of juice add an equal amount of sugar. Cook until some of the liquid, dropped on a cool plate, will form a jelly.

Crabapple Jelly

Cut crabapples into small pieces, leaving the skin on and the seeds intact. To every quart of crabapples use 1 quart boiling water. Cook 15 minutes in a kettle. Strain the juice through a sieve. To every cup of juice use 1 cup sugar. Cook until the juice, dropped on a saucer, forms a jelly. Pour into hot, sterilized glasses. Cover the top with melted paraffin.

Currant Jelly

Wash the currants. Leave the stems on. Mash them. Put in a kettle and cook 10 minutes. Strain through a sieve. To every cup of juice add 1 cup sugar. Cook until the liquid will form a jelly when dropped on a cool saucer. Pour into hot sterilized glasses and seal with melted paraffin.

Chili Sauce

Use 12 ripe peeled tomatoes or 1 quart canned tomatoes, 4 green peppers chopped, 2 onions chopped, 2 level tablespoons salt, 4 tablespoons sugar, 1 tablespoon cinnamon, 3 cups vinegar. Boil all together ½ hour. This may be kept in a sealed glass jar or in jelly glasses sealed with melted paraffin.

Olive Oil Pickles

Use 24 medium-size cucumbers sliced thin, 12 tiny onions sliced thin, 1 cup salt, 1 cup white mustard seed, 1 tablespoon celery seed, 1 cup olive oil and white vinegar as explained later. Cover the cucumbers and onions with salt. Let stand a few minutes. Drain and wash. Put a layer of pickles in a stone jar.

Add mustard seed, celery seed and olive oil. Repeat until all is used. Pour in white vinegar until all is covered. Keep in the jar.

Chopped Pickle

Use 12 green tomatoes chopped, 4 sweet red peppers chopped, 2 onions chopped. Add ⅓ cup salt. Let stand a few minutes, drain. Add 1 cup sugar, 2 cups vinegar. Mix in a kettle. Bring to a boil only. Seal in jars. It may be kept in a crock.

Ripe Tomato Pickle

Peel and chop 4 ripe tomatoes. Chop fine 1 green bell pepper. Chop fine 1 onion. Mix and drain until dry. Add to the drained vegetables a mixture of 1¼ cups sugar, 1¼ cups vinegar, 1 level tablespoon salt. Do not cook. If a larger amount is made, it may be put in glass jars and stored in a cool place. This recipe may be varied by adding 1 teaspoon curry powder.

Sweet Fruit Pickles

Plums, crabapples, peaches, pears or watermelon rind are used for these pickles. The fruit is left whole, except in the case of watermelon rind, which is peeled and cut into inch cubes. Parboil whichever fruit you use in salted water. This means just bring to a boil. Drain and combine with the sweet pickle sauce given below:

Sweet Pickle Sauce

To 2 cups of fruit use ½ cup brown sugar, ½ cup vinegar, 2 teaspoons whole spices of mace, cinnamon and cloves. Boil this in a saucepan 5 minutes. Pour the sauce over the fruit. Keep in a stone jar or seal in glass jars.

Sweet Vegetable Pickles

Use any vegetables in season, such as green beans, tiny cucumbers, pearl onions or cauliflower. Clean and remove tough skins or seeds. Cut into convenient pieces. Bring to the boiling point in salted water. Drain and combine with either the sweet pickle sauce given above or mustard sauce made as follows:

Mustard Pickle Sauce

Use 2 cups vinegar, 1 ounce mustard, 1 teaspoon turmeric (which may be purchased at any drug store), 2 tablespoons flour, ¼ to ½ cup sugar. The amount of sugar depends upon whether you want a sharp mustard pickle or a sweet one. Mix the mustard, sugar, flour and turmeric. Add the vinegar. Cook in a double boiler until thickened. Combine with the vegetables.

Red Cinnamon Apples

Peel and core 8 small apples. Make a syrup of 2 cups of sugar, 1½ cups of water. Add ½ cup of red cinnamon candies and cook until the apples are tender, but not broken. This should take about 30 minutes.

CHAPTER L

COFFEE, TEA AND CHOCOLATE

Filtered Coffee

Use 2 tablespoons of finely ground coffee for each cup of boiling water. Filtered coffee is made in a special coffee pot which has a sieve-like container to hold the coffee. The boiling water is poured over the coffee, a little at a time. Cover closely and keep in a warm place while the coffee is filtering.

Percolated Coffee

Use 2 tablespoons of ground coffee for every cup of water. Place the coffee in the strainer. Measure the water. Put into the percolator. Let percolate 5 minutes after the water sprays over the coffee. Do not percolate longer or the coffee will lose its flavor.

Boiled Coffee

Measure the water and heat it in the coffee pot. Use 2 tablespoons of coffee for every cup of water. When the water is boiling stir in the coffee. Remove the coffee pot from the heat. Let stand 2 minutes. Pour ½ cup of cold water in to settle the grounds.

For boiled coffee made with egg use the same proportion of water and coffee. Use an egg to mix the coffee with and a little cold water. Put into the coffee pot with 1 cup of cold water. Let this just come to the boiling point. Add the desired amount of boiling water. Let boil 3 minutes. Add ½ cup of cold water to clear. Let stand a few minutes.

Tea

Make tea in a china, glass or earthen pot. Scald the tea pot. Pour the water out. Put in 1 teaspoon of tea for every cup in the warm teapot. Pour freshly boiling water—water that is boiling hard—over the tea. Let it steep 3 minutes, no longer. A tea ball or tea bag is a convenience and has the advantage of not allowing the tea to stand on the grounds, for the ball can be removed when the tea has steeped 3 minutes.

Chocolate

Heat 4 cups of milk and 2 cups of water in a double boiler. Add ½ cake bitter chocolate. When it is dissolved beat occasionally with a Dover egg beater. Sweeten to taste. Add ¼ teaspoon salt and 1 teaspoon vanilla. Beat until frothy. You may add whipped cream sweetened and flavored with vanilla to each cup.

SECTION SIX

THE MECHANICAL REFRIGERATOR

CHAPTER LI

CARE AND USE OF THE MECHANICAL ICE BOX

The initial cost of mechanical refrigerators has been reduced very considerably since their first appearance on the market. Their operating cost is trifling and the actual saving of money by practising efficient and economical handling and storing of food is well worth considering. Any housekeeper who needs and can afford a new refrigerator will be wise to consider the proved performances of the several leading mechanical types.

The mechanical refrigerator maintains a constant safety temperature of 50° F. in its general storage cabinet and new models have in addition special cabinets of lower temperature for the storage of foods which need more cold. There are beside, in them all, the freezing trays which produce the ice cubes that are so convenient and find so many new and delightful uses.

There are many foods which can be bought cheaper in larger quantities than the housewife could accommodate before the mechanical refrigerator came into being. Butter is a good example. A pound costs less than a half pound. Many of the fresh vegetables are somewhat cheaper in 2 pound lots and the same is true of berries in season. With the mechanical refrigerator in which to store the surplus it is possible to save the pennies and cut down the amount of time and effort spent in shopping.

There is another manner in which economy can be practised with the mechanical refrigerator and that is in the preservation of left over foods. The wholesalers and retailers of our food supplies have gone to great lengths to prevent spoilage of food in transit and it is only good business sense not to waste what is not actually used for a meal in the home.

It is also a great convenience to have emergency supplies and prepared dishes on hand. The unexpected guest or impromptu entertainment becomes a much simpler problem when your mechanical refrigerator will furnish forth the necessary dishes.

Among the prepared foods which can safely be kept for considerable time in a modern mechanical refrigerator are:

Salad Dressing in covered jars
Prepared Salad Vegetables, in wax paper or covered dish
Dough for Ice Box Rolls, covered in waxed paper
Pastry, covered in waxed paper
Aspic Jelly, in jars
Vegetables prepared for cooking, in container dish or wax paper wrapping
Chilled and Frozen Desserts
Soups, prepared in advance.

Various items for an emergency luncheon or party can be safely kept in the mechanical refrigerator. Among them are:

Tomato or Clam Juice Cocktails, bottled
Sandwich Supplies
Anchovies
Caviare
Olives
Pickles
Relishes
Meat Pastes
Pimentos in covered jar

Parsley in covered jar or pan
Dessert Sauces in covered jars.

In hot weather the mechanical refrigerator is a great convenience since menus for the day can be prepared in advance and stored for use. Also it allows us to have cold soups and crisp, fresh salads and delicious frozen desserts.

All manner of frozen desserts may be prepared in this way. It is well to bear in mind that the old time recipes for ice cream, mousses and similar dishes must be modified to meet the dry air atmosphere of the mechanical refrigerator.

By the use of whipped cream and beaten egg whites more smoothly frozen desserts can be obtained. Evaporated milk well scalded then chilled can be whipped and will blend smoothly. It is necessary to remember however that this should be used only in such preparations as mayonnaise where a sharp flavor added to the recipe covers the taste of the milk. A small amount of gelatine added to the frozen desserts insures evener freezing. In many of the recipes given in the section following it is recommended that the ingredients be stirred *during* the freezing process. I wish to emphasize this direction again since it is highly necessary that mousses and similar frozen delicacies should be velvety in quality.

The care of a mechanical refrigerator is exceedingly simple and based on several basic laws.

The inside of these modern machines is finished usually in a beautiful heavy porcelain applied to metal. It can be kept spotless as simply as any fine china dish.

The mechanical refrigerator should be kept clean, of course, and every dish placed in it should be clean.

Do not place for storage foods wrapped in bags or covers of ordinary absorbent papers. This stores heat and makes the problem of refrigeration more difficult. Use waxed paper wherever paper wrapping is recommended.

The circulation of air in the mechanical refrigerator

should be constant. Cold air drops from the chilling unit and warm air from the stored food rises. Do not overcrowd the shelves or place articles too tightly against the walls. Let the air pass freely and better results will be insured.

The moisture from the fresh air admitted when the door is opened as well as the moisture given off by food collects on the sides of the freezing unit in form of frost. Frost prevents the unit working at complete efficiency when too thick. The makers of mechanical refrigerators always caution users to de-frost the machine regularly and enclose instructions how this is to be done. Careful attention must be given to these directions.

Ice cubes can best be taken from the trays in which they are frozen by setting the tray in a dish of cold water for 30 seconds. This will loosen the cubes. Still more convenient is the flexible rubber tray for ice cubes. It is true the ice freezes more slowly in the rubber tray, but it will remain frozen longer and it is very simple, by bending the tray, to disengage one or more cubes when wanted.

A vegetable pan of enamel is a most useful accessory for the mechanical refrigerator. All vegetables should be kept covered and the fruits too except such fruits as are protected by a thick skin. These pans are fitted with a specially designed cover.

Glass refrigerator dishes are convenient. The glass oven dish has been adapted to dual use now, but you must bear in mind that no glass dish can be taken from the refrigerator and put into the oven without warming first in warm, not hot water. If you disregard this warning you are pretty certain to have a broken dish. Nor should the glass dish be taken directly from the oven and put in the refrigerator. In that case it should be allowed to chill before transferring.

Various types of crockery bowls are made especially for use in the new refrigerators. They are useful and attractive and their flat lids make it possible to stack them and save in storage space, though it is well to keep in mind that air should move freely about each dish. The water bottle is another most useful accessory for the mechanical refrigerator. It insures a supply of cold, fresh drinking water at all times.

Because of the extremely dry air of the mechanical refrigerator food stored in it does not mingle its flavors or odors and bacterial growth is much slower. But it is a mistake to store food such as fruits or vegetables that have bad spots. Remove these spots before storage and of course never store food which has already deteriorated.

The recipes which follow will give you a very brief idea of some of the delicious desserts which may be prepared with very little labor by using the mechanical refrigerator. Recipes for other dishes especially adapted to the mechanical refrigerator will be found under the various classifications in this book.

CHAPTER LII

FROZEN REFRIGERATOR DESSERTS

Apricot Macaroon Mousse

Soak 1 cup of macaroon crumbs in 1 cup of apricot juice from canned apricots. Whip ½ pint of cream stiff. Combine with the crumb mixture. Freeze 3 hours in refrigerator pan. Serve with half an apricot on each dessert. Serves 4.

Pineapple Mousse

Heat 2 cups crushed pineapple. Add ¾ cup sugar and 2 teaspoons of gelatine that has been soaked in 4 tablespoons of cold water. Cool the mixture. Put in the refrigerator. When the mixture begins to set, fold in 2 cups of cream which has been beaten stiff. Pour into refrigerator pan. Stir occasionally as it freezes. Freeze for 3 hours. Serves 8.

Maple Parfait

Beat 3 eggs. Pour ¾ cup maple syrup over them. Beat. Cook in the double boiler, stirring constantly until thick. Cool. Put in refrigerator. When cold fold in 2 cups of cream beaten until stiff. Freeze in drawer of automatic refrigerator 3 hours. Stir occasionally as it freezes. Serves 6.

The white of the eggs may be saved and used for angel parfait.

Angel Parfait

Boil ¾ cup of sugar with ⅓ cup of water until it will

spin a thread. Pour in a thin, steady stream, beating constantly over the whites of 3 stiffly beaten eggs. Beat until cool. Add 1 pint of stiffly beaten cream. Freeze in the drawer of automatic refrigerator for 3 hours. This may be served in sherbet glasses with a tablespoon of crushed, sweetened berries in the bottom. Pile the parfait in the glasses. Put more crushed berries over the top. Serves 6.

Coffee Mousse

Whip 2 cups of cream stiff. Beat in ½ cup of sifted, powdered sugar. Add ½ cup of very strong cold coffee. Freeze in automatic refrigerator pan for 3 hours. Stir occasionally as it freezes. Serves 4.

Raspberry Mousse

Whip 1 pint heavy cream stiff. Add ½ cup sifted, powdered sugar. Add ¾ cup of raspberry juice and combine. Put in refrigerator pan and chill 3 hours. Serves 4. Any other fruit juice may be substituted for the raspberry.

Strawberry Mousse

Wash and stem 2 cups of strawberries. Crush them. Add 1 cup sugar. Just bring to the boiling point. Put through a sieve. Add 1 teaspoon gelatine dissolved in 2 tablespoons cold water. Chill. Add 1 pint of whipped cream, then the stiffly beaten whites of 2 eggs. Put in the drawer of automatic refrigerator. Freeze 3 hours. Stir occasionally as it freezes. Serves 6.

Cherry Ice Cream

Put ½ cup of cherry preserves through a sieve or a fruit press. Beat with a rotary beater with 1 pint of single cream.

Place in drawer of automatic refrigerator. Freeze to a mush. Remove to a chilled bowl. Beat with a rotary beater. Add ⅓ cup chopped candied cherries. Return to refrigerator pan and finish freezing. Any preserved fruit may be substituted for the cherries.

Vanilla Ice Cream

Place 1½ cups of rich milk in the double boiler. Heat it. Beat the yolks of 3 eggs. Add ½ cup of sugar sifted with 1 tablespoon flour and ⅛ teaspoon salt. Pour a little of the hot milk over the egg mixture. Add to the milk. Cook until the mixture coats the spoon. Add 2 teaspoons of vanilla and 1 teaspoon of gelatine dissolved in 2 tablespoons water. Cool. Put in the refrigerator pan. When frozen to a mush beat with a rotary beater in a chilled bowl. Add 1 cup of cream whipped. Return to pan and finish freezing. Serves 4.

Chocolate Ice Cream may be made from this recipe by cooking 1 square of chocolate in the custard.

Biscuit Tortoni

Soak ½ cup of fine macaroon crumbs in 1 cup of thin cream. Add ¼ cup sugar. Mix well. Let stand in refrigerator 1 hour. Whip 1 cup of cream until stiff. Add the macaroon mixture slowly, blending well. Flavor with ¼ teaspoon almond extract and ½ teaspoon vanilla. Place in paper cases. Dust the tops with fine macaroon crumbs. Freeze 2 hours in the pan of the automatic refrigerator.

Chocolate Ice Box Cake

½ Pound Cake Sweet Chocolate
4 Tablespoons Hot Water
4 Eggs
4 Tablespoons Sugar
Lady Fingers
Whipped Cream
1 Teaspoon Vanilla

Melt the chocolate with the hot water in a double boiler. Add the sugar. Add the beaten egg yolks. Cook over hot water, stirring constantly until smooth. Cool. Add vanilla. Stir in the stiffly beaten egg whites. Line a spring form mould with lady fingers, covering the sides and bottom. Cover with the chocolate mixture. Alternate cakes and filling until mould is full. Place in the ice box. Let stand for three or four hours. Unmould on a large cake plate. Decorate with flavored sweetened whipped cream.

Pineapple Refrigerator Cake

½ Cup Butter
1 Cup Sugar
1 Egg
2 Tablespoons Cream
2 Cups Drained, Crushed Pineapple

Pineapple Juice
3 Cups Graham Cracker Crumbs
½ Pint Whipped Cream
Candied Cherries

Cream butter and sugar together until light and fluffy. Add beaten egg, pineapple and cream. Put a layer ½ inch thick of graham cracker crumbs in the bottom of a buttered spring mould. Moisten with 4 tablespoons pineapple juice. Add a layer of pineapple mixture. Repeat, adding alternate layers of crumbs, pineapple juice and the pineapple mixture. Chill in the refrigerator 6 to 8 hours or longer. It may stay as long as 24 hours. Remove from the mould. Decorate with sweetened, flavored whipped cream. Garnish with candied cherries. Crushed berries and their juice may be substituted for the pineapple.

Lemon Sherbet

4 Tablespoons Lemon Juice
1 Cup Sugar

2 Cups Rich Milk

Stir the lemon juice and sugar until the sugar is dissolved.

Add the milk. Chill. Place in refrigerator pan. When the sherbet is cold enough to be mushy remove the pan and stir. Repeat the stirring twice at half hour intervals. Freeze 3 hours. Serves 4.

Orange Ice

⅔ Cup Sugar
⅓ Cup Light Corn Syrup
½ Cup Water

1⅔ Cup Orange Juice
3 Tablespoons Lemon Juice

Cook the sugar, corn syrup and water until it forms a soft ball when a little of the syrup is dropped from a spoon into a glass of cold water or until a candy thermometer registers 238° F. Remove from the stove. Add the fruit juices. Chill. Place in refrigerator pan. When it begins to freeze remove the pan and stir. Repeat stirring twice at half hour intervals. Finish freezing without any more stirring. Serves 6.

Orange Sherbet

1 Teaspoon Gelatine
¼ Cup Cold Water
¾ Cup Sugar
¼ Cup Confectioners' Sugar
¾ Cup Boiling Water

1 Egg
½ Cup Lemon Juice
¾ Cup Orange Juice
Grated Rind of 1 Orange

Soak the gelatine in cold water. Dissolve sugar and gelatine in the boiling water. Add the orange rind and fruit juices. Chill. Place in tray of refrigerator. Freeze to a mush. Beat cream stiff. Add confectioners' sugar. Beat egg white stiff. Add egg yolks and combine with the cream. Fold the cream mixture into the frozen mixture. Return to refrigerator pan. Stir twice at half hour intervals. Finish freezing without further stirring. Serves 4.

Pineapple Sherbet

1 Teaspoon Gelatine
¼ Cup Water
½ Cup Sugar
1 Cup Pineapple Juice

1 Cup Crushed Pineapple
2 Tablespoons Lemon Juice
2 Egg Whites

Soak the gelatine in the water. Heat the pineapple juice with the sugar. Add the gelatine. Chill. Add lemon juice and crushed fruit. Pour into freezing pan. Freeze for 1 hour. Remove, stir and fold in the beaten egg whites. Return to refrigerator. Stir twice at half hour intervals, then finish freezing without further stirring. Serves 6.

Cranberry Sherbet

1 Pound Cranberries
4 Tablespoons Lemon Juice
¾ Cup Water
1⅔ Cup Confectioners' Sugar

½ Cup Water
3 Tablespoons Gelatine
3 Egg Whites
½ Pint Whipping Cream

Cook the cranberries in 1 cup water for 5 minutes. Crush and put through a fruit press. Dissolve gelatine in ½ cup water. Boil sugar and water 3 minutes. Add the gelatine to this and cool. Add lemon juice. Add cranberries and chill. Put into freezing tray. When frozen to a mush add well beaten egg whites. Whip cream. Add. Stir twice at half hour intervals. Freeze. Serves 8.

Peppermint Ice Cream

¼ Pound Peppermint Candy
¾ Cup Milk
2 Tablespoons Gelatine

¼ Cup Water
2 Cups Whipping Cream

Dissolve the gelatine in water. Dissolve the candy in the milk in a double boiler. Add the gelatine. Chill. Whip the cream. Add the cream to the chilled mixture. Place in refrigerator pan. When frozen to a mush stir. Stir twice at half hour intervals. Continue freezing without further stirring. Serves 6.

Yellow Parfait

½ Cup Sugar
¼ Cup Water
4 Egg Yolks

1 Teaspoon Vanilla
1½ Cups Whipping Cream

Boil sugar and water until it spins a thread. Pour over well beaten egg yolks. Cook in a double boiler until smooth and slightly thickened. Chill. Pour into refrigerator pan. When this is beginning to freeze add whipped cream flavored with vanilla. Freeze for half hour, stir and stir again after another 30 minute interval. Finish freezing. Serves 6.

Chilled Fruit

Pour a medium sized can of fruit into the refrigerator tray. When it is partially frozen serve with whipped cream which has been flavored and sweetened. Decorate with maraschino cherries.

Coffee Mallow

20 Marshmallows
1 Cup Hot Coffee

1 Cup Cream
1 Teaspoon Vanilla

Melt the marshmallows in the coffee. Stir until smooth. Add vanilla and chill until slightly thickened. Beat whipped cream and add it. Freeze without stirring.

Banana Mallow

20 Marshmallows
1 Tablespoon Lemon Juice
⅔ Cup Boiling Water

1 Cup Crushed Bananas
1 Cup Whipping Cream

Melt the marshmallows in the boiling water. Add the bananas, after they have been put through a fruit press. Add the lemon juice and chill. When slightly thickened add whipped cream. Place in refrigerator tray and freeze without stirring.

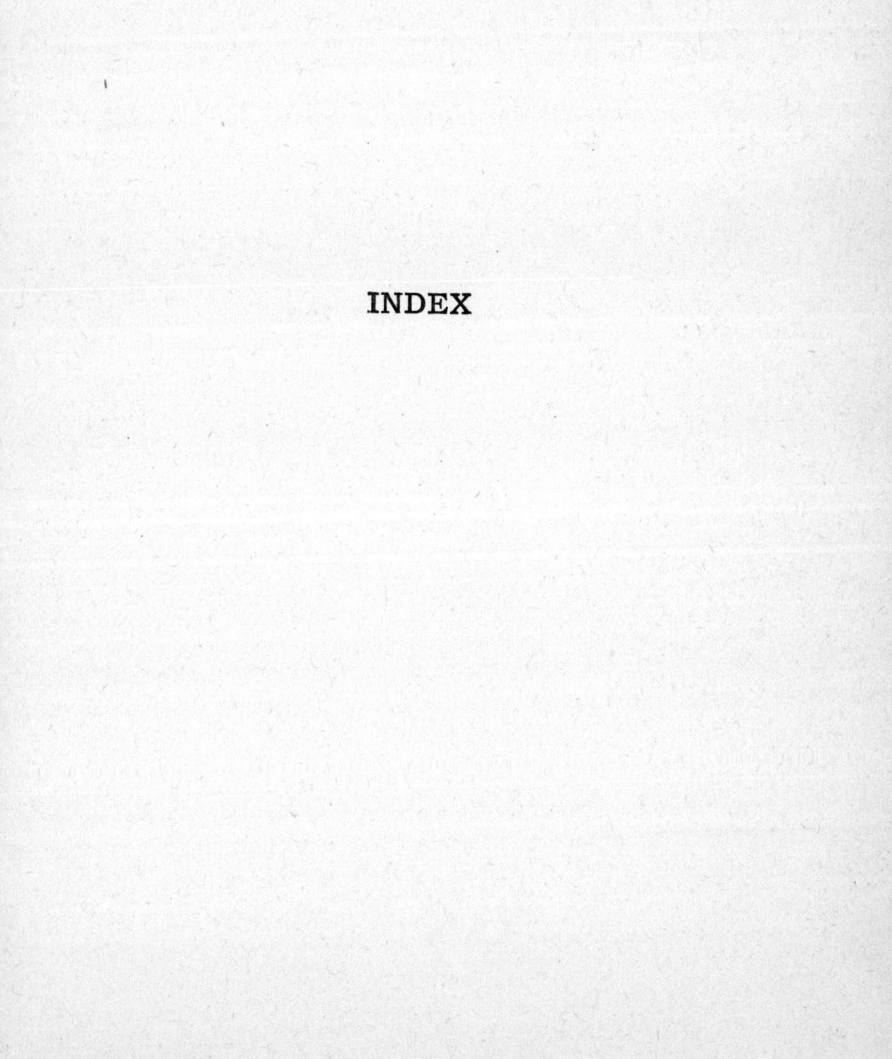

INDEX

INDEX

A

Alligator Pear with Orange Salad, 312
Alligator Pear Salad, 105, 143, 238
Alligator Pear Soup, 263
Aluminum Ware, Uses of, 25
Aluminum, Care of, 25
Ambrosia Salad, 314
Antipasto, 200
Anchovy Canapés, 205
Anchovy Sandwich, 226
Angel Food, 342
Angel Food Whip, 375
Angel Parfait, 395
Anchovy Salad, 314
Apple Dumplings, 364
Apple Butter and Pound Cake, 376
Apples and Cheese, 375
Apple Pie, 335
Apple and Onion Salad, 112-113
Apples in Syrup with Cream, 115-116
Apples, Fried, 111-112
Apple, Cabbage and Red Pepper Salad, 108-109
Apple and Raisin Conserve, 126-127
Apple and Cheese Canapé, 206
Apricot Skillet Cake, 370
Apricot Macaroon Mousse, 395
Apricots, Cooked, 384
Apricots, Cooked, 101-102
Artichokes, 296
Asparagus, 302
Asparagus with Lemon Butter Sauce, 120-121
Asparagus Tip Canapé, 204
Asparagus Salad, 259
Avocado and Crab Salad, 313
Avocado Canapés, 205
Avocado Sandwich, 227

B

Bacon and Vegetables, 305
Baked Red Bananas, 373
Banana Mallow, 401
Baked Custard, 371
Baked Pears, 371
Baked Rice Pudding, 367
Baking Powder Biscuit, 326
Banana Salad, 103-104
Bananas and Oranges, Baked, 112-113
Bananas, Baked, with Cream, 87
Bar-Le-Duc and Cream Cheese Sandwich, 231
Bavarian Cream, 369
Beef, Deviled Roast, 282
Beef Stew with Vegetables, 277
Beef with Vegetables, 90-91
Beef, Dried, with Scrambled Eggs, 92-93
Beef, Creamed Dried, 101-102
Beef, Roast, 174-175
Beef Filet, Planked, 187-188
Beef, How to Buy, 86
Berry Pudding, 137
Berry Pies, 336
Beets, Pickled and Stuffed, 202
Beet Salad, 144-145
Beet Soup, 269
Biscuits, Errors to Avoid, 85
Biscuit Tortoni, 397
Biscuits, 252
Birthday Cake Icing, 356
Birthday Cake, 356
Black Fruit Cake, 356
Blini Canapé, 208
Blueberry Pudding, 373
Blueberry Pancakes, 135
Boiled Custards, Common Mistakes in Making, 80
Boiled Icing, 351
Boiled Salad Dressing, 310

405

INDEX

Borsch (Russian Soup), 263
Bouillabaisse, 267
Boston Cream Pie Filling, 351
Bran Muffins, 243
Bread, Graham, 332
Bread, White, 330
Bread, Cinnamon, 330
Bread, Date, 331
Broccoli, 294
Broiling, Errors to Avoid, 84
Broilers, 58
Brownies, 359
Brown Sugar Fudge, 380
Brussels Sprouts, 153-154
Buffet Supper Menus, 257
Butterfly Cakes, 346
Butterscotch, 381
Butter Cake (Layer or Cup Cakes), 351

C

Cabbage and Apple Salad, 171-172
Cabbage, Creamed, 133
Cabbage Salad, 126-127
Cabbage Salad, Hot, 116-117
Cabbage with Apple, 302
Cabbage, Scalloped, 302
Cabbage, Stuffed, 288
Calves Liver and Bacon, 129

CAKES

Common Errors in Baking, 79
Angel Food, 342
Birthday Cake, 356
Black Fruit Cake, 356
Butterfly Cakes, 346
Butter Cake (Layer or Cup Cakes), 351
Caramel Cake, 345
Cinnamon Cake, 331
Cocoa Cake, 352
Cocoanut Cake, 343, 348
Chocolate Cake, 343, 353
Chocolate Ice Box Cake, 397
Devil's Food, 347
Frosted Raisin Spice Cake, 355
Fruit Cake, 354
Fruit Cake Steamed with Maple Sauce, 103-104
Gingerbread, Frosted, 136
Gingerbread, 350
Golden Cake, 353

Gommy's Cake, 353
Hallowe'en Orange Cake, 247
Hallowe'en Cake Decorations, 248
Holly Cakes, 252
Ice Cream Cake, 347
Lady Baltimore Cake, 346
Orange Cake, 247
Pineapple Ice Box Cake, 365
Pineapple Upside Down Cake, 366
Sponge Cake, 349
Sponge Cake Shortcake, 368
Strawberry Shortcake, 368
Waffle Cake, Chocolate, 320
Waffle Shortcake, Strawberry, Orange, 319
Waffle Cake, 321
Walnut Spice Cake, 344
White Almond Cake, 349

Candied Grapefruit or Orange Peel, 381
Cantaloupe Pickles, 383
Cantaloupe with Raspberry Sherbet, 377

CANAPÉS

Apple and Cheese, 206
Anchovy Canapé, 205
Asparagus Tip Canapé, 204
Avocado Canapé, 205
Blini, 208
Caviare Canapé, 204
Cheese and Mustard Butter Canapé, 206
Cheese and Onion Canapé, 205
Lobster Canapé, 207
Mushroom Canapé, 207
Peanut Butter and Bacon, 205
Pickled Mussels, 207
Prunes and Bacon, 206
Sardine Canapé, 205
Stuffed Olives and Bacon, 207
Surprise Canapé, 206
Water Cress and Shrimp, 207

CANDIES

Candy, Errors to Avoid, 82
Candy Making Temperatures, 15
Candy Thermometer, 14
Brown Sugar Fudge, 380
Butterscotch, 381

INDEX

Candied Orange Peel, 381
Cream Taffy, 379
Divinity Candy, 381
Fudge, 379
Mapleines, 382
Panocha, 380
Pineapple Creams, 382
Pralines, 379
Sugared Pecans, 382
Walnut Creams, 381

Carrots, Creamed, 127-128
Carrot Cups with Peas, 293
Casseroles, Various Types, 53
Caramel Frosting, 345
Casserole of Pork Chops, 289
Cauliflower au Gratin, 292
Cauliflower, 132, 301
Caviare Canapé, 204
Celery, Creamed, Minced Red Pepper, 133, 154-155
Celery and Avocado Hors D'Oeuvres, 204
Celery and Chicken Hors D'Oeuvres, 204
Celery and Shrimp Hors D'Oeuvres, 203
Chicken Bouillon Decoration, 249
Chicken Dinner Menu, 256
Chicken with Mushrooms and Sweetbreads, 259
Chicken Patties, 247
Chicken Almond Sandwich, 240
Chicken Sandwich, 229
Chicken Casserole, 191-192
Chicken, Broiled, 114-115, 171-172
Chicken, Braised, 177-178
Chicken, Baked with Mushrooms, 130
Chicken, Fried, 120-121, 284
Chicken with Vegetables, 109-110
Chicken Bouillon, 269
Chicken Casserole, 285
Chicken, Roast with Poultry Dressing, 284
Chicken Salad, 313
Chicken Pie, 289
Cheese Sandwich Loaf, 239
Cheese and Mustard Butter Canapés, 206
Cheese and Onion Canapé, 205

Cheese and Ginger Sandwich, 228
Cherry Pie, 335
Cherry Ice Cream, 396
Chopped Pickle, 386
Charlotte Russe, 369
Chocolate, 389
Chocolate Ice Cream, 397
Chocolate Nut Kisses, 358
Chocolate Pecan Squares, 360
Chocolate Icing, 352
Chromium Ware, Cleaning, 27
China and Glassware Essentials, 69
Chili Con Carne, 288
Chili Sauce, 385
Chops, Casserole of, 121-122
Chilled Fruit, 401
Clam and Chicken Bouillon, 268
Clam Bouillon, 268
Clam Juice Cocktail, 199
Clam Juice and Tomato Cocktail, 199
Club Sandwich, Glorified, 245
Caramel Tapioca, 373
Cookery Terms Explained, 15
Color and Charm in the Kitchen, 18
Color in Sandwiches, 225
Codfish, Creamed, 112-113
Combination Salad, 172-173
Coffee Mallow, 401
Coffee Jelly, 374
Coffee Mousse, 396
Coffee, Boiled, 388
Coffee, Percolated, 388
Coffee, Filtered, 388
Cornmeal Pancakes, 325
Corn Bread, 323
Corn Beef and Potato Cakes, 306
Corn Soufflé, 150-151
Cornmeal Dodgers, 90-91
Corn and Tomatoes, 97-98
Corned Beef Hash with Eggs, 184-185

COCKTAILS
Cranberry Cocktail, 197
Currant and Raspberry, 198
Grapefruit and Prune, 197
Grape Juice Cocktail, 197
Lime Cocktail, 198
Loganberry Juice, 198

408 INDEX

Pineapple Crème de Menthe, 198
Sauerkraut Juice, 198
Tomato Juice Cocktail, 198
White Grape Juice, 196

COOKIES
Brownies, 359
Chocolate Pecan Squares, 360
Chocolate Nut Kisses, 358
Cream Cookies, 358
Cry Babies, 361
Doughnuts, 359
Drop Spice Cookies, 361
Grandmother's Cookies, 360
Hermits, 359
Ice Box Cookies, 362
Pecan Macaroons, 361
Cream Cookies, 358

Cream Pie, 340
Cream Sponge Pudding, 370
Cranberry Relish, 383
Crushed Strawberries, 374
Cranberry Tart, 372
Cream Taffy, 379
Crabapple Jelly, 385
Cranberries, 384
Crabapples, Pickled, 386
Cranberry Sherbet, 400
Cranberry and Pineapple Pie, 336
Cranberry Pie, 336
Cream of Asparagus Soup, 267
Cream of Spinach Soup, 266
Cream of Celery Soup, 266
Cream of Onion Soup, 266
Crab Croquettes, 272
Cranberries, Cooked, 108-109
Crab Meat, Planked, 185-186
Cranberry Cocktail, 197
Cream Pistachio Sandwich, 230
Cream of Tomato Soup, 265
Cream of Mushroom Soup, 265
Croutons, 264
Crab Salad, 249
Cream Sauce, Common Errors in Making, 80
Custard Pie, 338
Cucumber Pickles, 383
Currant Jelly, 385
Currant and Mint Sauce, 384
Curry, East Indian, 280
Cucumbers and Onions, 102-103

Cucumbers, Baked, 177-178
Currant and Raspberry Cocktail, 198
Cucumbers Hors D'Oeuvres, 202
Currant Cup, 242
Cucumber Salad, Moulded, 238
Custards, Common Mistakes in Making, 80

D

Date Conserve, 121-122
Date Custard, 136
Date Pie, 340
Date Pudding, 371
Decorative Ice Cubes, 231
Deep Fat Thermometer, 14
Delight Sandwich, 241

DESSERTS
Apple Compote, 373
Apple Dumplings, 364
Apricot Skillet Cake, 370
Baked Custards, 371
Baked Pears, 371
Baked Red Bananas, 373
Baked Rice Pudding, 367
Bavarian Cream, 369
Blueberry Pudding, 373
Caramel Tapioca, 373
Charlotte Russe, 369
Coffee Jelly, 374
Cranberry Tart, 372
Cream Sponge Pudding, 370
Crushed Strawberries, 374
Date Pudding, 371
Floating Island, 366
Grapefruit and Strawberries, 369
Hard Sauce, 363
Honeydew Melon with Ice Cream, 371
Jelly Roll, 372
Loganberry Pudding, 368
Maple Custard, 374
Orange and Banana Compote, 369
Peach and Cherry Compote, 365
Peach Fluff, 372
Peaches in Honey, 374
Pears in Grenadine with Ice Cream, 367
Pears and Raspberries, 374

Pineapple Cream, 368
Pineapple Ice Box Cake, 365
Pineapple Upside Down Cake, 366
Plum Pudding, 363
Raspberry Compote, 370
Rice Pudding, 367
Sponge Cake Shortcake, 368
Strawberry Shortcake, 368
Velvet Sauce, 364
Velvet Sponge Pudding, 364

Deviled Ham Sandwich, 231
Devil's Food, 347
Devil's Food Icing, 348
Divinity Candy, 381
Doughnuts, 359
Dried Beef Hors D'Oeuvres, 203
Drop Biscuits, 123-124
Drop Spice Cookies, 361
Duck, Broiled, 168-169
Duckling, Broiled, 283
Duck Dinner Menu, 256
Duck, Roast, 181-182, 285
Dumplings, 191-192
Dutch Ovens, How to Season, 26

E

East Indian Curry, 280
Eggs à la King, 306
Eggs, Stuffed, 201
Egg Cookers, 49
Eggplant with Lamb, 307
Eggplant, Stuffed, 308
Eggplant, Broiled, 171-172, 304
Eggplant, Sauté, 114-115
Eggplant, Chopped, 302
Electric Utility Motors, 51
Electric Stoves, for Kitchen Use, 50
Electric Ranges, Costs, 28
Electric Table Stoves, 32
Electric Toasters, 49
Emergency Shelf, 62
Endive, Cooked with Cream, 91-92
Endive Salad with Roquefort Cheese Dressing, 115-116
Endive on Toast, 303
Endive Salad, 314
English Mutton Chops, 97-98

Envelope Biscuit, 327
Entertaining Without a Maid, 73
Enamel Ware, Uses of, 25

F

Fat Frying Temperatures, 15
Figs and Apple Sauce, 377
Fish Chowder, Curried, 108-109
Floating Island, 118-119, 366
Flounder with Tartar Sauce, 99-100
Flounder, Baked, 166-167
French Pancakes, 325
French Dressing, 235, 312
Fried Chicken, 259
Fritter Batter, 328

FROZEN REFRIGERATOR DESSERTS

Frozen Dessert Errors, 81
Angel Parfait, 395
Apricot Macaroon Mousse, 395
Banana Mallow, 401
Biscuit Tortoni, 397
Cherry Ice Cream, 396
Chilled Fruit, 401
Chocolate Ice Box Cake, 397
Chocolate Ice Cream, 397
Coffee Mallow, 401
Coffee Mousse, 396
Cranberry Sherbet, 400
Lemon Sherbet, 398
Maple Parfait, 395
Orange Ice, 399
Orange Sherbet, 399
Peppermint Ice Cream, 400
Pineapple Mousse, 395
Pineapple Refrigerator Cake, 398
Pineapple Sherbet, 400
Raspberry Mousse, 396
Strawberry Mousse, 396
Vanilla Ice Cream, 397
Yellow Parfait, 401

Frosting, Errors to Avoid, 82
Frozen Cheese with Fruit, 317
Frozen Fruit Salad, 316
Frosted Raisin Spice Cake, 355
Fruit Salad Dressing, 311
Fruit Cocktail, 239

INDEX

Fruitcake, Steamed with Maple Sauce, 103-104
Fruit Cake, 354
Fudge, 379

G

Giblet Gravy, 283
Ginger Cookies, 253
Ginger Bread, 350
Ginger Bread, Frosted, 136
Glass Oven Dishes, Care of, 55
Golden Cake Icing, 354
Golden Cake, 353
Golden Glow Drink, 233
Gommy's Cake, 353
Gooseberry Jam, 384
Grandmother's Cookies, 360
Grape Juice Cocktail, 197
Grapefruit with Raspberry Jam, 111-112
Grapefruit and Prune Cocktail, 197
Grape Juice and White Rock Drink, 232
Gravy, Common Errors in Making, 80
Grapefruit with Strawberries, 369
Grape Jelly, 385
Grenadine Delight Drink, 232

H

Hallowe'en Orange Cake, 247
Hallowe'en Cake Decorations, 248
Hallowe'en Parties, 244
Halibut, Baked, 157-158
Ham, Baked in Casserole, 286
Ham in Milk, 276
Ham, Spiced, 94
Ham and Potatoes, 129
Ham Creole, 155-156
Ham, Baked, 162-163
Ham and Eggs, 87
Ham and Chicken Mousse, 237
Hamburger Brochette, 290
Hamburg Steak, Planked, 186-187
Hard Sauce, 363
Hermits, 359
Hollandaise Sauce, 294

Holiday Cookies, 252
Holiday Emergency Stock, 251
Holiday Dinners, 255
Holly Cakes, 254
Honeydew Mellon with Ice Cream, 371
Honeydew Mellon with Green Grapes, 377

HORS D'OEUVRES

Antipasto, 200
Celery Stuffed with Avocado, 204
Celery Stuffed with Chicken, 204
Celery Stuffed with Shrimp, 203
Cucumber, 202
Dried Beef Hors D'Oeuvres, 203
Potato Chips with Pimento Cheese, 202
Salami or Smoked Salmon, 201
Sausage and Almond, 203
Stuffed Eggs, 201
Stuffed Pickled Beets, 202
Stuffed Radishes, 202
Stuffed Tomatoes, 201
Tiny Sausage Rissoles, 203

HOT BREADS

Baking Powder Biscuit, 326
Bran Muffins, 324
Corn Bread, 323
Cornmeal Pancakes, 325
Envelope Biscuit, 327
French Pancakes, 325
Fritter Batter, 328
Graham Muffins with Dates, 323
Maple Sugar Bread, 328
Muffins, 322
Pancakes, 324
Popovers, 327
Raisin and Nut Bread, 328
Scones, 326
Spoon Bread, 324

I

Ice Box Cookies, 362
Ice Box Rolls, 332
Iced Chocolate, 233
Ice Cream Cake, 347
Iced Tea, 234

INDEX

Indian Pudding, 116-117
Ironware, Seasoning, 26

J

Jelly Roll, 372
Jumbles, 135

K

Kale, 308
Kitchen Equipment Inventories, 59-61
Kidneys and Bacon on Toast, 102-103
Kidneys on Toast with Poached Egg, 91-92

L

Lady Baltimore Frosting, 346
Lady Baltimore Cake, 346
Last Minute Dessert, 376
Lamb, How to Buy, 86
Lamb Steak, Broiled, 146-147
Lamb Chops, Sauté, 105-106
Lamb Steak, Chopped, 189-190
Loin of Lamb, Roast, 172-173
Lamb Chops, 176-177
Lamb Cutlets, 286
Lamb Pot Roast, 290
Lamb Stew, 276
Leeks on Toast, 147-148
Lemon Meringue Pie, 338
Lemon Chiffon Pie, 340
Lemon Sherbet, 398
Lemon Pie, 337
Lemon Sauce for Vegetables, 301
Lettuce Salad, Russian Dressing, 111-112
Lettuce Hearts, Roquefort Cheese Dressing, 190-191
Lima Bean Soup, 264
Lima Beans with Mushrooms, 179-180
Lima Beans, Purée of, 184-185
Lima Beans and Tomatoes, 293
Lima Beans with Celery, 295
Lime Cocktail, 198
Lime Rickey, 241
Linen, Proper Equipment, 71
Liver, Braised, 151-152
Lobster Bisque, 264

Lobster Sandwich, 228
Lobster Canapé, 207
Lobster in Butter, 273
Lobster with Cauliflower, 273
Loganberry Punch, 232
Loganberry Juice Cocktail, 198
Loganberry Pudding, 368
Luncheon Soup, 268

M

Macaroni with Caper Sauce, 297
Macaroni Salad, 260
Mayonnaise, Errors to Avoid, 83
Mayonnaise, 310
Mayonnaise, Jellied, 311
Mayonnaise, Lemon, 311
Mackerel, Baked, 273
Maple Sugar Bread, 328
Maple Custard, 374
Maple Parfait, 395
Mapleines, 382
Marshmallow Fudge, 379-380
Marmalade Rounds, 378
Measures Used in Cookery, 13-16

MEATS

Meats, Allowance for Bone in Estimating Portions, 86
Meats, Selection of, 85
Meat Thermometer, 57
Baked Ham, Casserole, 286
Baked Ham, 287
Baked Steak, 281
Beef Roast, Deviled, 282
Beef Stew with Vegetables, 277
Chicken, Casserole, 285
Chicken, Fried, 284
Chicken Pie, 289
Chicken, Roast, 284
Chili Con Carne, 288
Duckling, Broiled, 283
Duck, Roast, 285
English Mutton Chops, 280
Giblet Gravy, 283
Hamburger Brochette, 290
Indian Curry, 280
Lamb Cutlets, 286
Lamb Pot Roast, 290
Lamb Stew, 276
Meat Loaf, 281

INDEX

Minute Steak, 276
Pork Chops, Casserole, 289
Pork Chops, Stuffed, 288
Pork Tenderloin, 281
Pot Roast, 278
Shepherd's Pie, 283
Steak with Onions, 286
Stuffed Cabbage, 288
Swiss Steak, 277
Tamale Pie, 287
Thick Steak, 277
Turkey, Roast, 282
Veal Cutlets, 278
Veal Fricassee, 279
Veal Kidney, 283
Veal and Olives, 289
Veal Roast, 279
Veal Steak, 280

Menu Making, 64
Menus, Variety in Foods, 65
Menu Making Chart, 66
Menus, an Improper Selection, 67
Meringue, 337
Meringues, Errors to Avoid, 82
Mistakes Common in Cooking, 79
Mulled Loganberry Juice, 254
Muffins, Bran, 324
Muffins, 322
Muffins, Graham with Dates, 323
Mussels, Pickled, 207
Mushroom Soup, 92-93, 263
Mushroom Canapé, 207
Mushroom Sauce, 270, 303
Mushrooms, 303
Mustard Pickle Sauce, 387

N

New Potatoes in Cream, 165-166
New Potatoes with Peas, 169-170
Noodles with Butter, 94
Noodles in Cream, 144-145
Nut Fudge, 379-380

O

Olives and Bacon Canapés, 207
Olive Oil Pickles, 386

Omelet, Creole, 103-104
Omelets, Errors to Avoid, 82
Omelet with Mushrooms, 95-96
Omelet Soufflé, 305
Onion and Cucumber Salad, 151-152
Onions, Glazed, 293
Onions, Sauté, 144-145
Onions, Scalloped, 133
Onion Soup, 102-103, 265
Onions, Stuffed, 295
Orange and Banana Compote, 369
Orange Cream in Orange Baskets, 246
Oranges with Cocoanut, 127-128
Orange Compote, 94
Orange Frosting, 248
Orange Ice, 399
Orange Peel, Candied, 381
Orange Pie, 336
Orange Sauce, 284
Orange Sauce for Pancakes, 325
Oven Temperature, 15
Oven Thermometer, 14
Oyster Dressing, 282
Oyster Loaf, 270
Oyster Patties, 247
Oyster Sandwich, 307
Oysters, Scalloped, 116-117
Oyster Soup, 264

P

Pancakes, 324
Panocha, 380
Pâté de Fois Gras Sandwich, 227
Peanut Butter and Bacon Canapé, 205
Peaches, Cooked, 384
Peach and Cherry Compote, 365
Peach Fluff, 372
Peaches in Honey, 374
Peach Pickles, 386
Pears with Cream Cheese and Currant Jelly, 177-178
Pears in Grenadine with Ice Cream, 367
Pears, Pickled, 386

Pear and Pineapple Cocktail, 236
Pears and Raspberries, 374
Pecan Macaroons, 361
Peppermint Ice Cream, 400
Peppers, Stuffed, 308

PICKLES
Cantaloupe Pickles, 383
Chili Sauce, 385
Chopped Pickle, 386
Cranberry Relish, 383
Cucumber Pickles, 383
Currant and Mint Sauce, 384
Mustard Pickle Sauce, 387
Olive Oil Pickles, 386
Ripe Tomato Pickle, 386
Sweet Fruit Pickle, 386
Sweet Pickle Sauce, 387
Sweet Vegetable Pickles, 387

PIES
Apple Pie, 335
Berry Pies, 336
Cherry Pie, 335
Cranberry and Pineapple Pie, 336
Cranberry Pie, 336
Cream Pie, 340
Custard Pie, 338
Date Pie, 340
Lemon Chiffon Pie, 340
Lemon Meringue Pie, 338
Lemon Pie, 337
Meringue, 337
Orange Pie, 336
Pie Crust, 334
Pie Crust, Causes for Failure, 80
Puff Paste, 334
Rhubarb Pie, 337
Rich Pumpkin Pie, 339

Pimento Cheese and Nut Sandwich, 228
Pimento Salad, 165-166, 237
Pimentos, Stuffed for Salad, 174-175
Pineapple Cream, 368
Pineapple Creams, 382
Pineapple Crème de Menthe Cocktail, 198

Pineapple and Honey Dew Salad, 315
Pineapple Ice Box Cake, 365
Pineapple Mousse, 395
Pineapple Refrigerator Cake, 398
Pineapple Salad, 162-163
Pineapple Sherbet, 400
Pineapple Upside Down Cake, 366
Plate Dinners, Method, 138
Plums, Pickled, 386
Plum Pudding, 363
Popovers, 327
Potatoes, Baked and Stuffed, 301
Potatoes, Baked, Errors to Avoid, 84
Potato Balls, 183-184
Potatoes, Browned, 118-119, 172-173, 299
Potatoes in Butter, 297
Potato Cakes, 298
Potatoes in Casserole, 299
Potato Chips with Pimento Cheese, 202
Potatoes, Creamed, 105-106, 299
Potatoes, Diced, 179-180
Potatoes with Egg Sauce, 143-144
Potatoes with Lemon Butter, 296
Potatoes, Lyonnaise, 131
Potatoes, Mashed, 111-112, 297
Potatoes, Mashed, Errors to Avoid, 83
Potatoes, Mashed Sauté, 298
Potatoes, Minced, 298
Potatoes O'Brien, 132, 298
Potatoes with Onions, 89-90
Potatoes with Parsley, 112-113, 300
Potato Salad, Moulded, 236
Potatoes, Savory, 99-100
Potatoes, Scalloped, 124-125, 300
Potatoes, Steamed, 97-98
Potato Soufflé, 298
Potato Soup, 131, 266
Pork, How to Buy, 86
Pork Chops with Apple Rings, 159-160
Pork Chops, Broiled, 165-166

INDEX

Pork Chops with Dressing, 126-127
Pork Chops, Floured, 123-124
Pork Chops, Stuffed, 288
Pork Tenderloin, 163-164
Pork Tenderloin Frenched, 130, 281
Pork Tenderloin, Roast, 127-128
Pork Tenderloin, Whole with Dressing, 179-180
Pot Roast, 278
Poultry, How to Buy, 86
Pralines, 379
Prunes and Bacon Canapé, 206
Prune Whip, 376
Puff Paste, 334
Pumpkin Pie, 339

R

Radishes, Stuffed, 202
Raisin Nut Bread, 328
Raspberry Compote, 370
Raspberry Mousse, 396
Raspberry Soda, 233
Red Cinnamon Apples, 387
Red Peppers, Stuffed, 315
Rhubarb Pie, 337
Rice, Browned, 146-147
Rice, Buttered, 157-158
Rice, Creamed, 131
Rice Pudding, 367
Rich Pumpkin Pie, 339
Ripe Tomato Pickle, 386
Rolled Salamagundi, 252
Romaine Salad, 89-90
Roasted Clams, 271
Roasters, Various Types, 57
Roasting, Errors to Avoid, 84
Russian Dressing, 311
Russian Steak, 106-107

S

Salmon, Boiled, 274
Sally Lunn, 331
Sandwich Biscuit, 252
Sardine Canapé, 205
Sausage and Almond Hors D'Oeuvres, 203
Sausage Rissoles, 203
Sauerkraut Juice Cocktail, 198

Salmon Broiled, Sauce Tartare, 169-170
Scones, 135, 326
Scallops, Fried, 271

SEA FOOD

Baked Shad, 274
Baked Mackerel, 273
Baked Shrimps, 272
Boiled Salmon, 274
Crab Croquettes, 272
Filet of Sole, 274
Fried Scallops, 271
Lobster in Butter, 273
Lobster with Cauliflower, 273
Oyster Loaf, 270
To Open Oysters and Clams, 271
Roasted Clams, 271
Tartar Sauce, 275
Shad Roe with Bacon, 143-144
Shrimps, Baked, 272

Shepherd's Pie, 283
Silverware, 70
Snappy Sandwich, 252
Southern Sandwich, 251

SOUPS

Alligator Pear Soup, 263
Beet Soup, 269
Bouillabaisse, 267
Borsch, 263
Chicken Bouillon, 269
Clam and Chicken Bouillon, 268
Clam Bouillon, 268
Cream of Asparagus Soup, 267
Cream of Spinach Soup, 266
Cream of Onion Soup, 266
Cream of Tomato Soup, 265
Cream of Mushroom Soup, 265
Croutons, 264
Fish Chowder, 267
Lima Bean Soup, 264
Lobster Bisque, 264
Luncheon Soup, 268
Mushroom Soup, 263
Onion Soup, 265
Oyster Soup, 264
Potato Soup, 266
Quick Method Stock, 262
Soup Stock, 262
Tomato Soup, 265
Vegetable Soup, 265

INDEX

Spinach with Mushroom Sauce, 303
Spoon Bread, 324
Spaghetti with Meat Sauce, 296
Sponge Cake, 349
Sponge Cake Shortcake, 368
Spinach, 118-119
Steak, Roast, 124-125
Steak with Cream Gravy and Waffles, 98-99
Steak, Broiled Ground, 89-90
Steak with Tomato Sauce, 153-154
Steak, Spitted with Oysters, 147-148
Steak, Broiled, 144-145
Steak, Baked, 281
Steak, Planked, 183-184
Steaks, Thin Sirloin, 88
Steak with Onions, 286
Step-by-Step Cooking, 141
String Beans in Pimento Cups, 183-184
Stonewall Jackson Drink, 233
Strawberry Shortcake, 120-121
Stuffed Tomato Salad, 161-162
String Beans, Green, 296
Strawberry Mousse, 396
Strawberry Jam, 384
Strawberry Shortcake, 368
Summer Squash, 134
Summer Squash in Casserole, 293
Sugared Pecans, 382
Summer Club Sandwich, 230
Surprise Canapé, 206
Sweet Potatoes, Scalloped, 123-124
Sweet Potatoes in Honey, 126-127
Sweet Potatoes, Browned, 159-160
Sweet Potatoes, Candied, 132, 301
Sweet Potatoes with Apples, 300

Swiss Steak, 277
Sweetbreads en Brochette, 307
Sweet Fruit Pickle Sauce, 387
Sweet Vegetable Pickles, 387
Sweet Fruit Pickles, 386
Sweetbread and Cucumber Salad, 241

Sweet Red Pepper Sandwich, 229
Sweet Potatoes, Broiled, 168-169
Sweet Potatoes, Baked, 181-182
Sweet Potatoes, Mashed, 127-128
Swiss Chard, 181-182

T

Table Decorations, 74
Table Setting, 71
Tamale Pie, 287
Tartar Sauce, 275
Tea, 389
Tea Wagon, Use at Table, 140
Thick Steak, 277
Tomato Soup, 265
Tomato Salad, Frozen, 242
Tomato Cocktail, 235
Tomatoes, Stuffed, 201
Tomato Juice Cocktail, 198
Tomatoes, Baked, 151-152
Tomatoes with Mint, 158-159
Tomatoes, Onions and Anchovy Salad, 106-107
Tomatoes Sauté, 99-100
Tomato Salad, 95-96
Tomatoes, Peppers and Onions Sauté, 87
Tomatoes, Sliced, 302
Tomato and Bacon, 306
Tomatoes, Stuffed, 309
Tomatoes, Scalloped, 309
Tomato Salad, Jellied, 312
Tomato Salad, Frozen, 316
Tomatoes, Baked, 295
Tomato and Mushroom Salad, 317
Turkey Dinner Menu, 255
Turkey, Roast, with Oyster Dressing, 282
Turkey Sandwich, Hot, 306

V

Vanilla Soufflé, 134
Vanilla Ice Cream, 397
Veal Chops, Breaded, 150-151
Veal Steak with Vegetables, 161-162
Veal Pot Roast, 118-119

INDEX

Veal and Olives, 289
Veal Kidney, 283
Veal Steak, 280
Veal, Roast Leg, 279
Veal Fricassee, 279
Veal Cutlets, 278
Vegetable Salad, 258
Vegetable Soup, 265
Vegetables for Salads, 312

VEGETABLES
Artichokes, 296
Asparagus, 302
Baked Tomatoes, 295
Broccoli, 294
Cabbage, Scalloped, 302
Cabbage with Apple, 302
Carrot Cups with Peas, 293
Cauliflower, 301
Cauliflower au Gratin, 292
Eggplant, Broiled, 304
Eggplant, Chopped, 302
Endive on Toast, 303
Green String Beans, 296
Hollandaise Sauce, 294
Lemon Sauce, 301
Lemon Butter Potatoes, 296
Leeks, 292
Lima Beans and Tomatoes, 293
Macaroni with Caper Sauce, 297
Mushrooms, 303
Onions, Stuffed, 295
Onions, Glazed, 293
Potatoes, Baked and Stuffed, 301
Potatoes, Creamed, 299
Potatoes, Browned, 299
Potatoes, Scalloped, 300
Potatoes with Parsley, 300
Potatoes, Mashed Sauté, 298
Potatoes, Minced, 298
Potatoes O'Brien, 298
Potatoes, Casserole, 299
Potato Soufflé, 298
Potato Cakes, 298
Potatoes, Mashed, 297
Potatoes in Butter, 297
Spaghetti with Meat Sauce, 296
Spinach with Mushroom Sauce, 303
Summer Squash, Casserole, 293

Sweet Potatoes with Apples, 300
Sweet Potatoes, Candied, 301
Tomatoes, Sliced, 302
Tiny Lima Beans with Celery, 295

Velvet Sauce, 364
Velvet Sponge Pudding, 364

W

Waffles, 98-99, 318
Waffle Cake, 321
Waffle Cake, Chocolate, 320
Waffles, Cornmeal, 319
Waffles, Errors to Avoid, 84
Waffles, Gingerbread, 321
Waffle Iron, Care of, 318
Waffles, Maryland Cream, 320
Waffles, Raised, 319
Waffle Short Cake, 319
Waldorf Salad, 316
Walnut Creams, 381
Walnut Icing, 344
Walnut Spice Cake, 344
Water Cress Salad, 94
Water Cress and Shrimp Canapés, 207
Watermelon Pickles, 386
Welsh Rarebit, Common Mistakes in Making, 81
White Almond Cake, 349
White Almond Icing, 350
White Grape Juice Cocktail, 196
Whole Wheat, Ground Cooked, 106-107

Y

YEAST BREADS
Cinnamon Bread, 330
Cinnamon Cake, 331
Date Bread, 331
Graham Bread, 332
Ice Box Rolls, 332
Sally Lunn, 331
White Bread, 330

Yellow Parfait, 401
Yorkshire Pudding, 124-125
Young Onions, Boiled, 168-169